全国工程硕士专业学位教育指导委员会推荐教材

工程硕士研究生英语
基础教程
学生用书

罗立胜 何福胜 主编

庞红梅 王宏利 郭 茜
罗承丽 周允程 王敬慧 编写

萧家琛 审校

清华大学出版社
北京

内 容 简 介

本教材以最新《全国工程硕士专业学位研究生英语教学要求》为主要依据编写,在原有《工程硕士研究生英语教程》(第二版)的基础上,结合编者多年的教学实践经验,进行了适当的增删、修订、补充和完善,使之更加适合现今工程硕士研究生的实际水平,符合此类研究生在外语教学中的实际需求。

版权所有,侵权必究。举报:010-62782989,beiqinquan@tup.tsinghua.edu.cn。

图书在版编目(CIP)数据

工程硕士研究生英语基础教程学生用书/罗立胜,何福胜主编. —北京:清华大学出版社,2006.6(2022.1重印)
ISBN 978-7-302-13045-1

Ⅰ. ①工… Ⅱ. ①罗…②何… Ⅲ. ①英语－研究生－教材 Ⅳ. H31

中国版本图书馆 CIP 数据核字(2006)第 050477 号

责任编辑:蔡心奕
责任印制:沈　露

出版发行:清华大学出版社
网　　址:http://www.tup.com.cn,http://www.wqbook.com
地　　址:北京清华大学学研大厦 A 座
邮　　编:100084
社 总 机:010-62770175
邮　　购:010-62786544
投稿与读者服务:010-62776969,c-service@tup.tsinghua.edu.cn
质量反馈:010-62772015,zhiliang@tup.tsinghua.edu.cn
课件下载:http://www.tup.com.cn,010-83470410

印 装 者:三河市铭诚印务有限公司
经　　销:全国新华书店
开　　本:185mm×230mm
印　　张:16
字　　数:337 千字
版　　次:2006 年 7 月第 1 版
印　　次:2022 年 1 月第 31 次印刷
定　　价:68.00 元

产品编号:021115-09

Preface 前言

本教材《工程硕士研究生英语基础教程》的编写以最新《全国工程硕士专业学位研究生英语教学要求》为主要依据,在原有《工程硕士研究生英语教程》(第二版)的基础上,结合编者多年的教学实践经验,进行了适当的增删、修订、补充和完善。参加编写的人员都是长期担任此项教学并具有丰富教学经验的英语教师。

本教材是全国工程硕士专业学位教育指导委员会批准立项的专项教材编写项目,也是清华大学出版社的重点教材项目。

《工程硕士研究生英语基础教程》分为学生用书和教师用书,共需 64 学时,一个学期完成。全书有 15 个单元,每个单元包括 Part A 正课文、Part B 语法和 Part C 副课文。每个单元可安排 4 至 6 学时。

本教材具有以下主要特点:

1. 严格按照《工程硕士研究生英语教学要求》编写。注重该类研究生的英语基础和英语运用能力的培养。

2. 在选材方面力求做到内容新颖丰富、题材广泛,从而拓宽工程硕士研究生在英语方面的视野及知识面。

3. 语言规范、难度适中、针对性强,适合工程硕士研究生的实际水平,符合此类研究生在外语教学中的实际需求。

4. 本教材的课文以及练习形式多样,以实用为目的,难度安排循序渐进,重视基础。在帮助工程硕士研究生打下较好的英语基础的同时,提高他们的英语实践能力。

5. 本教材不但适用于工程类硕士研究生,还适用于其他各类研究生课程班学员、在职人员申请硕士学位的自学人员等。

本教材在编写过程中得到了全国工程硕士专业学位教育指导委员会、清华大学出版社、清华大学外语系等单位的热情支持与帮助。萧家琛教授和外籍教师 Mary Tarrant 对初稿进行了审阅和修改。在此一并表示感谢。

由于编者水平有限，时间紧迫，错误和疏漏之处在所难免，衷心希望广大读者批评指正。

编　者

2006 年 3 月

Contents 目录

前言 ·· 1

UNIT 1 ·· 1
   Part A   Text（My First Job）··· 1
   Part B   Grammar（时态）·· 9
   Part C   Supplementary Reading
             （Four Words That Changed a Life）·················· 14

UNIT 2 ·· 18
   Part A   Text（Future of Net Economy）································ 18
   Part B   Grammar（语态）·· 26
   Part C   Supplementary Reading
             （Advertisements）··· 28

UNIT 3 ·· 34
   Part A   Text（Preserving Our Planet）································· 34
   Part B   Grammar（比较级）·· 42
   Part C   Supplementary Reading
             （Art for Sale）··· 45

UNIT 4 ·· 51
   Part A   Text（A Time for Apologies）·································· 51
   Part B   Grammar（不定式）·· 59
   Part C   Supplementary Reading
             （Life and Times of Bill Clinton）······················ 61

UNIT 5 ⋯⋯ 66
Part A Text（Teach Your Child to Wonder）⋯⋯ 66
Part B Grammar（分词）⋯⋯ 74
Part C Supplementary Reading
（Benchmarking Practices at Xerox）⋯⋯ 77

UNIT 6 ⋯⋯ 82
Part A Text（Engineering）⋯⋯ 82
Part B Grammar（动名词）⋯⋯ 90
Part C Supplementary Reading
（This *TITANIC* Floats!）⋯⋯ 93

UNIT 7 ⋯⋯ 98
Part A Text（The Land of the Lock）⋯⋯ 98
Part B Grammar（定语从句）⋯⋯ 107
Part C Supplementary Reading（Beyond the *Right* to Die, Will It Become a *Duty* to Die?）⋯⋯ 109

UNIT 8 ⋯⋯ 115
Part A Text（Perfume）⋯⋯ 115
Part B Grammar（状语从句）⋯⋯ 123
Part C Supplementary Reading
（Travelling Pamphlet）⋯⋯ 126

UNIT 9 ⋯⋯ 134
Part A Text（Managers for the Twenty-first Century）⋯⋯ 134
Part B Grammar（名词性从句）⋯⋯ 142
Part C Supplementary Reading
（Announcement Letters）⋯⋯ 145

UNIT 10 ⋯⋯ 150
Part A Text（How the Rich Got Rich—and You Could Too）⋯⋯ 150
Part B Grammar（强调句）⋯⋯ 158
Part C Supplementary Reading
（The Irresponsibility That Spreads AIDS）⋯⋯ 160

UNIT 11 ⋯⋯ 165
Part A Text（Kicking the Big-car Habit）⋯⋯ 165
Part B Grammar（倒装句及反意问句）⋯⋯ 173

Part C　Supplementary Reading
　　　　　　（An Impression of Zhu Diwen—A Nobel Physics Prize
　　　　　　Winner of Chinese Descent）…………………………………… 178
UNIT 12 …………………………………………………………………………… 184
　　　Part A　Text（The Advertising of a Product）………………… 184
　　　Part B　Grammar（虚拟语气）………………………………… 190
　　　Part C　Supplementary Reading
　　　　　　（Dividing a Kingdom）……………………………………… 193
UNIT 13 …………………………………………………………………………… 199
　　　Part A　Text（A Simple Truth About Happiness）…………… 199
　　　Part B　Grammar（直接引语和间接引语）………………………… 207
　　　Part C　Supplementary Reading
　　　　　　（To Win at Marriage, Learn to Lose）…………………… 209
UNIT 14 …………………………………………………………………………… 215
　　　Part A　Text（The Coming Age of Talking Computers）…… 215
　　　Part B　Grammar（倒装句）…………………………………… 223
　　　Part C　Supplementary Reading
　　　　　　（Bill Gates' Speech to Tsinghua University）…………… 225
UNIT 15 …………………………………………………………………………… 230
　　　Part A　Text（Mind Games）…………………………………… 230
　　　Part B　Grammar（插入语）…………………………………… 239
　　　Part C　Supplementary Reading
　　　　　　（When to Say No to Your Kids）………………………… 241

UNIT 1

Part A   Text (My First Job)
Part B   Grammar (时态)
Part C   Supplementary Reading
          (Four Words That Changed a Life)

Part A   Text

Warm-up Questions:

1. *What was your first job? Do you still have the same job?*
2. *Did you like your first job? Why (not)?*
3. *What have you learned from your first job?*

My First Job

Two noted Americans explain why
it's not what you earn—it's what you learn.
Compiled by Daniel Levine

The Auto Prepper (Jay Leno)

I acquired a very strong work ethic from my parents, both of whom lived through the Great Depression. They couldn't understand people who didn't work regularly. I once told my mom that Sylvester Stallone was getting $12 million for ten weeks of work. "What's he going to do the rest of the year?" she asked.

I took my parents' work ethic into my first job at Wilmington Ford near my hometown of Andover, Mass., when I was 16. I worked until five or six o'clock on school days and put in 12-hour days during the summer as a prepper. This meant washing and polishing the new cars, and making sure the paper floor mats were in place. Another responsibility was taking off the hubcaps at night, so they wouldn't get stolen, and replacing them the next day. This was hard work because we had about seven acres of cars.

One day, carrying an armful of hubcaps around a corner, I almost bumped into our new general manager. Startled, I dropped them all. He fired me on the spot.

I was too ashamed to tell my parents. Every day for about two weeks, I stayed busy until evening. Then I would go home and say I had a great day at work.

Desperate, I wrote a letter to Henry Ford II and told him what happened. I said that we were a loyal Ford family and that when I was old enough, I was going to buy a Mustang. Eventually the owner of the dealership called. "I don't know who you know in Detroit," he said, "but if you want your job back, you got it."

Later, during college, I wanted to work at a Rolls-Royce dealership, but the owner said there were no openings. So I started washing cars there anyway. When the owner noticed me, I said I was working until he hired me. He did.

It takes persistence to succeed. Attitude also matters. I have never thought I was better than anyone else, but I have always believed I couldn't be outworked.

The Cashier (Jill E. Barad)

I was ten when I first sat with my grandmother behind the register in her Manhattan pharmacy. Before long, she let me sit there by myself. I quickly learned the importance of treating customers politely and saying "thank you".

At first I was paid in candy. Later I received 50 cents an hour. I worked every day after school, and during the summer and on weekends and holidays from 8 a.m. to 7 p.m. My father helped me set up a bank account. Watching my money grow was more rewarding than anything I could have bought.

Grandma, a tough taskmaster, never gave me favorable treatment. She watched me like a hawk yet allowed me to handle high-pressure situations such as working during the lunch rush. Her trust taught me how to handle responsibility.

By the time I was 12, she thought I had done such a good job that she promoted me to selling cosmetics. I developed the ability to look customers directly in the eye. Even though I was just a kid, women would ask me such things as "What color do you think I should wear?" I took a genuine interest in their questions and was able to translate what they wanted into makeup ideas. I ended up selling a record amount of cosmetics.

The job taught me a valuable lesson: that to be a successful salesperson, you didn't need to be a rocket scientist—you needed to be a great listener. Today I still carry that lesson with me: I listen to customers. Except they are no longer women purchasing cosmetics from me; instead, they are kids who tell me which toys they would like to see designed and developed.

NEW WORDS

prepper /ˈprepə/ *n.*	给新车清洗和擦亮的小工
acquire /əˈkwaiə/ *vt.*	obtain, gain 获得,得到
ethic /ˈeθik/ *n.*	systems of moral principles; rules of conduct 道德观,道德标准
polish /ˈpɔliʃ/ *vt.*	cause sth. to become smooth and shining by rubbing 磨光,擦亮; improve (sth.) by correcting, making small changes or adding new material 修正,修改,修饰,加以润色
mat /mæt/ *n.*	席,垫
hubcap /ˈhʌbkæp/ *n.*	(车轮的)毂盖
replace /ri(:)ˈpleis/ *vt.*	put (sth.) back in its place 将(某物)放回原处; take the place of 代替,取代
acre /ˈeikə/ *n.*	英亩
armful /ˈɑ:mful/ *n.*	一抱
bump /bʌmp/ *v.*	碰撞或敲击某物,与某物相撞
startle /ˈstɑ:tl/ *vt.*	frighten, scare 使……受惊吓/吓一跳
desperate /ˈdespərit/ *a.*	feeling and showing great despair and ready to do anything regardless of danger 铤而走险的,不顾一切的
dealership /ˈdi:ləʃip/ *n.*	经营店
anyway /ˈeniwei/ *ad.*	nevertheless, anyhow 无论如何,即便如此
persist /pə(:)ˈsist/ *v.*	not give up, be determined 坚持; persistence *n.*
outwork /autˈwə:k/ *vt.*	工作比……做得更好/快/勤
cashier /kæˈʃiə/ *n.*	出纳员
register /ˈredʒistə/ *n.*	记录器;登记
v.	登记,注册;(仪表等)自动记下;挂号邮寄

pharmacy /'fɑ:məsi/ n.　　　　药房；药剂学
rewarding /ri'wɔ:diŋ/ a.　　　worth doing, satisfying　值得做的；令人满意的
taskmaster /'tɑ:sk,mɑ:stə/ n.　　工头，监工
hawk /hɔ:k/ n.　　　　　　　鹰
handle /'hændl/ v.　　　　　deal with, manage　处理，对付
　　　　　　　　　 n.　　　柄，把手
promote /prə'mout/ vt.　　　raise to a higher position or rank　提升，提拔；encourage or support　增进，鼓励
cosmetic /kɔz'metik/ n.　　　化妆品
　　　　　　　　　 a.　　　化妆用的；装饰性的，装门面的
genuine /'dʒenjuin/ a.　　　real, authentic　真的，非伪造的；sincere　真诚的
makeup /'meikʌp/ n.　　　　化妆品
rocket /'rɔkit/ n.　　　　　　火箭
purchase /'pə:tʃəs/ vt.　　　buy　购买
　　　　　　　　　 n.　　　buying　购买；a thing bought　购买之物

PHRASES

put in: give (time or effort) to sth.　花费(一段时间或精力)做某事
in place: 在平常的或应在的地方
on the spot: 当场，立即
set up: establish, build or raise　建立，开创；竖起(纪念碑、雕像等)
end up: finish (in a particular way)　结束，结果

NOTES

Jay Leno: the former auto prepper who is the host of NBC's "The Tonight Show"
Jill E. Barad: the former cashier who is the chairman and CEO of Mattel, Inc., the world's largest toy maker
the Great Depression: 大萧条(1929—1939年北美、欧洲及其他工业化国家发生的经济衰退)
Sylvester Stallone: 西尔维斯特·史泰龙，美国电影明星
Wilmington Ford: 福特汽车公司在威尔明顿(马萨诸塞州的一个镇)的专营店。福特

汽车公司由亨利·福特创建于1903年,为世界最大的汽车公司之一。

Andover, Mass.:美国马萨诸塞州安多佛镇

Henry Ford II:亨利·福特二世,1940年起任福特汽车公司的高级管理人员,其中1960—1980年为该公司的总裁

Mustang:野马,福特汽车公司出品的跑车和敞篷跑车品牌

Detroit:底特律,美国密歇根州最大的城市,被称为"世界汽车之都"

Rolls-Royce:英国的罗尔斯-罗伊斯(或译作劳斯莱斯)汽车有限公司。由查尔斯·斯图尔特·罗尔斯与亨利·罗伊斯共同创建于1906年。

Manhattan:曼哈顿,美国纽约市的五个行政区之一。曼哈顿虽然位于纽约市最小的岛上,却是该市真正的中心。

EXERCISES

I. *Reading Comprehension*:

Choose the best answer to each question.

The Auto Prepper

1. It can be inferred from the passage that the author's parents used to _____.
   A. be very rich   B. suffer from hardship
   C. spoil their children   D. hate working

2. The author's first job was to _____.
   A. drive and sell cars   B. wash and paint cars
   C. clean and brighten cars   D. polish and paint cars

3. It may be inferred from the passage that Detroit was where the author _____.
   A. grew up   B. got his first job
   C. went to college   D. got help from

The Cashier

4. All the following can be used to describe the author's grandmother EXCEPT _____.
   A. rewarding   B. trustful
   C. strict   D. knowing her employees' abilities

5. The word "they" (last sentence) refers to _____.
   A. salespersons   B. rocket scientists
   C. good listeners   D. customers

II. Getting Information:

Answer the following questions in English.

The Auto Prepper

1. How did the author's parents feel about people who didn't work regularly?
   _____

2. How did the author manage to get his job back?
   _____

The Cashier

3. Did the author prefer to save money or spend money? How do you know?
   _____

4. What's the important lesson the author learns from her first job?
   _____

5. In which field is the author now working?
   _____

III. Vocabulary and Structure:

A. Choose the correct word/phrase to fill into each sentence, using the proper form.

end up	handle	favorable	replace	put in
promote	regular	desperate	on the spot	make sure

1. They made _____ visits to the park on the suburbs during the weekends.
2. She was _____ to division manager last year.
3. We tried to walk to the park but _____ taking a taxi there.
4. His _____ of these important issues was highly praised.
5. Thomas bought a new hat to _____ the one he had lost.
6. The movie received generally _____ reviews.
7. Thank you for all the time and effort you _____.
8. _____ you're home by midnight.
9. He was hit by a falling tree and killed _____.
10. The earthquake survivors are in _____ need of help.

B. Find the proper forms of the following words according to the given word class.

1. open   (n.)   _____

Unit 1

2. persist   (*n.*) _____
3. succeed   (*n.*) _____
4. succeed   (*a.*) _____
5. important   (*n.*) _____
6. promote   (*n.*) _____
7. depress   (*n.*) _____
8. value   (*a.*) _____
9. loyal   (*n.*) _____
10. favor   (*a.*). _____

C. Use words/phrases from the passage to replace the italicized words/phrases in the following sentences.
1. We can *obtain* knowledge by reading books, newspapers, and by watching TV.
2. When all her other friends deserted her, Steve remained *constant*.
3. New York is a city *famous* for its shopping and nightlife.
4. You *frightened* me—I thought you were in the garden.
5. He accepted the *blame* for the mistake in the government report.
6. Teaching is not very *worth doing* financially.
7. She showed *sincere* sorrow at the news.
8. Guess whom I *encountered* today?
9. Tickets must be *bought* two weeks in advance.
10. We all hope that an agreement can be reached *at the end*.

IV. *Translation*:

A. Translate the following into Chinese.
1. Two noted Americans explain why it's not what you earn—it's what you learn.
2. I have never thought I was better than anyone else, but I have always believed I couldn't be outworked.
3. Watching my money grow was more rewarding than anything I could have bought.
4. I took a genuine interest in their questions and was able to translate what they wanted into makeup ideas.
5. I ended up selling a record amount of cosmetics.

B. Translate the following into English.

1. 她计划自己创业。(set up)

_____

2. 态度也很重要。(matter)

_____

3. 她在客人们到达之前把所有的家具都擦亮了。(polish)

_____

4. 有些经理不知道如何与人打交道。(handle)

_____

5. 我们完成那项工作的时间打破了纪录。(record)

_____

6. 她喜欢东西都摆好以后再开始工作。(in place)

_____

7. 她常常一天工作12个小时。(put in)

_____

8. 他是从报纸上得到这一信息的。(acquire)

_____

9. 我们部门有一个助理的职位空缺。(opening)

_____

10. 该组织旨在促进各国之间的友谊。(promote)

_____

V. *Writing Task*:

Write about 120 words on the topic "**My Job**". Try to cover the following points:

1. what job you do;
2. what it takes to succeed on your job;
3. what you have gained from your job.

VI. *Oral Practice*:

What do you think are the three most important characteristics that the following people should have? Working in pairs, tell each other what you think and give brief explanations.

1. engineers: _____; _____; _____
2. teachers: _____; _____; _____
3. doctors: _____; _____; _____

4. lawyers：_____；_____；_____
5. business people：_____；_____；_____
6. government officials：_____；_____；_____

Part B　Grammar

时态（Tenses）

英语中最基本的语法现象是时态。常见的时态有：一般现在时、现在进行时、现在完成时、一般过去时、一般将来时等。下面就常用时态的形式及用法作一简单的介绍。

I. 一般现在时

一般现在时通常表示习惯性的动作、一般状态、客观规律和永恒的真理。在这一时态中需要用动词原形，第三人称单数后面的动词需加-s 或-es。另外，在时间状语和条件状语从句中，通常用一般现在时代替一般将来时。请看下面各句中的一般现在时。

- He works in a factory.
- Does he study very hard?
- It seldom rains there.
- Light travels faster than sound.
- The train leaves at seven every Sunday.
- We'll go to see her as soon as she comes back from the hospital.

以上六句基本上反映了一般现在时的常用方法及基本形式。另外，动词 be 和 have 有特殊的人称形式，主要有以下几种：

- I am a graduate.
- She is an engineer.
- They are scientists.
- I have two books.
- She has a book.
- They have pens.

第三人称单数 be 需变成 is；第一人称用 am；其他情况则用 are。在使用 have 时，除了第三人称单数用 has，其他情况都用 have。

II. 现在进行时

现在进行时主要表示正在或目前这一阶段正在进行的动作；也可以用来表示将来的动作，但主要指按计划、安排将要发生的事情等。这一时态是由助动词 be 的人称形式加现在分词构成。如：

- She is learning English now.
- Are they building a big bridge over there?
- He's leaving for London tomorrow.
- Who's speaking first at the meeting?

III. 现在完成时

现在完成时通常表示目前已经完成的动作或刚刚完成的动作，也可表示到现在为止这段时间内发生的情况。其构成形式是 have 的人称变化形式 + 过去分词。以下各句表示了这一时态在不同情况下的使用。

- He has been sick for four days.（表示一段时间内的状态）
- We have always worked until eight o'clock in the evening.（习惯性动作）
- The train has left.（动作已完成）
- Up till now we have finished five lessons.（到现在为止这段时间内发生的情况）

IV. 一般过去时

一般过去时表示在过去某一特定的时间内发生的动作；这一动作不强调对现在的影响。动词 be 有 was 和 were 两个形式，was 用于第一、第三人称单数，were 用于其他情况。在构成否定及疑问句时，一般借助助动词 did。如：

- When did they start the research project?
- They often came to help us.
- He was a teacher in 1980.
- They did not come last night.

V. 一般将来时

一般将来时由助动词 shall 或 will 加动词原形构成，shall 用于第一人称，will 用于第二、第三人称。这一时态表示将来要发生的动作或情况。如：

- The agreement will come into force next week.
- When shall we have supper this evening?
- Who will look after the sick?

- He will be a manager next year.

除了一般将来时之外，还有一些其他的结构和时态也可表示将要发生的动作或情况。如：

- We are going to do this experiment tomorrow.（be going + 不定式，表示将来的动作）
- When is the school to be built?（be + 不定式，表示将来的动作）
- We're having a lecture tonight.（进行时，表示按计划将要发生的事情）
- He will write to you if he has time.（从句中用一般时，表示将来的动作）
- An accident is about to happen if one is careless.（be + about，表示将来）

VI. 将来进行时

将来进行时表示将来某时正在发生或持续的动作。这一时态由 will + be + 动词的现在分词构成。如：

- They will be cleaning the room this time tomorrow.

VII. 过去进行时

过去进行时由 be 的过去式和现在分词构成，主要表示过去某时正在发生或进行的动作。如：

- What were the students doing at eight last night?
- I was reading a newspaper when she came in.
- At that time he was talking to his client in the office.

VIII. 过去完成时

过去完成时由 had 加过去分词构成，表示过去某时之前已发生或完成的动作。如：

- The concert had already started when we got there.
- They had completed the work before 5 yesterday.

IX. 将来完成时

将来完成时表示将来某个时间已经发生的动作或情况；由 will + have + 过去分词构成。如：

- They will have learned about 4,000 words by the end of next month.

X. 现在完成进行时

现在完成进行时表示从过去某时开始一直持续的动作或情况，此动作或情况可能会继续下去。其构成形式为 has (have) + been + 现在分词。如：

- It has been snowing for two hours.

- They have been reading the textbook for three hours.

练 习

1. 用括号内动词的适当形式填空。

   (1) I think I _____ (see) your teacher twice this week.

   (2) The fire _____ (start) at seven last night.

   (3) When the old lady entered the apartment, the thief _____ (escape) already.

   (4) We did not catch what the stranger _____ (say).

   (5) When they finally got to the hotel, night _____ (fall) already.

   (6) The visitors _____ just _____ (arrive) from America.

   (7) By the time he gets home, his father _____ (leave) for Shanghai.

   (8) We will not start the project before he _____ (come) back from the United States.

   (9) He lost his new knife shortly after he _____ (buy) it.

   (10) The fire _____ (burn) for three hours before the firemen arrived.

   (11) I told him that he _____ (can go) there after school.

   (12) Irene _____ (teach) English at our school for two years. She will renew her contract tomorrow.

   (13) He is ill. He _____ (not eat) any food since last night.

   (14) This time tomorrow we _____ (plant) trees in the park.

   (15) From 3 to 5 yesterday, they _____ (repair) the car on the way to the park.

2. 选择适当的时态填空。

   (1) According to the time table, the train for London _____ at seven o'clock in the evening.

       A. was leaving   B. has left   C. leaves   D. will leave

   (2) You needn't hurry her. She _____ it by the time you are ready.

       A. will have finished   B. would finish

       C. will have been finishing   D. will be finishing

   (3) Darwin proved that natural selection _____ the chief factor in the development of species.

       A. has been   B. had been   C. was   D. is

Unit 1

(4) While Peggy _____, her brother is playing records.
    A. reads   B. is reading
    C. has read   D. has been reading

(5) It's been a long time since I _____. How are you?
    A. had last seen you   B. saw you last
    C. have last seen you   D. last was seeing you

(6) We _____ on it for several hours, but we have not yet reached any conclusion.
    A. work   B. are working
    C. have been working   D. have been worked

(7) He said that he _____ for Shanghai the next day.
    A. will leave   B. has left
    C. would leave   D. had left

(8) This is the first time I _____ this kind of refrigerator.
    A. saw   B. have seen
    C. am seeing   D. see

(9) He _____ this job before he moved into this city.
    A. found   B. would find
    C. was finding   D. had found

(10) I think this time yesterday he _____ an English class in No. 3 Classroom Building.
    A. was having   B. will have   C. had   D. would have

(11) By 2008, the university _____ 20,000 postgraduates.
    A. will be trained   B. trains
    C. will have trained   D. will be training

(12) Since 1970, he _____ in this bank and he loves the job very much.
    A. has worked   B. has been working
    C. is working   D. will be working

(13) I don't like to be disturbed if I _____.
    A. am working   B. will work
    C. work   D. have worked

(14) Before long, she _____ all about the matter.
    A. will have forgotten   B. will forget
    C. will be forgotten   D. will have been forgetting

(15) You can see the house _____ for years.
    A. isn't painted   B. hasn't painted
    C. hadn't been painted   D. hasn't been painted

Part C Supplementary Reading

Four Words That Changed a Life

"Are you too stupid to do anything right?" These words—said by a woman to a little boy who was evidently her son—were spoken because he had walked away from her. And they were said at a volume high enough that all the strangers nearby could hear. Chastised, the boy returned quietly to the woman's side, his eyes downcast.

Not a big moment, perhaps. Yet small moments sometimes last a very long time. And a few words—though they mean little at the time to the people who say them—can have enormous power. "Are you too stupid to do anything right?" Words like that can echo.

I recently heard a story from a man named Malcolm Dalkoff. He's 48; for the last 24 years he has been a professional writer, mostly in advertising. Here is what he told me:

As a boy in Rock Island, Ill., Dalkoff was terribly insecure and shy. He had few friends and no self-confidence. Then one day in October 1965, his high-school English teacher, Ruth Brauch, gave the class an assignment. The students had been reading *To Kill a Mockingbird*. Now they were to write their own chapter that would follow the last chapter of the novel.

Dalkoff wrote his chapter and turned it in. Today he cannot recall anything special about the chapter he wrote, or what grade Mrs. Brauch gave him. What he does remember—what he will never forget—are the four words Mrs. Brauch wrote in the margin of the paper: "This is good writing."

Four words. They changed his life.

"Until I read those words, I had no idea of who I was or what I was going to be," he said. "After reading her note, I went home and wrote a short story, something I had always dreamed of doing but never believed I could do."

Over the rest of that year in school, he wrote many short stories and always brought them to school for Mrs. Brauch to evaluate. She was encouraging, tough and honest. "She was just what I needed," Dalkoff said.

He was named co-editor of his high-school newspaper. His confidence grew; his horizons broadened; he started off on a successful, fulfilling life. Dalkoff is convinced that none of this would have happened had that woman not written those four words in the margin of his paper.

For his 30th high-school reunion, Dalkoff went back and visited Mrs. Brauch, who had retired. He told her what her four words had done for him. He told her that because she had given him the confidence to be a writer, he had been able to pass that confidence on to the woman who would become his wife, who became a writer herself. He told Mrs. Brauch that a young woman in his office, who was working in the evenings toward a high-school-equivalency diploma, had come to him for advice and assistance. She respected him because he was a writer—that is why she turned to him.

Mrs. Brauch was especially moved by the story of helping the young woman. "At that moment I think we both realized that Mrs. Brauch had cast an incredibly long shadow," he said.

"Are you too stupid to do anything right?"

"This is good writing."

So few words. They can change everything.

NEW WORDS

volume /ˈvɔlju(:)m/ n.	音量；卷册；体积
chastise /tʃæsˈtaiz/ vt.	punish severely, scold, criticize 严惩；责备，批评
downcast /ˈdaunkɑːst/ a.	looking downwards 目光向下的；depressed, sad 沮丧的,悲哀的
echo /ˈekəu/ v.	发出回声
n.	回声
insecure /ˌinsiˈkjuə/ a.	not feeling safe or protected, lacking confidence 缺乏安全感的,信心不足的；unsafe, risky 不保险的,不安全的
assignment /əˈsainmənt/ n.	作业,任务；分配,指派
mockingbird /ˈmɔkiŋbəːd/ n.	模仿鸟
recall /riˈkɔːl/ vt.	remember, bring back into the mind 回忆起,记起；order to return 召回
margin /ˈmɑːdʒin/ n.	页边空白,边缘；余地,余裕
evaluate /iˈvæljueit/ vt.	judge, estimate 评估,估计
horizon /həˈraizn/ n.	[常用复数]眼界,见识；地平线
fulfill /fulˈfil/ vt.	satisfy, accomplish 满足,实现；perform 履行,使……实现 fulfill oneself: fully develop one's abilities and character 充分发挥自己的才能
equivalency /iˈkwivələnsi/ n.	相等物

diploma/diˈpləumə/ *n.* 毕业证书,毕业文凭
incredible/inˈkredəbl/ *a.* extraordinary, amazing 难以置信的,不可思议的,惊人的; unbelievable 不可信的 **incredibly** *ad.*

PHRASE

turn to sb.：向某人寻求帮助,请教某人

NOTES

Rock Island, Ill.：美国伊利诺伊州（Illinois）洛克岛
To Kill a Mockingbird：《杀死模仿鸟》,美国作家哈珀·李（Harper Lee）1960 年的作品

EXERCISES

I. *Reading Comprehension*：
Answer the following questions in English.

1. Why did the woman say her son was "stupid"?

2. What is meant by "words like that can echo" (Para. 2, last sentence)?

3. How old was Dalkoff when he started his career as a professional writer?

4. What was Dalkoff like when he was a boy?

5. What did Mrs. Brauch ask her students to do after they finished reading *To Kill a Mockingbird*?

6. What had Dalkoff "always dreamed of doing but never believed [he] could do"?

7. How did Mrs. Brauch help Dalkoff with his short story writing?

8. To what did Dalkoff owe his success in life?

9. Why did the young woman come to Dalkoff for advice?

10. What is meant by "Mrs. Brauch had cast an incredibly long shadow" (Para. 11)?

II. *Vocabulary and Structure*:

Choose the correct word/phrase to fill into each sentence, using the proper form.

| echo | name | evident | insecure | fulfill | horizon |
| evaluate | recall | start off | enormous | turn to | convince |

1. We shall need to _____ how the new material stands up to wear and tear.
2. The full extent of the damage only became _____ the following morning.
3. Just _____ the time and I'll be there on the dot.
4. Brownell's comments _____ the opinion of the majority of the commission members.
5. I'd like to _____ by thanking you all for coming today.
6. You've been an _____ help.
7. Spending her junior year abroad has broadened her _____.
8. He still feels _____ about his ability to do the job.
9. She _____ seeing him outside the shop on the night of the robbery.
10. Without someone to _____ for advice, making the most appropriate choice can be difficult.
11. I've finally found a job in which I can _____ myself.
12. I hope this will _____ you to change your mind.

Part A　Text (Future of Net Economy)
Part B　Grammar (语态)
Part C　Supplementary Reading
　　　　(Advertisements)

Part A Text

Warm-up Questions:

1. *What do you know about the Net economy?*
2. *Have you ever tried Internet shopping? What do you think of it?*
3. *How is the Net economy going in our country?*

Future of Net Economy

By Pete Dowden

　　As we have entered the new century, human society is beginning its move from the industrial economy into the knowledge-based economy. In more specific terms, the application of information to the economy is best used in the networking of communication, or the so-called Net economy. This Net refers to the computer network of satellites, optic fibers, and telephone lines that connect the whole world. With the click of a mouse, information from the other end of the globe will be transported to your computer screen at the extremely fast speed of seven-and-a-half times around the earth per second. Generally, there are two aspects of the Net. One is the networking between businesses and their customers. The other is the networking between individual businesses, or the regional and even global networking between industrial production and scientific research. Internet shopping belongs to the first aspect.

From a long-term perspective, Internet shopping is but a low-level aspect of the Net, and it is not very likely to become the most important trend. After all, most commodities are unsuitable for Internet shopping. Besides, if everyone shops on the Net, what will happen to the hundreds and thousands of shopping malls? Therefore, the second aspect of the Net will be more important. Its significance goes beyond that of connecting businesses. There have been reports of immediate consultation of doctors from all over the world on the Internet. These are early examples of high-level networking.

It is estimated that the new interaction between computers and Net technology will have significant influence on the industry of the future. The huge power of electronic commerce (e-commerce) will change the face of trade dramatically. Sporting goods company Puma was on the verge of bankruptcy back in 1992. From 1993, Puma began to scatter its production, logistics and marketing divisions to 80 Net enterprises worldwide, and the results were spectacular. Puma was transformed from a common company into a magnificent one. The reason for this transformation is that intra and inter-business electronic links greatly increase the efficiency of production, planning, the collecting of information and data exchange. As the business is rapidly being rationalized, production figures go up while costs come down.

The development of e-commerce may well bring the world into a brand new era of "electronic currency". With the emergence of an electronic currency, everyone of us would be affected. At the moment, developed areas in Europe, the United States and Asia have already started studying the possibility of an electronic currency. Electronic currency is not only about currency. It refers to an entire finance system on the Net. It includes a virtual numeric currency, an electronic system of withdrawals, transfers and loans, and Smartcards (electronic purses) of all shapes and sizes. The appearance of an electronic currency system implies the emergence of "virtual banks" and "virtual enterprises". Actually, the original beginnings of a virtual bank appeared in the US in 1995 as the Security First Network Bank, the world's first Internet bank. Although it is a small and insignificant bank, it represents the trend of the future. In time to come, we may even have to abandon the familiar paper currency.

As the Net pushes the economy ahead rapidly, the economy is also bringing the Net market forward, resulting in the Internet itself becoming the world's largest emerging market. Of course, this is just the beginning. Although there are many companies, which made huge profits investing in the Internet market, they tend to be small companies, like Yahoo (at that time).

To date, most companies are making losses. The Net and e-commerce will foster a large number of free-lancers, and this will affect social structure in a big way. The competition for technological superiority in the era of the knowledge-based economy will also be more intense. This will definitely promote greater (even global) and more efficient cooperation to maintain competitiveness. The highly efficient research and development work will be conducted worldwide. The Net is best suited for small and medium enterprises to band together and break the monopolies of the "giants".

NEW WORDS

commodity /kəˈmɔdəti/ n.   something bought or sold   商品，货物

mall /mɔːl/ n.   a large building with a lot of shops, restaurants and so on   大型购物中心

consultation /kɔnsəlˈteiʃən/ n.   the process of getting advice from experts   请教，咨询，磋商；[医]会诊

perspective /pəˈspektiv/ n.   a way of thinking about something; viewpoint, view   观点，想法

scatter /ˈskætə/ v.   spread; throw over a wide area in an irregular way   分散，传播；漫射，扩散

logistics /ləˈdʒistiks/ n.   study of or department dealing with supplying, equipping and so on   后勤学，后勤

rationalize /ˈræʃənəlaiz/ vt.   make reasonable   使合理

virtual /ˈvəːtʃuəl/ a.   made or done on the Internet or computer rather than in the real world   虚拟的；实质的；[物]有效的，事实上的

withdrawal /wiðˈdrɔːəl/ n.   the act or process of withdrawing or taking away from   提款

original /əˈridʒənəl/ a.   of or belonging to the first   初步的，根本的；未发展的

emergence /iˈməːdʒəns/ n.   appearance   出现

superiority /sjuːpiəriˈɔrəti/ n.   high quality or excellence   优势，优越性

abandon /əˈbændən/ v.   desert, give up   放弃，抛弃

free-lancer /friː-laːnsə/ n.   a writer or artist whose service is not sold to a particular person   自由职业者，自由投稿人，自由作家

intense /inˈtens/ a.   having great force   激烈的

maintain/meinˈtein/*vt.*　　　　keep in existence　保持,维持
foster/ˈfɔstə/*vt.*　　　　　　train, cultivate　培养
efficient/iˈfiʃənt/*a.*　　　　　effective　有效的
medium/ˈmiːdiəm/*a.*　　　　intermediate degree or condition　中型的
enterprise/ˈentəpraiz/*n.*　　a company, organization or business　企业
monopoly/məˈnɔːpəli/*n.*　　having complete control of　垄断,垄断者

PHRASES

in more specific terms: to be more exact　具体地说
from a long-term perspective: in a long run　从长远来看
after all: all in all　毕竟,终究
on the verge of: on the brink of; almost　濒于,接近于
push ahead: push forward　推动,推进
bring forward: promote; propose　促进,提出
to date: up to now　到目前为止,迄今
make losses: lose money　赔钱

NOTES

Puma: the company manufacturing sports goods　彪马体育用品公司
Smartcard: a kind of credit card　智能卡,灵通卡
Yahoo: the address of an Internet　雅虎网站

EXERCISES

I. Reading Comprehension:

Choose the best answer to each question.

1. Internet shopping belongs to _____.
   A. the networking between individual businesses
   B. the regional and global networking between industrial production and scientific research
   C. the networking between businesses and their customers
   D. the networking between big enterprises and small ones

2. _____ is the more important aspect as to the Net economy.

   A. Internet shopping

   B. Shopping malls

   C. Connecting business

   D. Simultaneous consultation on the Internet

3. Electronic currency does not include _____.

   A. a virtual numeric currency

   B. electronic purses

   C. an electronic system of withdrawals, transfers and loans

   D. paper currency transfer on the Internet

4. The world's first Internet bank _____.

   A. is a small and insignificant one

   B. appeared in the developed areas in Europe

   C. is an international bank

   D. is the First Network Bank

5. According to the author's opinion, most companies which invest in the Internet market _____.

   A. are giant companies.

   B. are making losses

   C. have made huge profits

   D. have broken the monopolies

II. **Getting Information**:

Answer the following questions in English.

1. What does the Net refer to?

2. What is the reason for Puma's transformation?

3. What does electronic currency mean?

4. What does the appearance of an electronic currency system imply?

5. How can small and medium enterprises break the monopolies of the "giants"?

Unit 2

III. *Vocabulary and Structure*:

A. Choose the correct word/phrase to fill into each sentence, using the proper form.

| emergence | perspective | medium | intense | superiority |
| promote | on the verge of | to date | foster | trend |

1. Frequent cultural exchange will certainly help _____ friendly relations between our two universities.
2. The competition among these companies at the printing market has become very _____ in this city.
3. _____, we have not received any replies from them.
4. In this competitive world, it is better for any firm to gain technology _____.
5. The organization works to _____ friendship between nations.
6. It is reported that the Far East area is now _____ war again.
7. There is an obvious _____ that young people like less formal clothing.
8. We should look at these events which happened two hundred years ago from their historical _____.
9. The outstanding businessman agreed that the last decade was favorable for the _____ of new and promising enterprises in IT field.
10. The witness proved that the killer of the student was a man of _____ height.

B. Find the proper forms of the following words according to the given word class.

1. significance   (*a.*) _____
2. connect   (*n.*) _____
3. transform   (*n.*) _____
4. withdrawal   (*v.*) _____
5. rationalize   (*a.*) _____
6. efficiency   (*a.*) _____
7. superior   (*n.*) _____
8. emerge   (*n.*) _____
9. promotion   (*vt.*) _____
10. cooperative   (*n.*) _____

C. Complete the following sentences with the missing prepositions or adverbs.

1. It is estimated that the new interaction between computers and Net technology will have significant influence _____ the industry of the future.
2. In more specific terms, the application of information _____ the economy is best used in the networking of communication.
3. This Net refers _____ the computer network of satellites, optic fibers, and telephone lines that connect the whole world.
4. According to the author's opinion, Internet shopping belongs _____ the first aspect.
5. Some people argued that most commodities were unsuitable _____ Internet shopping.
6. As a result, Puma was transformed _____ a Common company into a magnificent one.
7. The development of e-commerce may well bring the world _____ a brand new era of "electronic currency".
8. _____ the moment, developed areas in Europe, the United States and Asia have already started studying the possibility of an electronic currency.
9. As the Net pushes the economy _____ rapidly, the economy is also bringing the Net market forward.
10. Net is best suited for small and medium enterprises to band _____ and break the monopolies of the "giants".

IV. *Translation*:

A. Translate the following into Chinese.

1. With the click of a mouse, information from the other end of the globe will be transported to your computer screen at the extremely fast speed of seven-and-a-half times around the earth per second.

2. Besides, if everyone shops on the Net, what will happen to the hundreds and thousands of shopping malls?

3. The huge power of electronic commerce (e-commerce) will change the face of trade dramatically.

4. The development of e-commerce may well bring the world into a brand new era of "electronic currency".

5. As the Net pushes the economy ahead rapidly, the economy is also bringing the Net market forward, resulting in the Internet itself becoming the world's largest emerging market.
_____

B. Translate the following into English.
1. 今晚她很可能给我打电话。(likely)
_____

2. 我看不懂这篇文章。(beyond)
_____

3. 新刷的一层油漆可使房间焕然一新。(transform)
_____

4. 做事不先考虑总会导致失败。(result in)
_____

5. 他估计那项工作需要三个月。(estimate)
_____

6. 我们相信这个协议将会积极地促进两国之间的贸易。(promote)
_____

7. 新机场必将推动这个地区的旅游业。(push ahead)
_____

8. 网络经济将对人们的生活产生重要的影响。(have significant influence on)
_____

9. 在昨天的会议上,他提出了一个新的经济发展计划。(bring forward)
_____

10. 到目前为止,他们还没有找到遇难的渔船。(to date, wrecked)
_____

V. *Writing Task*:
Write about Internet in some 120 words. Try to cover the following points.
1. How do you like Internet surfing?
2. What do you think is the future development of Internet?
3. How does Internet change your life?

VI. *Oral Practice*:
Form a pair, and then talk about the present situation of Net economy in our country.

Present your opinions to each other.

Part B Grammar

语态（Voice）

英语中的语态分为主动态和被动态。在这里将扼要地介绍一下被动语态。被动语态常表示动作的承受者，对动作的执行者无需指明。被动语态的构成是 be + 过去分词；其被动形式主要有：

- A table is made.（一般现在时的被动语态）
- A table has been made.（完成时的被动语态）
- A table will be made.（将来时的被动语态）
- A table is being made.（现在进行时的被动语态）
- A table was made.（过去时的被动语态）
- A table will have been made.（将来完成时的被动语态）
- A table would be made.（过去将来时的被动语态）
- A table was being made.（过去进行时的被动语态）

除了上面的几种被动语态的形式外，还有一些特殊的被动结构。如：

- This instrument must be handled with great care.（带情态动词的被动结构）
- The program has to be changed as soon as possible.（带不定式的被动结构）
- The sick were looked after in the hospital.（动词短语的被动结构）
- He was asked several questions in English.（带双宾语的被动结构）

练 习

1. 将下面的主动态句子变成被动态。

    (1) Many people speak English.

    (2) He is watching TV now in the room.

    (3) The criminal murdered the lady.

    (4) The teacher will punish Henry for coming late.

(5) Susan has eaten three apples.
(6) Citizens should obey the law.
(7) Where did the farmer first see the wolf?
(8) The watchman must have heard the noise.
(9) Parents ought to teach children good behavior.
(10) We shall make use of every minute and second.
(11) I never heard Nabey speak Japanese.
(12) Who will look after the children?
(13) We are to put off the sports meet.
(14) Mary realized they were making fun of her.
(15) The customs officer requested us to show our passports.

2. 选择适当的被动语态填空。

(1) That man _____ to tell a lie.
    A. was never known   B. has never known
    C. will never know   D. is never known

(2) The children _____ many times not to go near the street.
    A. have told   B. told
    C. have been told   D. were being told

(3) The new type of computer is going to _____ the month after next.
    A. turn out   B. be turned out
    C. will be turn out   D. will turn out

(4) After the synthetic _____, engineers had a better choice for materials for construction.
    A. had been developed   B. had developed
    C. to be developed   D. being developed

(5) After being tested in many ways, this newly-designed machine will _____ in the near future.
    A. be taken action   B. come to use
    C. be put into use   D. take its place

(6) His parents died when he was young, so he _____ by his grandma.
    A. was bred   B. was fed
    C. was brought up   D. was grown up

(7) Lead _____ as a material for sculpture since the time of the early Greeks.

A. being used　　B. has used　　C. is to use　　D. has been used

(8) We heard that Mary _____ a raise by her employer.

A. gave　　B. had been given　　C. will give　　D. has given

(9) He ordered the work _____.

A. started at once

B. to be started at once

C. to start at once

D. at once to start

(10) He was _____ to be clever but dishonest.

A. thought as　　B. thinking　　C. thought　　D. to think

Part C Supplementary Reading

　　以下是两则英文广告。在英语中,广告是一种常见的文体,也是日常生活中经常遇见的文字材料。广告有多种类型,如招聘广告、产品广告、旅游广告、租赁广告等。其主要特点是:1)文体比较简练,文字通俗易懂;2)经常使用一些不完整的句型,但是突出关键词,使其非常醒目。

　　了解广告英语具有一定的实用意义。在我们的生活环境中,会见到不同类型的以英语撰写的广告。如果具有这方面的阅读能力,我们可以直接理解广告的意义。

Advertisements

Passage 1

BORED? LONELY? OUT OF CONDITION? WHY NOT TRY THE CAMDEN SPORTS CENTER	
TENNIS	**SKIING**
Indoor and outdoor courts.	Smooth lanes.
Coaching from beginners to Advanced, every day not Evenings.	Instructors at weekends and Fridays. Daytime practice.
Children only—Sat. mornings.	8 years upwards.

续表

SWIMMING 2 pools, 1 heated. Olympic length. Tuition available. Women: Tuesday and Thursday. Men: Monday, Wednesday and Friday. Children: Saturday. Family day: Sunday.	**GOLF** 9-hole practice course. Professional coaching. Lessons must be booked in advance in daytime. Evening practice. Minimum age—9 years.

GYMNASTICS

Maximum age 18 years.

Children aged 5-10.

Mondays and Wednesdays 4:00-6:00 p.m.

10-18 years olds Friday evenings.

Bar on Sunday mornings.

AND MUCH MORE:
TABLE TENNIS, SNOOKER, DARTS, CHESS (EVERY DAY AND EVENING),
CAFE (ALL DAY), BAR (LUNCHTIME AND EVENINGS),
CRECHE (WEEKDAYS AND WEEKENDS, NOT EVENINGS).
CENTER OPEN 10:00 a.m.-10:00 p.m. DAILY.
INTERESTED? MORE DETAILS INSIDE.

Passage 2

A	B
Quiet student offered room in private house. Share bath and kitchen. $ 50 weekly excluding gas/electricity.	Professional couple, 3 children, 2, 4 and 6, offer single room, rent-free, to student willing to baby-sit 3 evenings weekly, occasional weekends. Live as family.

续表

C	D
Double room suitable 2 students sharing. Cooking facilities, share bathroom. Non-smokers only. $70 each weekly, excluding gas/electricity.	Teacher going on 3-month study course abroad willing to let comfortably furnished flat in prestige block to responsible students. 2 double bedrooms, 1 single. Use of garden. Rent $70 each, weekly, inclusive. No late parties.

INTERESTED? CONTACT: Joan Benson, Student accommodation officer. Room 341 Moff Building, Fri. 10 a.m.–5 p.m.

NEW WORDS

tennis /'tenis/ n.　　a game played by striking a ball back and forth with rackets over a net　网球

skiing /'ski:iŋ/ n.　　act or sport of one who skis　滑雪

court /kɔ:t/ n.　　a level space laid out for tennis　网球场

pool /pu:l/ n.　　a swimming pool　游泳池

book /buk/ vt.　　preserve　预定

minimum /'minimǝm/ a.　　least quantity, amount, or degree　最小的

gymnastics /dʒim'næstiks/ n.　　art or practice of physical exercises　体操

maximum /'mæksimǝm/ a.　　greatest quantity, amount, or degree　最大的

snooker /'snukǝ/ n.　　game played with a stick hitting balls into holes at the table　一种台球

dart /da:t/ n.　　thin or pointed thing to be thrown or shot　飞镖

tuition /tju:'iʃǝn/ n.　　instruction; charge or payment for formal instruction　指导;学费

facility /fǝ'siliti/ n.　　equipment provided for particular purpose　设备

prestige /pre'sti:ʒ/ n.　　having high reputation or importance　有声望

block /blɔk/ n.　　urban area　街区

inclusive /in'klu:siv/ a.　　including　包括的

PHRASES

in advance：before hand　提前,预先
rent-free：without rent　不付房租
baby-sit：look after a baby　照看小孩

NOTES

1 **pool heated**：一个游泳池内的水是加温的
Bar work on Sunday mornings：酒吧周日上午开门
Instructors at weekends and Fridays：周五和周末有教练指导

EXERCISES

I. *Reading Comprehension*：

1. The first passage is probably taken from _____.
   A. a local government document
   B. a page in a local newspaper
   C. an advertisement in a car magazine
   D. a poster in a classroom

2. In the first passage which sport would be most suitable for a young married woman with a baby? She doesn't want anything too tough.
   A. Daytime tennis.
   B. Tuesday evening swimming.
   C. An afternoon golf session.
   D. Skiing at the weekend.

3. In the first passage which day and time would be the best for a family with two children aged 6 and 8, who all want tuition (指导)?
   A. Sunday afternoon.
   B. Saturday morning.
   C. Friday evening.
   D. All day Saturday.

4. In the first passage to obtain coaching in golf, you must _____.
   A. not be over nine
   B. only practice in the daytime
   C. make a prior booking
   D. book nine lessons

5. From the information given in the first passage, which sport seems the most suitable for young children of pre-school age?

A. Golf.　　　B. Swimming.　　　C. Gymnastics.　　　D. Skiing.

6. In the second passage, the information may come from _____.
   A. an advertisement in a formal newspaper
   B. a college notice board
   C. a leaflet from a travel agency
   D. a notice in the window of an estate agent

7. In the second passage, the single room offered in A would be suitable for a student _____.
   A. in need of relaxation
   B. doing intensive study
   C. anxious to make new friends
   D. wanting self-contained accommodation

8. A student accepting the offer in B _____.
   A. must have had some experience of child care
   B. would have no free time at all
   C. must be a member of this large family
   D. would be able to live everyday cheaply

9. For two students D would be more economical than C because _____.
   A. they would share a room
   B. the basic expenses are cheaper
   C. there are no extras except for food
   D. there is free use of the garden

10. The flat offered in D _____.
    A. is expensively furnished
    B. is on the first floor
    C. can only accommodate four people
    D. only available for a short period

II. *Vocabulary and Structure*:

Choose the correct word/phrase to fill into each sentence, using the proper form.

| include | details | furnished | maximum | in advance |
| book | prestige | advanced | responsible | exclude |

Unit 2

1. After careful discussion doctors _____ the food poisoning as the cause of the illness in this area.
2. The breakfast and dinner are _____ in the fee you have paid for the accommodation.
3. He is the author of great _____ for the romantic fiction.
4. The _____ technology in machine manufacturing will be adopted to this plant.
5. This kind of plane can fly at a(n) _____ altitude of 25,000 meters.
6. He said that all the seats in the theater for this play had been _____.
7. The rent for the _____ apartment is usually $150 per week in this region.
8. If you want to terminate the agreement on your own, you must let him know at least two weeks _____.
9. According to the law in this country, parents are _____ for the welfare of their children.
10. The likeness between the two models of the cars is just perfect in every _____.

UNIT 3

Part A   Text (Preserving Our Planet)
Part B   Grammar (比较级)
Part C   Supplementary Reading
         (Art for Sale)

Part A   Text

Warm-up Questions:

1. *Do you know how much damage human activity is doing to the environment?*
2. *What kinds of environmental problems have appeared on our planet in recent years?*
3. *Have you got some ideas about how to preserve our planet?*

Preserving Our Planet

Despite decades of scientific research, no one yet knows how much damage human activity is doing to the environment. Humans are thought to be responsible for a large number of environmental problems, ranging from global warming to ozone depletion. What is not in doubt, however, is the devastating effect humans are having on the animal and plant life of the planet.

Currently, about 50,000 species become extinct every year. "If this carries on, the impact on all living creatures is likely to be profound," says Dr Nick Middleton, a geographer at Oxford University. "All species depend in some way on each other to survive. And the danger is that, if you remove one species from this very complex web of interrelationships, you have very little idea about the knock-on effects on the ecosystem. So, if you lose a key species, you might cause a whole flood of other extinctions."

Complicating matters is the fact that there are no obvious solutions to the problem. Unlike global warming and ozone depletion—which, if the political will was there, could be reduced by cutting gas emissions—preserving bio-diversity remains an intractable problem.

The latest idea is "sustainable management". This means humans should be able to use any species of animal or plant for their benefit, provided enough individuals of that species are left alive to ensure its continued existence.

Sustainable management is seen as a practical and economical way of protecting species from extinction. Instead of depending on largely ineffective laws against illegal hunting, it gives local people a good economic reason to preserve plants and animals. In Zimbabwe, for instance, there is a sustainable management project to protect elephants. Foreign tourists pay large sums of money to kill these animals for sport. This money is then given to the inhabitants of the area where the hunting takes place. In theory, locals will be encouraged to protect elephants, instead of hunting them illegally—or allowing others to do so—because of the economic benefit involved.

This sounds like a sensible strategy, but it remains to be seen whether it will work. With corruption popular in many developing countries, some observers are suspicious that the money will actually reach the people it is intended for. Others wonder how effective the locals will be at stopping illegal hunters.

There are also questions about whether sustainable management is practical when it comes to protecting areas of great bio-diversity such as the world's tropical forests. In theory, the principle should be the same as with elephants—allow logging companies to cut down a certain number of trees, but not so many as to completely destroy the forest.

Sustainable management of forests requires controls on the number of trees which are cut down, as well as investment in replacing them. Because almost all tropical forests are located in countries which desperately need income from logging, there are few regulations and incentives to do this. In fact, for loggers, the most sensible economic approach is to cut down as many trees as quickly as possible.

One reason is the stable price of most commercial tree species in tropical forests. Typically, they rise in value annually by, at most, four to five per cent. Contrast this with interest rates in most developing countries, where investors can typically expect returns of 15 per cent or more, and sometimes zero return. Clearly, it makes no economic sense to delay harvests.

One solution might be to verify wood which comes from sustainably managed forests. In theory, consumers would buy only this wood and so force logging companies to go "green" or go out of business. Unfortunately, unrestricted logging is so much more profitable that wood from managed forests would cost up to five times more—an increase that consumers, no matter how "green", are unlikely to pay.

For these reasons, sustainable management of tropical forests is unlikely to become widespread in the near future. This is disheartening news. It's estimated that these forests contain anything from 50 to 90 per cent of all animal and plant species on Earth. In one study of a five-square-kilometre area of rain forest in Peru, for instance, scientists counted 1,300 species of butterfly and 600 species of bird. In the entire continental United States, only 400 species of butterfly and 700 species of bird have been recorded.

Scientist Professor Norman Myers sees the situation as a tremendous "experiment we're conducting with our planet". "We don't know what the outcome will be. If we make a mess of it, we can't move to another planet... It's a case of one planet, one experiment."

NEW WORDS

preserve /prɪˈzəːv/ *v.*　　keep safe from harm or danger　保护
despite /disˈpait/ *prep.*　　in spite of　尽管
decade /ˈdekeid/ *n.*　　a period of 10 years　十年
ozone /ˈəuzəun/ *n.*　　[U] form of oxygen with a sharp and refreshing smell; (popular use) pure refreshing air as at the seaside　臭氧;(通俗用法)新鲜空气
depletion /dɪˈpliːʃən/ *n.*　　using up, little remaining　用尽
devastating /ˈdevəsteitɪŋ/ *a.*　　ruinous　破坏性极大的,毁灭性的
species /ˈspiːʃiːz/ *n.*　　[*pl.* unchanged 复数不变] division of a genus（生物之）种
extinct /ikˈstiŋkt/ *a.*　　no longer in existence　绝种的;extinction n.
profound /prəˈfaund/ *a.*　　deep; needing much thought or study to understand　深刻的;深奥的
survive /səˈvaiv/ *v.*　　continue to live　继续存在;survival n.
ecosystem /ˌiːkəˈsistəm/ *n.*　　生态系统
emission /iˈmiʃən/ *n.*　　sending out or giving off (of light, heat, smell, etc.) 发出,排放
intractable /inˈtræktəbl/ *a.*　　hard to manage　难处理的,难对付的

Unit 3

sustainable/sə'steinəbl/*a.*	able to keep up or maintain 能维持的;可持续的
effective/i'fektiv/*a.*	able to bring about the result intended 有效的;奏效的; ineffective *a.*
inhabitant/in'hæbitənt/*n.*	person living in a place 居民
involve/in'vɔlv/*vt.*	have as a necessary consequence 牵涉;包含
corruption/kə'rʌpʃən/*n.*	腐败
sensible/'sensəbl/*a.*	reasonable; practical 明智的;切实的
suspicious/sə'spiʃəs/*a.*	inclined not to believe 怀疑的;多疑的
tropical/'trɔpikəl/*a.*	热带的
logging/'lɔgiŋ/*n.*	work of cutting down forest trees for timber 伐木工作;伐木业
investment/in'vestmənt/*n.*	putting money into a business 投资;投资额
desperately/'despəritli/*ad.*	not caring what happens because hope is gone 绝望地;不顾一切地
typically/'tipikəli/*ad.*	usually, generally 通常;一般情况
incentive/in'sentiv/*n.*	sth. that incites or has a tendency to incite to determination or action 刺激;动机;鼓励
annually/'ænjuəli/*ad.*	every year 每年
verify/'verifai/*vt.*	test the truth or accuracy of 鉴定;查对
disheartening/dis'hɑ:tniŋ/*a.*	causing to lose courage or confidence 使沮丧的;使气馁的
tremendous/tri'mendəs/*a.*	very great; enormous 极大的,巨大的
mess/mes/*n.*	state of confusion; or disorder 混乱;杂乱

PHRASES

do damage to: do harm to 使……受到损害
be responsible for: 对……有责任的,对……应负责任的
be in doubt: be uncertain 怀疑的;未确定的
have an impact on: have an effect in 对……产生影响;对……产生效果
depend on: rely on 依赖,依靠
protect… from: keep safe… from 防卫,保护
in theory: good as an idea, but not possible in fact 理论上

as well as: in addition to 除……以外；并；也
at most: not more than 至多
out of business: stop operating as a company 停业的（地）；破产的（地）
up to: as far as 直到
make a mess of: put into disorder or confusion 使……成一团糟；弄乱；破坏

NOTES

global warming: a general increase in world temperatures 全球气温上升
ozone depletion: the reduction of the amount of ozone 臭氧大大减少。臭氧是一种氧气，它停留在大气层外围边缘，从而能防止来自太阳的不良射线到达地球表面。
knock-on effects: a process in which each part is directly influenced by the one before it 连锁作用
bio-diversity：由 biology 和 diversity 两个词构成，意指所有的生物
Zimbabwe：津巴布韦，位于非洲东南部的国家
Peru：秘鲁，位于南美洲西部的国家

EXERCISES

I. *Reading Comprehension*：

Choose the best answer to each question.

1. This passage mainly talks about _____.
    A. the great damage human activity is doing to the environment
    B. the sustainable management that is seen as a practical and economical way of protecting species from extinction
    C. the ways of preserving bio-diversity of our planet
    D. humans who are experimenting with our planet

2. All the following are correct statements about species EXCEPT that _____.
    A. removing one species from the planet might cause 50,000 species extinct every year
    B. removing one species from the planet might cause the extinctions of other species
    C. all species are members of a very complex web of interrelationships
    D. we haven't found satisfactory solutions to the problem of preserving bio-diversity

3. It can be inferred from Para. 3 that _____.

A. the political will might help reduce global warming and ozone depletion
B. preserving bio-diversity is still a great problem
C. preserving bio-diversity is more difficult than dealing with global warming and ozone depletion
D. preserving bio-diversity is less difficult than dealing with global warming and ozone depletion

4. It is true that sustainable management _____.
A. proves to be a sensible way of protecting species from extinction
B. is also practical to protect areas of great bio-diversity
C. remains to be seen whether it will work
D. might become widespread in the near future

5. The tone of this passage is _____.
A. humorous   B. serious   C. optimistic   D. pessimistic

II. *Getting Information*:

Complete the following table, using the information given in the passage.

Environmental problems humans should be responsible for	
Number of extinct species every year	about
Animal protected in Zimbabwe	
The latest idea of protecting species from extinction	
The phenomenon occurring in many developing countries	
The area of great bio-diversity	
The annual rise-rates of most commercial tree species in tropical forests	at most
The general annual interest rates in most developing countries	or more

III. *Vocabulary and Structure*:

A. Choose the definition from Column (B) that best matches each italicized word or phrase in Column (A).

(A)   (B)
1. *sustainable* management   a. reasonable
2. *despite* the terrible flood   b. enormous

3. during the past *decade*   c. continue to live
4. a pure and healthy *environment* d. in spite of
5. *extinction* of a disease   e. doubtful
6. *survive* in the desert   f. able to keep up
7. *effective* measures   g. surroundings
8. *sensible* advice   h. dying out
9. a *suspicious* glance   i. ten years
10. a *tremendous* scientific achievement j. having an effect

B. Find the opposites of the following words in the text.

1. damage _____   2. manageable _____   3. increase _____
4. extinction _____ 5. shallow _____   6. rare _____
7. trusting _____   8. limited _____   9. producer _____
10. safety _____

C. Choose the correct word/phrase to fill into each sentence, using the proper form.

preserve	environment	sensible	in doubt	species
suspicious	in theory	involve	tropical	investment
desperately	out of business	up to	tremendous	

1. The man became rich through making a wise _____.
2. That strange animal belongs to a(n) _____ that I haven't seen before.
3. Bananas grow best in _____ climates.
4. He is getting _____ of my staying away so long.
5. A child's character is greatly influenced by his home _____.
6. If you are _____ about his ability to do the task, don't entrust him with it.
7. The Mexican minority in the southwestern part of the United States numbers _____ three million.
8. There was a(n) _____ explosion, and the building fell down.
9. The company went _____ because it couldn't sell its products.
10. A political dispute _____ six nations may be settled by an agreement between them.
11. All this occurred in an already _____ poor country.
12. Why don't you do something _____ in your spare time?

13. She dieted constantly in order to _____ her youthful figure.
14. The government plans seem good _____ but I doubt if they'll work in practice.

D. Complete the following sentences, using the words given in brackets.
1. A _____ earthquake left thousands homeless. (devastate)
2. Efforts have been made to prevent the _____ of the buffalo. (extinct)
3. His _____ is still uncertain; he has been very badly hurt and may die. (survive)
4. The new interest rate becomes _____ next month. (effect)
5. The rocket _____ long streams of flame and smoke. (emission)

IV. *Translation*:
A. Translate the following into Chinese.
1. So, if you lose a key species, you might cause a whole flood of other extinctions.

2. Instead of depending on largely ineffective laws against illegal hunting, it gives local people a good economic reason to preserve plants and animals.

3. With corruption popular in many developing countries, some observers are suspicious that the money will actually reach the people it is intended for.

4. Sustainable management of forests requires controls on the number of trees which are cut down, as well as investment in replacing them.

5. In theory, consumers would buy only this wood and so force logging companies to go "green" or go out of business.

B. Translate the following into English.
1. 这场特大洪水给长江中下游地区造成了严重的灾害。(do damage to)

2. 这本畅销书对读者产生了深刻的影响。(impact on)

3. 这辆旧自行车,我最多能付你5美元。(at most)

4. 他们的经济利益及政治权利都应当受到保护。(as well as)
   _____

5. 这场突发疾病把我的假期计划搞得一团糟。(make a mess of)
   _____

6. 如果你明智的话,你就再学习一年。(sensible)
   _____

7. 倘若这本书没有其他人想借的话,你可以再续借一个礼拜。(provided)
   _____

8. 报界纷纷指责专题电视节目中使用的粗鄙语言。(a flood of)
   _____

9. 她的任务是把货物整齐地排列在商店橱窗里。(range)
   _____

10. 校长鼓励参加全国数学竞赛的选手们争取取得最好的成绩。(encourage)
    _____

V. *Oral and Writing Tasks*：

A. Work in groups of 3 or 4 to talk about the environmental problems which occurred on our planet in recent years. Try to cover the following points.
   1. 近年来,地球环境遭到严重破坏
   2. 原因及危害
   3. 应采取的措施

B. You are also expected to write on the topic you have talked about. Your composition should be about 120 words.

Part B   Grammar

比较级 (Comparative Degree)

英语中的形容词和副词常常用于比较结构。在表达这一结构时要有特别的形式,叫做"比较级"和"最高级"。原来的形式称为原级。比较级和最高级的构成方式:1) 在单音节和少数双音节的词尾加-er 和-est;2）在多数多音节词的前面加 more 和 most;3）一些少数词以特殊的方式构成比较级和最高级，如 good—better—best；little—less—least；bad—worse—worst 等。常见的比较级和最高级的句型结构如下：

- He is <u>as tall as</u> his brother.
- He is <u>not as tall as</u> his brother.
- This report is <u>as important as</u> that one.
- This report is <u>the most important of</u> the three.
- This table is <u>heavier than</u> that one.
- It takes <u>less</u> time to get there by bus <u>than</u> by train.
- He works <u>the hardest</u> in the class.
- He <u>doesn't</u> study <u>so hard as</u> his sister.

除了以上构成形式以外，表达方式也需给予重视。

1. 比较级中，如果是两个相同的事物或人进行比较，形容词前需加 the，如：
   - He is <u>the cleverer</u> of the two.
   - This book is <u>the more interesting of</u> the two.

2. 表示"越……越……"的比较结构中要用 the，如：
   - <u>The more</u> one earns, <u>the more</u> one has to pay income tax.
   - <u>The faster</u> you can finish the work, <u>the earlier</u> you can go home.

3. 少数形容词的比较级不用连词 than，如：
   - His experience <u>is superior</u> to mine.
   - His position <u>is inferior</u> to his wife's.

4. 比较级前有一个表示程度的状语，如：
   - My sister is <u>two years</u> older than I.
   - Grain output this year is <u>10 percent</u> higher than that of the last year.

练 习

1. 选择适当的比较级形式填空。

   (1) Peter's record was _____ on the team.
       A. not so good as all the players
       B. not good as the players
       C. not so good as any other player's
       D. so good as not that of any player's

(2) The team is good, but not as good as _____.
   A. ours   B. us   C. we   D. ourselves

(3) This tool is _____ that one.
   A. as useful almost as   B. as almost useful as
   C. almost as useful as   D. almost as useful than

(4) He will not be _____ to vote in this year's election.
   A. old enough   B. as old enough
   C. enough old   D. enough old as

(5) Bob's work proved _____ than that of others.
   A. not much better   B. not more better
   C. no more as good   D. not much as good

(6) They are _____ my other neighbors.
   A. as friendly   B. friendly than
   C. friendlier as   D. more friendly than

(7) I think he is _____ than I.
   A. elder three years   B. old three years
   C. three years elder   D. three years older

(8) Can we do our work better with _____ money and _____ people?
   A. lesser…few   B. less…fewer
   C. little…less   D. few…less

(9) She is _____ beautiful of the two sisters.
   A. younger and more   B. more young and more
   C. youngest and most   D. the younger and more

(10) He can run _____ I do.
   A. as faster than   B. faster as
   C. as fast as   D. so fast that

(11) _____, the worse I seem to feel.
   A. When I take more medicine   B. The more medicine I take
   C. Taking more of the medicine   D. More medicine taken

(12) Why is there _____ traffic on the streets in February than in May?
   A. less   B. fewer   C. few   D. little

(13) Prices for cars in the US can run _____ $20,800.
   A. as high as   B. so high as
   C. as high to   D. so high to

(14) This room is _____ that one.
   A. three times big than   B. three times as big as
   C. three times bigger   D. bigger three times than
(15) This year, the grain production was three times _____ last year.
   A. as much as   B. as many as
   C. as more   D. as much

2. 将下面的短句译成英语。
   (1) 这座城市的人口要比那座城市的人口多。
   (2) 你读的英语文章越多,就能够读得越快。
   (3) 在这三条铁路中,这条是最长的。
   (4) 这个工厂比那座工厂大二倍。
   (5) 这项工作与去年我们完成的那项工作一样难。
   (6) 他在研究中取得的成就比我们的多。
   (7) 这两个公园中,这个更整洁,更干净。
   (8) 他讲英语是我们班上讲得最好的。
   (9) 这座工厂的产量比1990年增长了百分之十。
   (10) 我们完成这项工作需要的人比他们少。

Part C Supplementary Reading

Art for Sale

London is the centre of the international art market and Sotheby's, which has its headquarters there, is the world's biggest and oldest seller of art and antiques. If you were lucky enough to own a priceless "Old Master", or a valuable antique, and you wanted to sell it, you would probably put it up for auction at Sotheby's.

Sotheby's auctions are attended by some of the world's richest people, who spend millions of pounds on art and antiques each year. Consequently, the company is very proud of its status and its 250-year-old reputation. But, earlier this year, that reputation came under threat, when a journalist accused Sotheby's staff of bringing art treasures to London illegally. If these allegations are true, they will severely damage London's credibility as a centre of the world's art trade.

As if that weren't bad enough, London's art dealers and auction houses are facing an even bigger threat from European Union regulations. If passed in Britain, the EU laws would make London a much less attractive place to purchase art treasures. Buyers and sellers would then look elsewhere for the best prices and could stop coming to London altogether.

The problems began earlier last year, when a journalist from Britain's Times newspaper, Peter Watson, claimed that senior staff at Sotheby's were at the centre of a widespread smuggling operation. He made his allegations in a book and television programme, which used hidden cameras to film Sotheby's staff. Watson says the programme, which was shown last February, proves that art treasures were being illegally exported to London on a regular basis, and the international art trade needs to be cleaned up.

In the programme, a woman is filmed going to Sotheby's Milan office in Italy with a valuable painting. She pretends she wants to sell it and a member of staff offers to smuggle the painting out of Italy and put it up for auction at Sotheby's in London. According to Italian law, special permission is needed to export any work of art which is more than 50 years old and this permission can be very difficult to get.

"Sotheby's organized the whole thing," says Watson. "They gave us instructions to set up a false address in London, which we did, and then the painting was delivered. We took it into Sotheby's. It came up for auction last summer and we bought it back and returned it to Italy, where it belonged."

After the programme was broadcast, Sotheby's was quick to start its own internal inquiry and it admitted that rules had been broken. But the company rejected Watson's charge that smuggling is widespread.

Sotheby's Managing Director in Europe, George Bailey, said that the incident was an "isolated case". Later, once the internal inquiry was complete, a member of staff who was identified in the programme resigned. Bailey also questioned the reliability and honesty of the investigators, and he accused Peter Watson of inducing staff to break the company's rules.

It is widely acknowledged that the art world often turns a blind eye to the kind of practices highlighted by Peter Watson, but the bad publicity was still very damaging for Sotheby's. However, the reaction from other dealers and auction houses in London was muted—probably because they are facing a much bigger threat from EU regulations.

As far as the EU is concerned, the art market is like any other kind of business, and it wants all member countries to operate according to the same laws. On the positive side, this would put an end to smuggling within the EU because dealers and buyers would be free to move art treasures from country to country. However, the regulations would also make London a less attractive place to buy and sell art.

The EU is putting pressure on the British government to adopt three crucial regulations. One is the imposition of a tax on the resale of new works of art. This would affect contemporary art, which is very profitable—£ 300 million worth of 20th-century paintings were sold in London last year.

Dealers are also concerned that Britain will have to put the same rate of VAT on imported art as other EU countries. This would mean that VAT on imports would be doubled to five per cent.

Finally, the British government is being urged to sign an EU treaty which would make it easier for owners to claim back stolen art, after it had been sold abroad. This would probably create big delays and complications, potentially threatening London's advantage over other art centres.

London's art dealers are convinced that, if these measures are implemented, the art market will move to places like New York and Switzerland, and the British economy will lose out. But it is going to be very difficult for the British government to try and block the EU regulations while Britain's most famous auction house is tainted by scandal.

NEW WORDS

headquarters /ˌhedˈkwɔːtəz/ n. pl.　place from which operations are controlled　总部；司令部

antique /ænˈtiːk/ n.　material thing, relic, esp. a work of art, of old times　古物,古董

auction /ˈɔːkʃən/ n.　public sale at which goods are sold to the persons making the highest bids (or offers)　拍卖

allegation /ˌæliˈgeiʃən/ n.　statement, esp. one made without proof　宣称,声称(尤指无证据的)

credibility /ˌkrediˈbiliti/ n.　the state or quality of being trusted　信誉

journalist /ˈdʒəːnəlist/ n.　a person engaged in journalism, esp. newspaper work　从事新闻业者,新闻记者

widespread /ˈwaidspred/ a.　found, or distributed, over a large area　广泛的,普及的

smuggling/'smʌglɪŋ/*n.*   getting (goods) secretly and illegally   走私

broadcast/'brɔːdkɑːst/*v.*   send out in all directions   广播；播送

reliability/rɪˌlaɪə'bɪlɪti/*n.*   可靠性

induce/ɪn'djuːs/*vt.*   persuade or influence; lead or cause (sb. to do sth.)   劝诱；促使

acknowledge/ək'nɔlɪdʒ/*vt.*   agree or admit the truth of   承认

highlight/'haɪlaɪt/*v.*   give prominence to   使显著

mute/mjuːt/*vt.*   to make a sound quiet, to reduce the intensity of   减弱(消除)……声音；缓解

positive/'pɔzətɪv/*a.*   practical and constructive; that definitely helps   实际而有建设性的；有益的

crucial/'kruːʃəl/*a.*   decisive; critical   决定性的；关系重大的

imposition/ˌɪmpə'zɪʃən/*n.*   laying or placing (a tax, duty, etc. on)   加强（课税）

contemporary/kən'tempərəri/*a.*   of the present time   目前流行的

claim/kleɪm/*n.*   a demand for something due or believed to be due   要求，请求

complication/ˌkɔmplɪ'keɪʃən/*n.*   state of being complex, confused or difficult   复杂；混乱；困难

implement/'ɪmplɪmənt/*vt.*   carry out; fulfill   实现；履行

taint/teɪnt/*v.*   make or become infected   变污；感染

scandal/'skændl/*n.*   public disgrace, revelation of wrongdoing   丑闻；丑行

PHRASES

put up: offer for sale   提供以供出售

accuse...of: say that (sb.) has done wrong   控告

on a... basis: （常作行为方式状语用）on a daily/weekly/regular basis = every day/every week/regularly; on the basis of... = because of a particular fact or situation

clean up: put in order   整理

turn a blind eye to: pretend not to see   视若无睹，假装看不见

as far as... be concerned: 就……而言

put an end to: finish; get rid of 结束;消除
lose out: suffer defeat or loss 失败;亏损

NOTES

Sotheby's：索斯比拍卖行,世界著名的艺术品、古玩拍卖行
"Old Master"：指历史上著名画家的作品
VAT：value added tax 增值税

EXERCISES

Reading Comprehension：

A. Decide whether the following statements are true or false. Mark "T" before a true statement and "F" before a false one.

_____ 1. London is the centre of the world's art trade.

_____ 2. The headquarters of Sotheby's is located in London.

_____ 3. London is now a more attractive place for art dealers.

_____ 4. Sotheby's is proud of itself partly because a lot of rich people attend its auctions.

_____ 5. Sotheby's is proud of itself partly because a lot of art treasures are being exported to London and then put up for auction there.

_____ 6. Other dealers and auction houses in London are angry at Sotheby's scandal.

_____ 7. The art world often pretends not to notice the smuggling operation.

_____ 8. George Bailey rejected Watson's charge completely.

_____ 9. The British economy will not be affected even if the art market moves to some other places.

_____ 10. The British government is unwilling to accept the EU regulations.

B. Choose the best answer to each of the following questions.

1. The main idea of this passage is that _____.

   A. Britain's most famous auction house, Sotheby's, is tainted by scandal

   B. EU regulations would make London a less attractive place to buy and sell art

   C. London's art market is facing threat from scandal and tougher regulations

49

D. The British government is urged to adopt some regulations
2. Buyers and sellers would stop coming to London altogether if _____.
   A. it is true that Sotheby's staff help bring art treasures to London illegally
   B. London's credibility is severely damaged as a centre of the world's art trade
   C. smuggling is widespread in London
   D. EU regulations are passed in Britain
3. All the following were Sotheby's reactions towards Peter Watson's allegations EXCEPT that it _____.
   A. was quick to start its own internal inquiry
   B. denied the idea that rules had been broken
   C. rejected Watson's charge that smuggling is widespread
   D. accepted the resignation of one of its staff
4. The positive effect of the EU is that it would _____.
   A. make all member countries to operate according to the same laws
   B. stop smuggling within the member countries
   C. make London a more attractive place to buy and sell art
   D. be easier for owners to claim back stolen art
5. It's UNTRUE that the British government is urged to _____.
   A. impose a tax on the resale of new works of art
   B. impose the same rate of VAT on exported art as other EU countries
   C. sign a treaty to make it easier for owners to claim back stolen art
   D. sign a treaty to create big delays and complications

Part A   Text (A Time for Apologies)
Part B   Grammar (不定式)
Part C   Supplementary Reading
          (Life and Times of Bill Clinton)

Part A Text

Warm-up Questions:

1. *Is it easy for you to apologize for past wrongs? Why or why not?*
2. *Why do heads of state feel the need to apologize, and why now?*
3. *Do world leaders take risks when saying sorry for past wrongs?*

A Time for Apologies

Throughout history, saying sorry is not something political and religious leaders have felt comfortable about. Some see it as a sign of weakness; for others it's an admission that they are liable to make errors—something religious institutions are particularly careful to avoid.

But as political systems have become more sophisticated, the idea that governments or churches are faultless has become increasingly difficult to defend. The response of some people in positions of authority has been to stand up and apologize for past wrongs.

The trend began in earnest in 1995, when the Queen of England admitted that the Maori people of New Zealand had been shamefully treated, when the country was a British colony. Since then, what started as trickle of apologies has turned into something of a flood. Last year alone, apologies were issued by three of the world's most powerful nations. The US President, Bill Clinton, apologized for medical experiments which his government carried out on black A-merican men in the 1930s; the British Prime Minister, Tony Blair, apologized for Britain's failure to help victims of the Irish potato famine, which killed over a million people last century; and French Catholic Bishops apologized for the role of their predecessors during World War II.

But why do heads of state feel the need to apologize, and why now? One answer has to do with the recent 50th-anniversary of the end of World War II. Three years ago, governments around the world wanted to mark this historic event with some acts. But those countries which had been on the winning side found that simple celebrations of victory were no longer appropriate. Many political leaders, like most of their citizens, belong to post-war generations, who now look on the conflict as more than simply the victory of good over evil. Also, the passing of time has erased much of the propaganda of the period. In its place, recently declassified documents reveal that many of the victors either profited, or turned a blind eye to the sufferings of the war.

In the event, the 50th-anniversary celebrations emphasized the re-creation of harmony and the desire never to repeat the cruelties and suffering of World War II. But amid the general goodwill, the few remaining survivors of cruelties like the Holocaust, and military occupation, called for their personal suffering to be admitted, and for compensation to be paid.

But the renewed investigation of crimes committed during World War II is only one reason for the apology phenomenon. Other governments, notably the US, have also realized that if they want to demand high standards of moral behaviour from other nations, they can only do so if they admit their own past wrongs.

But it's not just a sense of conscience, nor demands from pressure groups, which lies behind these apologies. A well-timed apology can do a lot to promote a head of state's public image—in the 1990s, caring and sympathetic leaders are better vote winners than proud and determined ones.

However, playing the public-relations game with apologies is dangerous, as some politicians have found to their cost. The Swiss government is still trying to put right the public-relations disaster that resulted from their partial apology for Switzerland's dealings with the Nazis in the 1930s and the 1940s.

But, in Britain, Tony Blair has gained a different kind of political advantage through his apology for the Irish potato famine. His statement has helped improve relations between the parties involved in the difficult peace negotiations over Northern Ireland. He is now thought to be considering an official apology for the 1972 killing of Northern Irish Catholics by the British

Army on what has become known as "Bloody sunday".

Before he issues an apology, however, Tony Blair will have to consider the possibility that victim's families might issue claims for compensation. The cost of fulfilling or fighting such claims could outweigh any political advantages. Also, because this event happened relatively recently, relations between the different sides in Northern Ireland could suffer.

These points illustrate some of the risks that leaders take when saying sorry for past wrongs. But, for most leaders, these risks have been purely academic. So academic, in fact, that there is a concern that "sorry" might turn out to be the easiest word after all.

NEW WORDS

apology/əˈpɔlədʒi/ n.	statement of regret 道歉,谢罪
apologize/əˈpɔlədʒaiz/ vi.	make an apology (to sb., for sth., for doing sth.) 道歉
liable/ˈlaiəbl/ a.	likely 易于……的
sophisticated/səˈfistikeitid/ a.	having lost natural simplicity 复杂的;高级的
authority/ɔːˈθɔriti/ n.	power or right to give orders and make others obey 权利;权威;威信
trickle/ˈtrikl/ n.	weak or thin flow 滴;滴水;细流
issue/ˈiʃjuː/ vt.	give or send out 发出,宣布
famine/ˈfæmin/ n.	extreme scarcity (esp. of food) in a region 饥荒
Catholic/ˈkæθəlik/ a.	天主教的
bishop/ˈbiʃəp/ n.	主教
predecessor/ˈpriːdisesə/ n.	former holder of any office or position 前任
anniversary/ˌæniˈvəːsəri/ n.	yearly return of the date of an event; celebration of this 周年纪念日;周年纪念
historic/hisˈtɔrik/ a.	famous in history; associated with past times 历史上著名的;有历史意义的
celebration/ˌseliˈbreiʃən/ n.	sth. done to show that a day or an event is important 庆祝
appropriate/əˈprəupriit/ a.	right or suitable 应当的,合适的
generation/ˌdʒenəˈreiʃən/ n.	all the people about the same age (一)代
erase/iˈreiz/ vt.	rub or scrape out 擦掉,抹掉

propaganda /ˌprɔpəˈgændə/ *n.*　spreading of information, doctrines, ideas, etc.　宣传，传播

declassified /ˌdiːˈklæsifaid/ *a.*　removing from a state of being kept secret　销密的，解密的

suffering /ˈsʌfəriŋ/ *n.*　pain of body or mind　痛苦，苦难；sufferings *n.* (*pl.*) feelings of pain, unhappiness, etc.　痛苦、不幸等之感觉；苦恼

amid /əˈmid/ *prep.*　in or into the middle of　在其间，在其中

compensation /ˌkɔmpenˈseiʃən/ *n.*　something that constitutes an equivalent; payment　补偿；赔偿

renewed /riˈnjuːd/ *a.*　重新进行的

investigation /inˌvestiˈgeiʃən/ *n.*　careful and thorough inquiry　调查，审查

phenomenon /fiˈnɔminən/ *n.*　an observable fact or event　现象

descendant /diˈsendənt/ *n.*　offspring　后代，子孙

conscience /ˈkɔnʃəns/ *n.*　moral sense　良心，天良

sympathetic /ˌsimpəˈθetik/ *a.*　caring; compassionate　有同情心的；同情的

disaster /diˈzɑːstə/ *n.*　great or sudden misfortune; terrible accident　大灾难，灾祸；事故

academic /ˌækəˈdemik/ *a.*　of school, scholastic; scholarly, not practical　学校的，学术上的；学究式的，不切实际的

PHRASES

in earnest: in a determined manner; seriously　郑重地，认真地

turn into: become　变成

carry out: put into practice　实行，执行

have to do with: be connected with　与……有关系

belong to: be a member of　属于

look on... as: regard... as　把……视为

in the event: as it turns out　结果，到头来

find to one's cost: realize sth. is true from one's own very unpleasant experience　通过自己的痛苦经历认识到，亲自体验到

result from: happen as a natural consequence　发生，产生

turn out to be: prove to be 证明为

NOTES

the Maori people of New Zealand：新西兰的土著毛利人

the Irish potato famine：1845—1847 年，爱尔兰因土豆枯萎病而引发大范围饥荒。其间，由于饥馑和移民，爱尔兰的人口减少了 25%。

the Holocaust：大屠杀，指第二次世界大战中希特勒纳粹党对犹太人的残酷迫害和屠杀

EXERCISES

I. *Reading Comprehension*：

Choose the best answer to each of the following questions.

1. This passage mainly talks about that _____.
    A. nowadays, saying sorry is something political and religious leaders feel comfortable about
    B. governments and churches are likely to make errors now
    C. many world leaders have apologized for past wrongs due to some reasons
    D. many world leaders apologized for past wrongs to celebrate the 50th-anniversary of the end of World War II

2. "something" in the last sentence of the first paragraph refers to _____.
    A. saying sorry
    B. a sign of weakness
    C. an admission that they are liable to make errors
    D. that they are liable to make errors

3. Which of the following is NOT mentioned as one of the reasons for which leaders apologize for past wrongs?
    A. The reinvestigation of the crimes committed during World War II.
    B. A sense of conscience and demands from pressure groups.
    C. They want to show their high standards of moral behaviour.
    D. A well-timed apology can help improve their public images.

4. What does the word "academic" mean in the last paragraph?
    A. scholarly
    B. having no real effect

C. important   D. easy to do

5. It can be inferred from the last paragraph that _____.

   A. most leaders say sorry for past wrongs in words only

   B. "sorry" might be the easiest word for leaders to say

   C. leaders seldom say sorry for past wrongs

   D. leaders always say sorry for past wrongs

II. *Getting Information*:

Answer the following questions in English.

1. What makes the political and religious leaders reluctant to make apologies?

_____

2. What triggered the trend of making apologies?

_____

3. Complete the following table, using the information given in the passage.

Who		*Whom*	*Reasons*
Queen of England	apologized to	Maori people of New Zealand	They had been shamefully treated
The US president (Bill Clinton)	apologized to		
The British Prime Minister (Tony Blair)	apologized to		
French Catholic Bishops	apologized for		
Swiss government	apologized for		

4. What did the 50th anniversary celebrations of the end of WWII emphasize?

_____

5. What kind of leaders are more popular in the 90's?

_____

III. *Vocabulary and Structure*:

A. Find in the text the words or expressions which fit the following descriptions:

   1. expression of regret: _____   2. likely: _____

   3. power: _____   4. very serious lack of food: _____

   5. former holder of position: _____ 6. rub out: _____

   7. age group: _____   8. pain: _____

9. payment: _____
10. inquiry: _____
11. an observable event: _____
12. terrible accident: _____

B. From the list, choose the word which is closest in meaning to the italicized word(s) in each sentence, making any necessary changes.

| sympathetic | apologize | sophisticated | academic | issue |
| appropriate | historic | suffering | celebration | conscience |

1. To meet the needs of the war a general call for troops was *given*.
2. Next day was to be the great mass-meeting to *show the importance* of the Russian revolution.
3. John *was saying sorry to* Susan for having kept her waiting.
4. Plain, simple clothes are *suitable* for school wear.
5. I can't work this *complex* new equipment.
6. She refused to talk about her family's *pains and sorrows* during the war.
7. The freedom of speech under a dictatorship is *not very practical*.
8. Jean's got no *moral sense*, she'd steal anything from anybody.
9. She *showed understanding* when I failed my exam.
10. Japan and China signed a *famous* peace and friendship treaty in history.

C. Complete each sentence with one phrase from the given list, making any necessary changes.

| in earnest | turn into | carry out | turn out to be | belong to |
| look on... as | in the event | turn a blind eye to | find to one's cost | result from |

1. His failure _____ not working hard enough.
2. All the buildings had been _____ hospitals.
3. Though it looked like rain this morning, it has _____ a fine day.
4. Sandy and Mary began to discuss old times _____.
5. Over nine-tenths of the inhabitants there _____ the Han nationality.
6. A kind person will _____ trivial faults in others.
7. These children _____ their teachers _____ their friends.
8. The killings were said to have been _____ by members of the People's Temple.
9. I _____ that a broken leg can be very painful.

10. We were afraid he would be nervous on stage, but _____ he performed beautifully.

IV. *Translation*:

A. Translate the following into Chinese.

1. The trend began in earnest in 1995, when the Queen of England admitted that the Maori people of New Zealand had been shamefully treated, when the country was a British colony.

2. Many political leaders, like most of their citizens, belong to post-war generations, who now look on the conflict as more than simply the victory of good over evil.

3. But it's not just a sense of conscience, nor demands from pressure groups, which lies behind these apologies.

4. The Swiss government is still trying to put right the public-relations disaster that resulted from their partial apology for Switzerland's dealings with the Nazis in the 1930s and the 1940s.

5. So academic, in fact, that there is a concern that "sorry" might turn out to be the easiest word after all.

B. Translate the following into English.

1. 对战争带来的灾难视而不见
2. 50周年庆典
3. 向……做出公开道歉
4. 适时的道歉
5. 提升国家首脑的公众形象
6. 解决公共关系危机
7. 为过去的过错道歉
8. 新近解密的文件
9. 承认自己过去的错误
10. 支付战争赔偿费

C. Translate the following into English.

1. 我们要求日本政府对他们在第二次世界大战中对中国人民实行的暴行进行正式道歉。(make an apology for)
2. 后来证实有两名旅客丧生。(turn out)
3. 现在人们把电视机当作必备的生活用品之一。(look on... as)

4. 对人民的疾苦视而不见的政治领袖是不会受到人民的拥护的。（turn a blind eye to）
5. 那位勇敢的年轻人冒着生命危险把这个小孩从湖里救上来。（take risk）

V. *Writing Task*：

You are supposed to be at a very important presentation today. However, you miss it for some reason. Write a formal letter of apology in 120 words to your boss. You should cover the following points：
1. 表示道歉。
2. 解释原因。
3. 保证以后不会发生类似的事情。

VI. *Oral Task*：

Do you think the official apology is helpful in promoting a leader's public image？Work in groups of 3 or 4 to talk about it.

Part B Grammar

不定式（Infinitive）

不定式是英语动词的一种非限定形式，通常前面带有 to。不定式在句子中可用作：主语、宾语、定语、表语、状语。

· To complete this program needs at least two months.（主语）
· She wants to pass the test first.（宾语）
· They have too much homework to do this evening.（定语）
· My hope is to let the computer take over this boring work.（表语）
· They started to run in order to get there before 5.（状语）

除了不定式在句子中的语法作用外，不定式还有以下几点需给予重视。
1. 不定式的时态变化
· We are very glad to have received your letter.（完成时）
· The bridge seems to have been completed.（完成时的被动语态）
· They seem to be working very hard.（进行时态）

2. 不带 to 的不定式
- Let him take three apples.
- I heard him say that he would come.

类似的动词还有 make，see，have，watch，notice，feel 等。

3. 在复合结构中的不定式及不定式短语
- He told us how to write effectively.
- It is easy for her to cook a meal for five people.

第一句中的不定式作为宾语补足语，前面用连接副词 how；第二句中的不定式短语实际上是句子的主语，由 it 表示逻辑上的主语。

4. 带有 too 和 enough 的不定式结构
- He is too young to travel alone.（too 表示"太……而不能……"）
- The book is good enough to be published.（enough 的位置在形容词之后）

练 习

1. 选择适当的不定式填空。

（1）It seems very difficult _____.
　　A. to stop the child to cry　　B. stopping the child to cry
　　C. stop the child crying　　　D. to stop the child crying

（2）We are glad to _____ when you needed our help.
　　A. help　　　　　　　　　　B. having helped you
　　C. have helped　　　　　　　D. have helped you

（3）The teacher _____ their exercises.
　　A. made the students do　　　B. make the students doing
　　C. have made the students do　D. makes the students done

（4）The doctor found it difficult _____ this infection.
　　A. in treating　　　　　　　　B. to treat
　　C. for treating　　　　　　　 D. in treating

（5）He couldn't help but _____ when his toy car fell into the river.
　　A. cry　　B. to cry　　C. crying　　D. will cry

（6）What _____ next will be discussed at today's meeting.
　　A. can you do　　　　　　　　B. will you do
　　C. shall we do　　　　　　　　D. to be done

(7) He sent his son to the doctor _____ an X-ray check.
   A. gives   B. to give
   C. being given   D. to be given

(8) The story was said to _____ on the information from a reliable source.
   A. being based   B. have been based
   C. base   D. be based

(9) Mother warned _____ the electric lamp.
   A. not to touch   B. him not to touch
   C. him not touching   D. him not touch

(10) He finds it difficult _____ himself to the climate here.
   A. to adapt   B. accustomed
   C. get used   D. applying

2. 将下列短句翻译成英文。
（1）完成这项工作至少需要 10 人。
（2）我们的目的是通过英语考试。
（3）她还有许多作业要做，所以她不能同你去舞会。
（4）为了实现这一目标，我们必须努力工作。
（5）我叫他打扫房间。
（6）对他们来说扩大词汇量是非常必要的。
（7）他们自愿到工厂去工作。
（8）他的任务是照看病人。
（9）我们必须现在马上动身，以便在 5 点钟之前到达那里。
（10）我们需要 2 人录入这篇文章。

Part C   Supplementary Reading

Life and Times of Bill Clinton

Between the end of the Second World War and the early sixties, a baby boom occurred in the US, and people born during that period were known as the "baby boomers". Bill Clinton is no doubt a typical representative of that generation. Like the 1992 general elections, the presidential election of 1997 was not merely a skirmish between two political parties but also a generation war between the "baby boomers" and the G. I. generation represented by Bush and Dole. Clinton's triumph signaled a shift of US political power from the older generation to the younger one, and might reflect developments of far reaching significance in today's American politics.

William Jefferson Clinton was born on August 19, 1946, in the mountain city of Hope, Arkansas. In English, "Hope" means "xiwang". No wonder that later on Clinton' supporters often called him "the man from the city of hope".

The family circumstances of Clinton's childhood years were very unfortunate. Clinton's own father died in a traffic accident 3 months before Clinton was born. His stepfather, Roger Clinton, was a habitual drunkard, which caused discord in the family. Such an experience helped Clinton become a man who knew his own mind, had self-restraint and self-control, and was good at competition. Self-reliant, diligent and hard working, Clinton gained a good education. In the fall of 1964, he enrolled in Georgetown University in Washington D. C., and majored in international politics. After graduation, he won the famous Rhodes scholarship and pursued advanced studies for 2 years in England's Oxford University. In 1971 he entered Yale University's law college and obtained a doctorate in law two years later. During his university days, Clinton actively participated in the students' movement against the Vietnam War, avoided army enlistment, and took a trip to Moscow in 1970. These experiences helped him mature early, but left him vulnerable to political controversies later, and branded him as a young liberal.

After leaving Yale, Clinton returned to his hometown in Arkansas where he began his political career. In 1974, when he was not quite 28, he formally campaigned for congress. His vivid and dramatic first attempt greatly threatened his opponents. Though defeated in his campaign, his political talent received confirmation in news and political circles, winning him the title of "child prodigy". In 1976, Clinton won the post of State Attorney General. In 1978, he succeeded in his campaign for the Governorship and at 32 became the youngest governor in the history of the state of Arkansas. In 1980, he lost to the Republicans in his campaign for re-election but two years later he staged a comeback, which won him the nickname of "undefeatable kid". He kept the Governorship right up until January 1993, when he officially became the master of the White House. His first term of office expired in 1997, but he defeated republican Dole and was re-elected, and has served as President up until the present.

In October 1997, when China's President Jiang Zemin visited the US, he and President Clinton reached agreement in the setting up of a constructive, strategic partnership for the 21st century. President Clinton has announced this year that he will move up his visit to China to the end of June in order to give fresh stimulus to the development and improvement of Sino-US relations.

NEW WORDS

boom /buːm/ *n.*	sudden increase 激增;迅速增长
presidential /ˌpreziˈdenʃəl/ *a.*	of a president or his duties 总统的
skirmish /ˈskəːmiʃ/ *n.*	a minor battle; a short, sharp argument 小战斗;短期的尖锐争论
significance /sigˈnifikəns/ *n.*	[U] meaning; importance 意义;重要
stepfather /ˈstepˌfɑːðə/ *n.*	one's mother's later husband 继父
habitual /həˈbitjuəl/ *a.*	having a regular habit 有习惯的
drunkard /ˈdrʌŋkəd/ *n.*	man who is drunk, or who often gets drunk 醉汉,酒徒
discord /ˈdiskɔːd/ *n.*	disagreement, quarrelling 不一致;争吵
scholarship /ˈskɔləʃip/ *n.*	payment of money to a scholar so that he may continue his studies 奖学金
pursue /pəˈsjuː/ *vt.*	have as an aim or purpose 追求
doctorate /ˈdɔktərit/ *n.*	the highest degree given by a university 博士学位
enlistment /inˈlistmənt/ *n.*	engagement for duty in the armed forces 入伍,从军
vulnerable /ˈvʌlnərəbl/ *a.*	that is liable to be damaged; not protected against attack 易受伤害的;易受攻击的
brand /brænd/ *vt.*	give (sb.) a bad name 使蒙受……的污名
opponent /əˈpəunənt/ *n.*	one that takes an opposite position (as in a debate, contest, or conflict) 对手;敌手
confirmation /ˌkɔnfəːˈmeiʃən/ *n.*	证实;断言
prodigy /ˈprɔdidʒi/ *n.*	person who has unusual or remarkable abilities 不凡之人
nickname /ˈnikneim/ *n.*	name given in addition to or altered from or used instead of the real name 绰号,诨名
expire /ikˈspaiə/ *n.*	to come to an end （期限等）届满,到期
stimulus /ˈstimjuləs/ *n.*	motive 刺激;激励

PHRASES

know one's own mind: know and be sure about the things one wants, or intends to do 有自己的想法，有决断

stage a comeback: go back to a former position of strength, importance, or high rank, after a period of absence 卷土重来，东山再起

NOTES

baby boom：（尤指第二次世界大战后，1947—1961 年美国的）生育高峰；baby boomer 生育高峰期出生的人

the G. I.：美国兵

Bush：美国第 41 届总统（1989—1993）布什

Dole：共和党的总统候选人多尔，1997 年被克林顿击败

Rhodes scholarship：由英国人 Cecil J. Rhodes 创立于牛津大学，以英联邦各国和美国学生为一年一度主要授奖对象的罗兹奖学金

State Attorney General：美国司法部长

EXERCISES

I. *Reading Comprehension*：

A. Answer the following questions.

1. What happened to Clinton's own father before he was born?

2. Which factors helped Clinton gain a good education?

3. What did Clinton do during his university days?

4. At what age did Clinton formally begin his political career?

5. Why was Clinton nicknamed "undefeatable kid"?

B. Choose the best answer to each of the following questions.

1. The word "skirmish" (Para. 3) probably means _____.
   A. agreement   B. conflict   C. contract   D. contradiction
2. Clinton's childhood years were very _____.
   A. happy   B. unhappy   C. wonderful   D. unknown
3. It is UNTRUE that _____.
   A. Clinton's own father was a habitual drunkard
   B. Clinton's stepfather was a habitual drunkard
   C. Clinton was once the youngest governor in the history of the state of Arkansas
   D. Clinton won the presidential reelection in 1997
4. Which of the following is NOT mentioned as one of Clinton's characteristics?
   A. knowing his own mind
   B. having self-restraint and self-control
   C. being caring and sympathetic
   D. being good at competition
5. From the passage, we can draw the conclusion that the success of Clinton results from _____.
   A. the help of others
   B. the authority and influence of his family
   C. just fortune
   D. his self-reliant spirit and diligence

II. *Vocabulary and Structure*:

Choose the correct form of each word to fill in the sentence.

1. John took his _____ morning walk around the park. (habit)
2. You can not put the _____ stuff in the fridge. (expire)
3. Though _____, his political talent received confirmation in news. (defeat)
4. Farmers say they are being hurt by foreign _____. (compete)
5. Bill has done everything to avoid _____ to me. (talk)
6. They want an income that is _____ to both countries. (agree)
7. City leaders hope the amusement park will _____ tourism. (stimulus)
8. The suspect crossed the bridge, with four police cars in _____. (pursue)
9. There has been a _____ increase in temperature since yesterday. (drama)
10. Mr. King says he welcomes _____ criticism. (construct)

Part A   Text (Teach Your Child to Wonder)
Part B   Grammar (分词)
Part C   Supplementary Reading
         (Benchmarking Practices at Xerox)

Part A Text

Warm-up Questions:

1. What do you think "education" is: inputting information or allowing young minds to explore?
2. What should it be in your opinion?
3. How do you rate your school education on a scale of one to ten? Why?
4. "Education is what survives when what has been learned has been forgotten." Do you understand this statement? Do you agree with it?
5. Although "education" comes from a Latin word meaning "to draw out", nowadays it seems to mean "to accept". What do you think?

Teach Your Child to Wonder

Sadly, far too few schools make science appealing. Courses introduce more new vocabulary than foreign language courses. Textbooks are as dull as dictionaries. As a result, too many children think that science is only for people as clever as Einstein.

The irony is that children start out as natural scientists, instinctively eager to investigate the world around them. Helping them enjoy science can be easy—there's no need for a lot of scientific jargon or expensive laboratory equipment. You only have to share your children's curiosity.

Try these simply techniques:

1. _____

I once visited a class of seven-year-olds to talk about science as a career. The children asked me textbook questions—about schooling, salary, whether I liked my job. When I finished answering, we sat facing each other in silence. Finally I said, "Now that we've finished with your lists, have you got any questions of your own about science?"

After a long pause, a boy raised his hand. "Have you ever see a grasshopper eat? When I eat leaves like that, I will get stomachache. Why?"

This began a barrage of questions that lasted nearly two hours. "What makes tears?" "Where do little spiders get all the stuff to make their webs?" "Am I just a bag of blood? When I cut myself, I see blood."

You may not know the answers to your child's questions. It's all right to say, "I don't know but maybe we can find out." Then you can explore the questions together.

2. _____

Even if you know the answer to a child's question, resist the impulse to respond quickly, leaving no opening for discussion. That reinforces the misconception that science is merely a set of facts stored in the heads of adults. Science is about explaining. Science is not just facts but the meaning that people give to them—by weaving information into a story about how nature probably operates.

The best way to respond to a child's question is to begin that process of story-making together. If she asks why it's dark at night, try, "Let's think of what is different about night that would make it darker than day." If he wonders where bee live, say, "Let's watch and maybe we can see where they go." Always be ready with the answer, "Let's find out".

3. _____

Grown-ups are notorious for expecting quicker answers. Studies over the past three decades have shown that, after asking a question, adults typically wait only one second or less for a response—no time for a child to think. When adults increase their "wait time" to three seconds or more, children respond with more logical, complete and creative answers.

I once conducted a lesson in air pressure by pushing two rubber toilet plungers together until all the air was driven out and they were tightly suctioned. Two children had to tug them mightily to separate them. "How come you need so much force to pull them apart?" I asked.

After several minutes, a boy named Ron said, "The air is trapped in there and it finds a hole and it all goes out. That's what makes a popping sound". He went on to demonstrate his misconception, but I didn't say anything yet.

Another pupil then revealed what she'd been thinking: "No, it's because all the air is out of the plunger". She pushed it down on the floor until it stuck, showing that once the air was forced out of the cup, the air pressure was less on the inside than on the outside.

Rather than telling children what to think, give them time to think for themselves. If a child gets the answer wrong, be patient. You can help when needed with a few leading questions.

4. _____

Once you have a child engaged in a science discussion, don't jump in with "That right" or "Very good". These verbal rewards work well when it comes to encouraging good behaviour. But in conversing about science, quick praise can signal that the discussion is over. Instead, keep the ball rolling by saying, "That's interesting" or "I'd never thought of it that way before", or coming up with more questions or ideas.

Never exhort a child to "Think!" It doesn't make sense—children are always thinking without your telling them to.

Avoid asking "why" question. Most children are accustomed to hearing "why" when their behavior is criticized: "Why is your bedroom so messy?" "Why can't you behave?" Instead, I use "How come?"

5. _____

Real-life impressions of nature are far more memorable than any lesson children can extract from a book or TV program. Let children look at their fingertips through a magnifying glass, and they'll understand why you want them to wash before dinner. Rather than explaining what mould is, grow some on a piece of bread. Rather than saying water evaporates, set a pan to boil and let them watch the water level drop.

If you take your children to a "hands-on" science museum, don't manage their itinerary. Let them lead the way, and explore what interests them most.

6. _____

Everyday activities can provide fascinating lessons in science. Children can learn a great deal about physics and engineering simply by flying a kite.

Try making your own with light-weight wood, string and paper. By the end of the afternoon's "experiment", your children will get a basic lesson in scientific cause and effect. They'll discover how wind direction and intensity shift at different altitudes.

When buying toys, blocks of all kinds are great for construction projects. Choose toys with working parts. Even better, look for toys that children can safely take apart and put back together again.

By sharing your children's curiosity, you can give them a valuable lesson that extends far beyond the realm to experiment, in the face of difficulties.

And they will see clearly that learning is not drudgery or something that happens only in school. Learning is something to be enjoyed every day—for a lifetime.

NEW WORDS

appealing /əˈpiːliŋ/ a.   attractive, moving   吸引
jargon /ˈdʒaːgən/ n.   technical or special words/terms   （科学）术语
grasshopper /ˈgraːʃɔpə(r)/ n.   蚱蜢, 蝗虫
impulse /ˈimpʌls/ n.   sudden inclination to act without thought about the consequence   冲动
reinforce /ˌriːinˈfɔːs/ v.   make stronger   加强, 加深
misconception /ˌmiskənˈsepʃən/ n.   wrong idea   错觉
notorious /nəuˈtɔːriəs/ a.   臭名昭著的
suction /ˈsʌkʃən/ n.   action of sucking   吸
tug /tʌg/ v.   pull hard   拽, 曝
exhort /igˈzɔːt/ v.   urge, advise earnestly   力劝, 告诫
extract /iksˈtrækt/ v.   拔出, 抽出
mould /məuld/ n.   霉, 霉菌
evaporate /iˈvæpəreit/ v.   change into vapor   蒸发
itinerary /aiˈtinərəri/ n.   a detailed plan for a journey   旅行计划
intensity /inˈtensiti/ n.   strength or depth   强度
realm /relm/ n.   region   领域, 范围

PHRASES

a barrage of...: a large number/amount of   大量的
leading question: 启发性问题

keep the ball rolling: continue doing something 使……不中断
cause and effect: 因果关系
in the face of…: 面临

NOTES

toilet plunger: 厕所揣子
hands-on: providing practical experience of something by telling people do it themselves
亲自体会的，自己动手的

EXERCISES

I. Reading Comprehension:

Look at the headings below. Read the article and choose the most suitable heading for each of the gaps in the text numbered 1-6. There are more headings than you need.

A. Show, don't tell.

B. Give lots of praise.

C. Stop buying toys.

D. Watch your language.

E. Listen to their questions.

F. Give them time to think.

G. Fly a kite.

H. Direct their learning.

I. Tell stories, don't recite facts.

II. Interpretation:

Answer the following questions, either with factual answers based on the text or by interpreting the writer's ideas.

1. Who was the article written for?

2. Why do children often give illogical or incomplete answers to adults' questions?

3. Do you think the writer of the article is a professional journalist?

4. Is the writer a man or a woman in your opinion? Why?

5. The writer thinks science is an inevitably boring subject. True or false?

6. What's wrong with saying "Very good" when talking about science with a child?

7. What advice do you think the writer would give to school science teachers?

8. Is what the writer suggests closer to or further away from the original meaning of "education"?

III. *Vocabulary*:

Find words or phrase in the text (given below) that mean the same as or something very similar to the definitions given below. Write down the word or phrase in the space provided. Please note that there are some extra words in the bracket.

persist	appealing	misconception
drudgery	cause and effect	mould
jump in	keep the ball rolling	make sense
hands-on	in the face of	leading question
jargon	magnifying glass	a barrage of questions

Meaning	Word or phrase in the text
1. a type of question in which the words used suggest the answer	1.
2. a great number of questions suddenly directed at someone	2.
3. special words or phrases used in a particular profession or subject (often difficult for ordinary people to understand)	3.
4. a piece of curved glass which makes objects look larger than they really are	4.
5. a wrong idea based on failure to understand a situation	5.

续表

Meaning	Word or phrase in the text
6. the reason why something happens and the result it has	6. _____
7. describing something that someone has done or used personally rather than read or learned about	7. _____
8. keep doing something that you want lots of others to do	8. _____
9. hard, boring work	9. _____
10. soft green or grey growth that develops on old food	10. _____

IV. *Translation*:

A. Translate the following into Chinese.

1. The irony is that children start out as natural scientists, instinctively eager to investigate the world around them.

2. This began a barrage of questions that lasted nearly two hours.

3. Science is not just facts but the meaning that people give to them—by weaving information into a story about how nature probably operates.

4. Studies over the past three decades have shown that, after asking a question, adults typically wait only one second or less for a response—no time for a child to think.

5. Instead, keep the ball rolling by saying, "That's interesting" or "I'd never thought of it that way before", or coming up with more questions or ideas.

6. Real-life impressions of nature are far more memorable than any lesson children can extract from a book or TV program.

7. By sharing your children's curiosity, you can give them a valuable lesson that extends far beyond the realm to experiment, in the face of difficulties.

B. Translate the following into English.

1. 一大堆问题

2. 别冲动,不要急于回答问题

3. 不要给孩子规定去思考什么

4. 鼓励他们说下去(使……不中断)

5. 安排活动方案

6. 面临困难

C. Translate the following into English.

1. 解说员的讲解非常有吸引力。(make... appealing)

2. 简单点儿讲吧,别用那些专业术语了。(rather than)

3. 不要急于回答,留出一些讨论的余地。(opening for discussion)

4. 一些启发性的问题可以鼓励孩子思考。(leading question)

5. 面临困难的时候坚持下去就会取得回报。(in face of...; it pays...)

V. *Writing Task*:

Adding details is a very important way of giving color to your writing. Giving concrete examples can also relate your arguments to the real world. Writing with no detail tends to be boring to the reader.

Look at the following outline of a primary school experience. Where there are gaps, add the missing factual information for yourself. Where there are asterisks, add one or two sentences which give interesting details.

> When I was... years old I went to a primary school＊,...
>
> My first day at school ＊ was...
>
> I met a lot of other kids at school but I had one particular friend ＊ ...
>
> We used to play different games ＊ during the breaks between lessons...
>
> I can still remember our class teacher ＊ ...

VI. *Oral Practice*：

Pair-work：Join a partner and discuss your own primary school experiences. Also share your points about how you should teach your own children when they are still young.

Part B　Grammar

分词（Participles）

　　分词是动词的另一种非限定形式,分为现在分词和过去分词两种。如：breaking 和 broken。它们在句子中主要起形容词和副词的作用,可以用作定语、状语或表语。如：

　　·They will carry out the plan passed at the yesterday's meeting.（定语）

　　·The story is very amusing.（表语）

　　·Permitted by his boss, he left the office earlier than before.（状语）

　　现在分词和过去分词的主要区别是前者表示主动的意思,而后者则表示被动的意思。另外分词还有其自身的完成形式和被动形式。如：

　　·Not having made adequate preparations, they decided to put off the meeting until next week.

　　·Being repaired at this moment, the library cannot be opened to the students.

　　第一句中表示了完成时态,第二句表示了进行时的被动语态。除了分词的形式及语法作用外，另外一种与分词有关的语法现象是分词独立结构。在这一结构中，分词可以有自己的逻辑主语。这种主语常常是名词或代词主格，放置分词短语之前。它可以表示时间、原因、条件、伴随等。

- The problem being settled, they went back to rest. （时间）
- Weather permitting, they will go to the Great Wall. （条件）
- This paper deals with graduate education, with particular attention paid to Ph. D programs. （带有 with 的过去分词构成分词独立结构）

练 习

1. 选择适当的分词形式填空。

（1）Many things _____ impossible in the past are common today.
　　A. considered　　　　　　　　B. to consider
　　C. considering　　　　　　　　D. being considered

（2）The machine _____ in our factory these days is a new type of electronic computer.
　　A. to produce　　　　　　　　B. being produced
　　C. produce　　　　　　　　　　D. to be producing

（3）The noise of desks _____ could be heard out in the street.
　　A. being opened and closed　　B. be opened and closed
　　C. opening and closing　　　　D. having opened and

（4）_____ that Barton had been promoted, his friends came to congratulate him.
　　A. Having been heard　　　　B. Being heard
　　C. To have heard　　　　　　D. Having heard

（5）_____ by the police, the kidnappers had no choice but to surrender.
　　A. Surrounding　　　　　　　B. Having surrounded
　　C. Surrounded　　　　　　　　D. To surround

（6）Never _____ faith in himself, James Watt went on with his experiment.
　　A. losing　　B. to lose　　C. lost　　D. to be lost

（7）There are four factories in our institute, _____ over 100 workers.
　　A. with each have　　　　　　B. each having
　　C. each has　　　　　　　　　D. with each has over

（8）_____ a bomb on the road, the car was stopped.
　　A. Having seen　　　　　　　B. The driver seeing
　　C. Seeing　　　　　　　　　　D. After seeing a bomb

(9) The weather _____ fine, they decided to go out for a stroll.
   A. is   B. was   C. being   D. having

(10) _____ in all parts of the country, pines are the most common trees in this part.
   A. Found   B. Finding them
   C. To find them   D. They are found

(11) Commercial banks make the most of their income from interest _____ on loans and investments in stocks.
   A. earn   B. earned   C. to earn   D. was earned

(12) Returning to my apartment, _____.
   A. my watch was missing   B. I found my watch disappeared
   C. I found my watch missing   D. the watch was missed

(13) Having been served lunch, _____.
   A. the problem was discussed by the members of the committee
   B. the committee members discussed the problem
   C. it was discussed by the committee members the problem
   D. a discussion of the problem was made by the members of the committee

(14) The police pursued the criminal continuously, _____.
   A. and finally catch him   B. finally catching him
   C. to catch him in the final D. with a final catch

(15) She finished her work, _____.
   A. tiring and wearing out   B. tired and wear out
   C. tired and worn out   D. tiring and worn out

2. 以分词的适当形式填空。

(1) The baby was wakened by the _____ (deafen) sound.
(2) The _____ (wound) man was taken to hospital.
(3) This is a mistake often _____ (make) through negligence.
(4) A bus _____ (come) from the opposite direction knocked down the cyclist.
(5) He sent away the _____ (bark) dog at once.
(6) _____ (Stand) on the top of the hill, we came in sight of the whole waterfall.
(7) _____ (Drive) by despair, many unemployed school-leavers have degenerated into criminals.
(8) All the planes _____ (depart) for London are carefully searched and checked before taking off.

(9) A boy _____ (believe) to have killed a roommate has escaped from the city.
(10) Most cars _____ (import) from Japan are used as taxis.

Part C Supplementary Reading

Benchmarking Practices at Xerox

By Sophie Fox

   Benchmarking deserves credit for inspiring some legendary corporate turnarounds; Ford's resurgence with the Taurus and Sable models and Motorola's dramatic improvements in quality and cycle times are just two examples. Benchmarking has become a mainstream tool, used by many organizations to remain competitive in the global marketplace. To be effective, benchmarking not only needs solid support from top management, but must also become an integral part of the entire organization, cascading down to every employee.
   In today's business environment, benchmarking projects are numerous and cottage industries have sprung up to support them; in the last year alone, over half a dozen books on benchmarking have hit the stand and the number of benchmarking consultants has grown considerably.
   The formal definition of benchmarking is the continuous process of measuring products, services, and business practices against those of the toughest competitors or companies renowned as leaders. Xerox pioneered benchmarking in the late 1970s when it suddenly found that the Japanese had more than a 40 percent cost advantage in copiers and that Xerox's own market share in copiers had severely declined. Xerox CEO David Kearns initially launched the successful "Leadership through Quality" program to boost product quality and reduce manufacturing costs. Since then, Xerox senior management has required all organizations within Xerox to pursue benchmarking.
   There are four major types of benchmarking activities pursued at Xerox: internal, functional, generic, and competitive. The theory behind internal benchmarking maintains that, because large organizations have multiples of the same units set up to perform similar activities, information can easily be shared among similar units to the company's advantage. At Xerox, the company utilizes internal benchmarking as a device to transfer opinions, ideas, and information (regarding best internal practices) among its divisions. In keeping with this idea, for example, the

US customer operations division chose its sister affiliate in Canada as the benchmark for improving its customer service process.

Functional benchmarking is the story of Xerox's learning relationship with L. L. Bean. In the early 1980s, the members of Xerox's benchmarking review team asked, "Who's the best external benchmark for customer order processing?" Surprisingly, the answer was not other high-tech companies such as IBM, Cannon, or Minolta. Rather, it was L. L. Bean, which picked its orders manually as did Xerox. The big difference was that Bean was three times faster. Thus, Bean became Xerox's functional benchmark in the area of order processing. In essence, functional benchmarking focuses on determining and subsequently implementing best practices, regardless of the industry they are found in.

Generic benchmarking has become one of Xerox's most important focal points. Xerox identified numerous basic business processes, such as order taking, in which they sought improvement. One individual was assigned to oversee improvements in each of 10 areas encompassing the 67 identified processes. These process owners became responsible for documenting specific means of improving processes, overseeing implementation of organizational benchmarking activities regarding the individual processes, and resolving cross-functional disputes arising from resource allocation.

Finally, competitive benchmarking entails uncovering competitor practices that can then be implemented and improved upon within an organization. For example, prior to benchmarking, Xerox had four places where it stored and handled material. After reviewing top-competitor practices, Xerox changed its materials management structure to be more in line with that of its competitors. As a result, materials-handling operations have been significantly streamlined without any accompanying loss of service quality.

In total, has benchmarking paid off for Xerox? Well, consider this. Since embarking on its benchmarking quest, Xerox has been able to cut manufacturing costs in half, reduce inventories by two-thirds, increase overall organizational productivity significantly, and achieve almost 100 percent parts acceptance from customers. As a result, Xerox has been able to reclaim the market leadership position that had once been threatened.

NEW WORDS

benchmark/'bentʃmaːk/*n.*   a mark cut in some durable material in a line of survey for reference at a future time; anything that serves as a

Unit 5

		standard of comparison or point of reference 基准,基准点,基(准)标(记)
turnaround	/'tə:nə,raund/ *n.*	a complete change from a bad situation to a good one (营业、经济的)突然好转;(观点的)彻底改变
resurgence	/ri'sə:dʒəns/ *n.*	(esp. of ideas, beliefs, etc.) a return to power, life, and activity 复活,复兴
cascade	/kæs'keid/ *n.*	waterfall 瀑布
	v.	pour in quantity 倾泻,流注
spring	/spriŋ/ *v.*	(sprang, sprung) (up) appear; grow up quickly from the ground or from a stem 出现;发生;迅速长出
consultant	/kən'sʌltənt/ *n.*	person who gives expert advice (e.g. in medicine, surgery, business) 提供专家意见(如有关医药、外科、商业等方面)的人;顾问
renown	/ri'naun/ *n.*	fame 名望,声誉
	a.	famous; celebrated 有名的,著名的
pioneer	/,paiə'niə/ *v.*	open up (a way, etc.); show (new methods, etc.) to others 开辟(道路等);提倡(新法等)
boost	/bu:st/ *v.*	give (sb. or sth.) a push up; increase the value, reputation, etc. of (sb. or sth.) 将(某人或某物)推起;举起;为(某人或某事)吹嘘;捧
pursue	/pə'sju:/ *v.*	go on with; work at 继续做;做
multiple	/'mʌltipl/ *n.*	quantity which contains another quantity a number of times without remainder 倍数
utilize	/'ju:tilaiz/ *v.*	make use of; find a use for 利用;化为有用
regarding	/ri'ga:diŋ/ *prep.*	with reference to; concerning 关于;有关
affiliate	/ə'filieit/ *n.*	a branch organization 分支机构,分支联号,会员
implement	/'implimənt/ *v.*	carry an undertaking, agreement, promise into effect 实现;完成(任务等);履行(协定、诺言)
quest	/kwest/ *n.*	a search 探索,寻求
entail	/in'teil/ *v.*	make necessary; impose (expenses, etc. on sb.) 使必要;使负担(花费等)(与 on 连用,后接某人)
streamline	/'stri:mlain/ *v.*	make more efficient (by simplifying, getting rid of, wasteful methods, etc.) (借简化或废除不经济的方法等)使更为有效;提高效率

inventory/ˈinvəntri/ n.　　　　detailed list, e.g. of household goods, furniture, etc.
　　　　　　　　　　　　　　　详细目录(如动产、家具等的清单);财产清册;存货
reclaim/riˈkleim/ v.　　　　　demand that sth. be given back　要求归还

PHRASES

cottage industry: (an) industry whose labor force consists of people working at home with
　　　their own tools or machinery　家庭手工业
to sb.'s advantage: profitable or helpful to sb.　对某人有利;有助于某人
in essence: in its/one's nature　在本质上
focus on: concentrate　集中
regardless of: paying no attention to　不顾;不注意
arise from: result from　产生
prior to: before　在……之前
in line with: in agreement with　与……一致
pay off: to result in success　获得成功,见成效,(企业)有收益
embark on: start, take part in　开始;从事
in total: when all have been added up　总计,总体来看

EXERCISES

1. *Reading Comprehension*:
    1. What do the two examples—Ford and Motorola demonstrate?
        A. Large companies inspire corporate turnarounds.
        B. Benchmarking practices can only be carried out at large companies.
        C. Benchmarking is conducive to inspiring corporate turnarounds.
        D. Benchmarking practices were first carried out at Ford and Motorola.
    2. Which of the following is NOT mentioned in the second paragraph?
        A. Cottage industries support benchmarking projects.
        B. Books on benchmarking are difficult to understand.
        C. There are more and more benchmarking consultants.
        D. There exist many benchmarking projects.

3. What does benchmarking mean?

   A. A process of measuring how competitive a company is.

   B. A process of improving top management of a company.

   C. A process of measuring a company in reference to its competitor.

   D. A process of catching up with companies renowned as leaders.

4. What companies are most suitable for internal benchmarking?

   A. Companies which have many divisions.

   B. Companies which have many competitors.

   C. Companies where similar activities are performed in many of its units.

   D. Companies which are backward.

5. Which of the following shows that benchmarking has paid off for Xerox?

   A. Its manufacturing costs have been cut down considerably.

   B. Its inventories have been smaller than before.

   C. Customers totally accept their parts products.

   D. All of above.

II. *Multiple Choices*:

1. Benchmarking deserves credit for inspiring some legendary corporate turnarounds.

   A. belief　　　B. honor　　　C. praise　　　D. money

2. To be effective, benchmarking needs solid support from top management.

   A. unanimous　　B. strong　　　C. continuous　　D. dependable

3. Xerox CEO David Kearns initially launched the successful "Leadership through Quality" program to boost product quality.

   A. aid　　　　B. promote　　C. improve　　D. encourage

4. One individual was assigned to oversee improvements in each of 10 areas encompassing the 67 identified processes.

   A. examine　　B. inspect　　C. overlook　　D. supervise

5. Xerox has been able to reclaim the market leadership position that had once been threatened.

   A. cry out　　B. draw back　　C. call back　　D. demand back

UNIT 6

Part A Text (Engineering)
Part B Grammar (动名词)
Part C Supplementary Reading
        (This *TITANIC* Floats!)

Part A Text

Warm-up Questions:

1. *What is engineering? What's the content of it? What association could you make between engineering and our life? Please cite some examples.*
2. *In your opinion, what is the job of an engineer? Are you an engineer? What do you do in your work?*
3. *Do you know Industrial Revolution? Who are some famous representatives of the Industrial Revolution? What effect did the revolution have on people's life?*
4. *What abilities or traits may help a person become a successful engineer? Do you think that you are a successful engineer?*

Engineering

By Walter Monfried

Engineering is the profession that puts scientific knowledge to practical use. Engineers use principles of science to design structures, machines, and products of all kinds. They look for better ways to use existing resources and often develop new materials. Engineers have had a direct role in the creation of most of modern technology—the tools, materials, techniques, and power sources that make our lives easier.

The field of engineering includes a wide variety of activities. For example, engineering projects range from the construction of huge dams to the design of tiny electronic circuits. Engineers may help produce guided missiles, industrial robots, or artificial limbs for the physically handicapped. They develop complex scientific equipment to explore the reaches of outer space and the depths of the oceans. Engineers also plan our electric power and water supply systems, and do research to improve automobiles, television sets, and other consumer products. They may work to reduce environmental pollution, increase the world's food supply, and make transportation faster and safer.

The history of engineering is the record of human ingenuity through the ages. Even in prehistoric times, people adapted basic engineering techniques from things that were available in nature. For example, sturdy sticks became levers to lift large rocks, and logs were used as rollers to move heavy loads. The development of agriculture and the growth of civilization brought about a new wave of engineering efforts. People invented farming tools, designed elaborate irrigation networks, and built the first cities. The construction of the gigantic Egyptian pyramids at Giza during the 2500s B. C. was one of the greatest engineering feats of ancient times. In ancient Rome, engineers built large aqueducts and bridges and vast systems of roads. During the 200s B. C., the Chinese erected major sections of the monumental Great Wall of China.

Early engineers used such simple machines as the inclined plane, wedge, and wheel and axle. During the Middle Ages, a period in European history that lasted from the A. D. 400s to the 1500s, inventors developed machines to harness water, wind, and animal power. The growing interest in new types of machines and new sources of power to drive them helped bring about the Industrial Revolution of the 1700s and 1800s, during which, their role expanded rapidly. The practical steam engine developed by the Scottish engineer James Watt in the 1760s revolutionized transportation and industry by providing a cheap, efficient source of power. New iron-making techniques provided engineers with the material to improve machines and tools and to build bridges and ships. Many roads, railroads, and canals were constructed to link the growing industrial cities.

Distinct branches of engineering began to develop during the Industrial Revolution. The term civil engineer was first used about 1750 by John Smeaton, a British engineer. Mechanical engineers emerged as specialists in industrial machinery, and mining and metallurgical engineers were needed to supply metals and fuels. By the late 1800s, the development of electric power and advances in chemical processing had created the fields of electrical and chemical engineering. Professional schools began to be founded as the demand for engineers steadily increased.

Since 1900, the number of engineers and of engineering specialities has expanded dramatically. Artificial hearts, airplanes, computers, lasers, nuclear energy, plastics, space travel, and television are only a few of the scientific and technological breakthroughs that engineers have helped bring about in this century. Because science and technology are progressing and changing so rapidly, today's engineers must study throughout their careers to make sure that their knowledge and expertise do not become obsolete. They face the challenging task of keeping pace with the latest advances while working to shape the technology of the future.

The field of engineering offers a broad range of job opportunities. Engineers may work in factories, offices, and government laboratories or at construction sites. Some engineers are involved in the research and development of new products. Others are responsible for turning plans and specifications for new structures, machines, or systems into reality. Still others use their background and training to sell and service technical equipment. Many engineers work on projects in teams that include scientists, technicians, and other engineers, however, some engineers act as independent consultants who sell their services to people who need engineering assistance. Engineers may also hold teaching positions or move up into management positions in business.

Certain abilities and traits help qualify a person for an engineering career. Engineers must have technical aptitude and skill in mathematics and the sciences. They should be curious about the "how" and "why" of natural and mechanical things and creative in finding new ways of doing things, able to analyze problems systematically and logically and to communicate well—both orally and in writing, and willing to work within strict budgets and meet tight deadlines. In addition, skill in directing and supervising other workers is an important part of many engineering jobs.

NEW WORDS

engineering /ˌendʒiˈniəriŋ/ *n.* the application of scientific and mathematical principles to practical use 工程（学）

range /reindʒ/ *vt.* divide into classes 排列，归类于

n. place in a certain class or category 行列，范围；射程；山脉

dam /dæm/ *n.* a barrier constructed to hold back water and raise its

Unit 6

	level 水坝
circuit /'sə:kit/ *n.*	the complete path of an electric current 电路
handicapped /'hændikæpt/ *n.* *a.*	a physical or mental disability 残疾人 残废的
ingenuity /,indʒi'nju:iti/ *n.*	cleverness at making things 机灵;独创性;精巧
sturdy /'stə:di/ *a.*	strong 强健的;坚定的
lever /'li:və, 'levə/ *n.* *v.*	杆, 杠杆, 控制杆 抬起
irrigation /,iri'geiʃən/ *n.*	supplying land with water by means of channels or streams 灌溉
gigantic /dʒai'gæntik/ *a.*	huge 巨大的
feat /fi:t/ *n.*	achievement 业绩
aqueduct /'ækwidʌkt/ *n.*	channel for the conveyance of water 水渠
plane /plein/ *n.*	a tool for smoothing the surface of the object 刨
wedge /wedʒ/ *n.*	a V-shaped block 楔子,三角木
axle /'æksl/ *n.*	the pin, bar or shaft on which a pair of wheels rotates 轴
harness /'hɑ:nis/ *vt.*	to utilize (a river, a waterfall, natural forces) for motive power 利用
ironmaking /'aiən'meikiŋ/ *n.*	炼铁业
distinct /dis'tiŋkt/ *a.*	clear, obvious 清楚的;明显的;独特的
metallurgical /,metə'lə:dʒikəl/ *a.*	relating to the science of metals 冶金学的
mechanical /mi'kænikl/ *a.*	of a machine 机械的, 机械制的
speciality /,speʃi'æliti/ *n.*	专门,特性,特别
breakthrough /'breikθru:/ *n.*	advance 突破
obsolete /'ɔbsəli:t/ *a.*	out of date 荒废的,陈旧的
challenging /'tʃælindʒiŋ/ *a.*	full of challenge 有挑战性的
trait /treit/ *n.*	characteristic feature 显著的特点,特性
aptitude /'æptitju:d/ *n.*	natural tendency, or ability 智能,聪明,自然倾向
systematically /sistə'mætikəli/ *ad.*	in a systematic manner 系统地, 有步骤地
orally /'ɔ:rəli/ *ad.*	by, through, or with the mouth 口头上地, 口述地

PHARASES

range from... to...: cover from... to... 涵盖范围从……到……
in prehistoric times: at the time in human history before anything was written 在史前时期
bring about: cause to happen 导致，发生
keep pace with: keep up with 跟上……的步伐
qualify sb. for: make sb. qualified for 使某人有……的资格
be curious about: be eager to know or learn 对……充满好奇心
meet deadlines: finish by the deadline 在最后期限前完成

NOTES

Industrial Revolution: the mechanization of industry and the consequent changes in social and economic organization, esp. in Britain (the late 18th and early 19th centuries) 工业革命（亦称产业革命）
the Middle Ages: the period of European history from the fall of Roman Empire (476) to the late 15th century 中世纪
James Watt: 1736-1819, the Scottish engineer who made (1765) fundamental improvements to the Newcomen steam engine, leading to the widespread use of steam engine in mines, factories, etc. 詹姆斯·瓦特
the "how" and "why" of: ……的方式与方法

EXERCISES

I. Reading Comprehension:

Choose the best answer to each of the following questions.

1. This passage is mainly about _____.
    A. a general introduction of engineering
    B. a specific definition of engineering
    C. a classification of engineering
    D. functions of engineering

2. Which of the following statement best summarizes the main idea of the second paragraph?

   A. Both huge dams and tiny electronic circuits involve engineering.

   B. Engineering helps people deal with pollution.

   C. Engineers are of great importance.

   D. Engineering covers various kinds of activities.

3. Professional engineering schools were founded because _____.

   A. there were distinct branches of engineering

   B. it was advocated by John Smeaton

   C. engineering became more sophisticated

   D. more and more engineers were needed

4. Which of the following is NOT the invention of the 20th Century?

   A. Lever.　　　B. Artificial heart.　　　C. Laser.　　　D. Plastics.

5. Which of the following is NOT mentioned as a necessary characteristic that may enable a person to be a qualified engineer?

   A. Technical skill.　　B. Team spirit.　　　C. Curiosity.　　　D. Logic.

II. Getting Information:

Answer the following questions in English according to the text.

1. What is the definition of Engineering?

   _____

2. What do you know about the history of engineering through the ages?

   _____

3. When was the Industrial Revolution?

   _____

4. Who invented the steam engine?

   _____

5. Why should the engineers keep studying all the time?

   _____

III. Vocabulary and Structure:

A. Please give out the correct forms of the words. (note: There may be more than one possible answers.)

Noun	Verb	Adjective
	challenge	
	specialize	
		existing
		curious
emergency		
	qualify	
practice		

B. Identify one of the four choices (A, B, C or D) which would keep the meaning of the underlined word or phrase.

1. She had supposed human <u>ingenuity</u> would find ways to overcome food shortages and overpopulation.

    A. findings   B. cleverness   C. curiosity   D. inventions

2. Delicate Japanese trees were replaced by <u>sturdier</u> North American trees.

    A. stronger   B. taller   C. straight   D. heavier

3. The powers of the atom are about to be <u>harnessed</u> for ever-greater production.

    A. hardened   B. converted   C. changed   D. utilized

4. Her poverty was a <u>handicap</u> in her career.

    A. disadvantage   B. challenge   C. advantage   D. tool

5. He had a <u>distinct</u> feeling that something was wrong.

    A. different   B. clear   C. plain   D. vague

6. Those physicians and specialists' finding was a great <u>breakthrough</u> in their fight against heart disease.

    A. achievement   B. failure   C. pity   D. leak

C. Fill in each of the blank with the proper word in the box.

career	distinct	expand	load	monumental
practical	process	range	reduce	specification

1. The device is used to measure the _____ of the gun.
2. The artist spent many years on his _____ painting, which covered all the walls of the

exhibition hall.
3. The truck was carrying a(n) _____ of bananas.
4. The design is worthless for all _____ purposes.
5. This experienced editor is said to be able to _____ the misprints to almost nil.
6. The company has _____ its operations in Stanford by opening a new branch office there.
7. There is a(n) _____ improvement in your study, you must have put in more effort.
8. The firm is now in the _____ of moving the main equipment to a new place.
9. My grandfather was a(n) _____ teacher; it's the only job he'd ever done.
10. In system development, the _____ refers to a description of how the design of a system, device, or program is to be implemented.

IV. *Translation*:

A. Translate the following into Chinese.
1. Engineers have had a direct role in the creation of most of modern technology—the tools, materials, techniques, and power sources that make our lives easier.
2. They develop complex scientific equipment to explore the reaches of outer space and the depths of the oceans.
3. They may work to reduce environmental pollution, increase the world's food supply, and make transportation faster and safer.
4. The construction of the gigantic Egyptian pyramids at Giza during the 2500s B.C. was one of the greatest engineering feats of ancient times.
5. The growing interest in new types of machines and new sources of power to drive them helped bring about the Industrial Revolution of the 1700s and 1800s, during which, their role expanded rapidly.

B. Translate the following into English.
1. 一个健壮结实的孩子
2. 利用河流发电
3. 在史前时期
4. 使他成为合格的工程师
5. 对知识充满好奇心
6. 按时完成工作

C. Translate the following into English.
1. 很明显,与他争论无济于事。(it is no use…)
2. 他在我们学校演的剧中扮演老国王的角色。(play a role of)
3. 她在这张照片中显得很年轻。(make… look young)
4. 他帮助那位教授编了那本词典。(assist, compile)
5. 请你务必查清房间上锁后再离开。(make sure)

Part B Grammar

动名词(Gerunds)

动名词的形式是在动词原形后面加上-ing;在句子中起名词的作用,可作为句子的主语、表语和宾语。

- Driving a car is fun.(主语)
- My favorite sport is swimming.(表语)
- I enjoyed reading this novel very much.(宾语)

动名词的学习中,大家应该特别注意:

1. 动名词作宾语

有些动词只能接动名词做宾语,而不能接不定式。这些动词是:acknowledge、advice、admit、anticipate、appreciate、avoid、allow、bear、can't help、cease、commence、complete、confess、delay、deny、discourage、detest、dread、endure、enjoy、envy、escape、excuse、fancy、favor、figure、finish、imagine、involve、justify、keep、mind、miss、permit、postpone、practice、quit、recall、repent、require、resent、resume、risk、save 等。例如:

- Mark often attempts to escape being fined whenever he breaks traffic regulations.
  每当马克违反交通规则时,他常常企图逃避罚款。
- People appreciate working with him because he has a good sense of humor.
  因为他很有幽默感,所以大家喜欢和他一起工作。

2. 动名词的固定搭配

动名词在很多情形下用在固定搭配中,如:be busy doing sth.、have trouble doing sth.、have difficulty doing sth. 等;此外在"there/it is + 名词或形容词 + 动名词"和句型"动词 + it + 形容词或名词 + 动名词"结构中使用动名词。用于这个结构中的形容词和名词有:good、no good、nuisance、no use、senseless、use、useless、waste、worthwhile。例如：

- Sometimes very young children have trouble separating fact from fiction and may believe that such things actually exist.

  有时，小孩子分不清现实与虚幻，还认为这样的事是果真存在。

- Do you think it worthwhile investing a large sum of money in this project?

  你认为向该项目大量投资值得吗？

3. 有些动词，如 remember、forget、stop、regret、go on、afford、attempt、try 等动词的宾语既可是不定式，也可以是动名词，但意义有所不同：总的来说，不定式表示动作尚未发出或完成，而动名词则表示动作已经发出或完成。注意加以区分。例如：

- I remember having asked her to write us.

  我记得曾要她给我们写信。

- Remember to meet me tonight.

  记住今晚来见我。

练 习

1. 选择适当的形式填空。

(1) Many people favor _____ more nuclear power plants.

　　A. to build　　　B. built　　　C. build　　　D. building

(2) Professor Smith _____ about him and he pretended not to mind.

　　A. heard the students to talk　　　B. heard the talk by the students

　　C. heard the students talking　　　D. heard the students talked

(3) _____ to the office was very slow this morning because of the traffic.

　　A. To drive　　　　　　　　　B. Driving

　　C. Being driven　　　　　　　D. I drove

(4) I would appreciate _____ it a secret between us.

　　A. you to keep　　　　　　　　B. that you would keep

　　C. your keeping　　　　　　　D. that you are keeping

(5) The doctor has difficulty _____ this infection.

　　A. in treating　　　　　　　　B. to treat

　　C. for treating　　　　　　　　D. being treating

(6) This house needs _____. I will call the repair company tomorrow.

　　A. to be paint　　　　　　　　B. painting

　　C. to painting　　　　　　　　D. painted

(7) I _____ brushing my teeth twice a day.
　　A. used to be　　　　　　　　B. am in the habit of
　　C. make a rule of　　　　　　D. ought to

(8) Would you mind _____ the recorder? I am working on my paper now.
　　A. being turned off　　　　　B. turning off
　　C. to turn off　　　　　　　 D. turn off

(9) With _____ her do this, she will have no difficulty persuading them to accept her plan.
　　A. I help　　　　　　　　　　B. my helping
　　C. me helping　　　　　　　　D. mine helping

(10) You need to know that _____ arrest is a crime.
　　A. to resisting　　　　　　　B. the resisting
　　C. to be resisted　　　　　　D. resisting

(11) I have to tell you that it is no use _____ to him about this.
　　A. to talk　　　　　　　　　　B. talking
　　C. in talking　　　　　　　　 D. talk

(12) _____ work means moving a body through a distance by a force.
　　A. Having done　　　　　　　　B. To be done
　　C. Being done　　　　　　　　 D. Doing

(13) She regretted _____ a big mistake in the examination.
　　A. her having made　　　　　　B. to make
　　C. her was making　　　　　　 D. to have made

(14) Besides _____ the technology of designed ships, he also learned how to build them.
　　A. master　　　　　　　　　　 B. to master
　　C. having master　　　　　　　D. mastering

(15) It is a waste of time _____ about it with them.
　　A. to be argued　　　　　　　 B. to argue
　　C. arguing　　　　　　　　　　D. being argued

2. 将下面的短句翻译成英语(按括号中标明的语法要求用动名词)。

　　(1) 翻译这本书是很难的。(主语)

　　_____

　　(2) 现在往火车站赶没有用了,火车一定是开走了。(主语)

　　_____

（3）我们都知道他非常喜欢集邮。（be fond of 宾语）

（4）教室里禁止吸烟。（prohibit, forbid 宾语）

（5）我们的任务是增加产量。（表语）

（6）他们反对把会议推迟到下周。（介词宾语）

（7）我把窗户关上你介意吗？（宾语）

（8）他避免给我们一个明确的答复。（宾语）

（9）你有兴趣去看英语剧吗？（介词宾语）

（10）他组织这项工作的方法是非常有效的。（介词宾语）

Part C Supplementary Reading

This *TITANIC* Floats!

By Kathryn Johnson

Those of you who have enjoyed director James Cameron's science fiction hits such as *Aliens*, *The Abyss* and *The Terminator* may be surprised at his newest movie. Titanic is an old-fashioned romance with incredible special effects.

Titanic is an epic that women will love to cry at, with a leading man (Leonardo DiCaprio) that they will love to look at. However, men will also have a good time at this movie. There's plenty of action, from walls of water, to collapsing staircases, to falling smokestacks. Cameron also thoughtfully provided the beautiful Kate Winslet for the men to admire. In short, no one from eight to eighty will be bored watching *Titanic* (all three-plus hours of it)!

The plot is tried-and true. Kate Winslet plays Rose DeWitt Bukater. She is the only daughter of a Philadelphia society matron who has fallen on hard times. Rose and her domineering mother (Frances Fisher) are returning from vacation in Europe.

Cal Hockley (Billy Zane), Rose's finance is traveling with them. He is very rich, but very nasty. Only a self-centered, social-climbing mother could want this guy for a son-in-law.

As anyone could easily predict, Rose doesn't love Cal. Why should she? He treats her like a piece of property. She is only marrying him to please her mother. In addition, Rose feels trapped by the social rules of the upper class. At the beginning of the movie, Rose recalls her trip on the Titanic, as "... a slave ship, taking me back to America in chains."

Suddenly, we see Rose running across the deck to commit suicide by jumping off the ship. Cameron doesn't provide enough background for such a desperate act but he needed a way for Rose and the hero Jack Dawson (Leonardo DiCaprio) to meet. The scene is unrealistic but it gets the job done. Jack is a poor but bold artist who had already noticed Rose from afar.

This is where the film starts to take off. It has all of the elegance and romance of a 1940s Hollywood film. In true Hollywood fashion, Rose introduces young Jack to civilized upper-class society, horrifying her mother and making her finance very jealous. In return, Jack shows her that you don't have to be rich to have fun, and teaches her to spit like a man.

The romance between Jack and Rose takes up the first half of the movie. Then the iceberg hits and we see Cameron at his best. The special effects are the most amazing that he (or any other director) has ever put on the screen. This is his true strength as a director.

Of course, no film is without its faults. One major problem is that not enough is done with the minor characters. For example, Danny Nucci's role as Jack's friend is left completely undeveloped. And Kathy Bates is wonderful as Molly Brown, but we don't see enough of her. In addition, the main characters are stereotypes. Rose is beautiful and sweet. Jack is poor but honest. And Cal is thoroughly evil. However, despite these faults, you will find yourself caring about and believing in these people.

The computer-generated special effects are simply awesome. There will be no doubt in your mind that the Titanic is sinking. However, other scenes, such as crowd scenes, are not as believable. Cameron uses computer images most effectively to connect the past to the present. For example, he shows us the wreck of the Titanic lying on the floor of the ocean and then magically it becomes the ship moving through the sea.

No one knows if Titanic will make money or not. With a price tag of $200 million, it will have to do very, very well both in the United States and abroad. The simple story should help.

Movie-goers all over the world will be able to identify with Rose, Jack and the rest of the passengers on that unlucky ship. Whether or not the film is a financial success, Cameron has succeeded in making a wonderful romantic epic.

45　　Despite some flaws, this Titanic really does float. Don't miss it.

NEW WORDS

alien/ˈeiljən/ *n.*	foreigner　外侨;外星人
abyss/əˈbis/ *n.*	hole so deep as to appear bottomless; hell, or the lower world　深渊
terminator/ˈtəːmineitə/ *n.*	someone who put an end to…　终结者
epic/ˈepik/ *n.*	史诗
a.	史诗般的
smokestack/ˈsməukstæk/ *n.*	烟筒
matron/ˈmeitrən/ *n.*	married woman or widow　主妇
domineer/dɔmiˈniə/ *v.*	act or speak in a dominating manner　控制,支配
nasty/ˈnɑːsti/ *a.*	morally dirty and unpleasant　下流的,道德沦丧的
elegance/ˈeligəns/ *n.*	good taste, beauty and grace　品位高雅;优美,典雅
iceberg/ˈaisbəg/ *n.*	冰山
stereotype/ˈstiəriəutaip/ *n.*	fixed in form, used and repeated without change　老套路
awesome/ˈɔːsəm/ *a.*	引起敬畏的

PHRASES

science fiction: 科幻电影
tried-and-true: 真实可信
fall on hard times: have a difficult time in life　苦难
commit suicide: kill oneself　自杀
at one's best: showing one's strong point　显示长处,最佳状态
there will be no doubt in your mind: you will completely believe　完全相信

NOTES

The Abyss: a science fiction movie《深渊》
The Terminator: a science fiction movie《终结者》

special effect：电影特技
leading man：男主演
price tag：价格标签

EXERCISES

Reading Comprehension:

A. Answer the questions below about the different parts of the movie review.

1. Read the title and the first paragraph. What do you think the writer's opinion of the movie is? Why do you think so?

   _____
   _____

2. What is the purpose of Paras. 3-6?

   _____
   _____

3. How is paragraph 8 a little different from the rest of the review?

   _____
   _____

4. What is the purpose of Paras. 10-11?

   _____
   _____

5. What is the author's attitude towards the movie?

   _____
   _____

B. Complete the detailed information below about the movie *Titanic*.

1. Movie title: *Titanic*
2. Director: _____
3. Main characters   4. Played by
_____   _____
_____   _____

续表

5. Minor characters	6. Played by
_____	_____
_____	_____

7. Good points of the movie: _____
   _____
   _____
   _____

   Specific examples: _____
   _____
   _____

8. Criticism of the movie: _____
   _____
   _____
   _____

   Specific examples: _____
   _____
   _____

9. Comparisons with other movies: _____
   _____

10. Writer's overall opinion: _____

UNIT 7

Part A   Text (The Land of the Lock)
Part B   Grammar (定语从句)
Part C   Supplementary Reading
         (Beyond the *Right* to Die, Will It Become a *Duty* to Die?)

Part A Text

Warm-up Questions:
1. *In your opinion, what does "lock" stand for?*
2. *What do you think of the personal safety and security of property in China?*
3. *What kinds of safeguards do people use in China?*

The Land of the Lock

By Bob Greene

   Years ago in America, it was customary for families to leave their doors unlocked, day and night. In this essay, Greene regrets that people can no longer trust each other and have to resort to elaborate security systems to protect themselves and their valuables. Although the author is writing his opinion, he uses many examples to reinforce his ideas and to prove his thesis.

   In the house where I grew up, it was our custom to leave the front door on the latch at night. I don't know if that was a local term or if it is universal; "on the latch" meant the door was closed but not locked. None of us carried keys; the last one in for the evening would close up, and that was it.

Those days are over. In rural areas as well as in cities, doors do not stay unlocked, even for part of an evening.

Suburbs and country areas are, in many ways, even more vulnerable than well-patrolled urban streets. Statistics show the crime rate rising more dramatically in those allegedly tranquil areas than in cities. At any rate, the era of leaving the front door on the latch is over.

It has been replaced by locks, security chains, electronic alarm systems and trip wires hooked up to a police station or private guard firm. Many suburban families have sliding glass doors on their patios, with steel bars elegantly built in so no one can pry the doors open.

It is not uncommon, in the most pleasant of homes, to see pasted on the windows decals announcing that the premises are under surveillance by this security force or that guard company.

The lock is the new symbol of America. Indeed, a recent public-service advertisement by a large insurance company featured not actuarial charts but a picture of a child's bicycle with the now-usual padlock attached to it.

The ad pointed out that, yes, it is the insurance companies that pay for stolen goods, but who is going to pay for what the new atmosphere of distrust and fear is doing to our way of life? Who is going to make the psychic payment for the transformation of America from the Land of the Free to the Land of the Lock?

For that is what has happened, we have become so used to defending ourselves against the new atmosphere of American life, so used to putting up barriers, that we have not had time to think about what it may mean.

For some reason we are satisfied when we think we are well-protected; it does not occur to us to ask ourselves: Why has this happened? Why are we having to barricade ourselves against our neighbors and fellow citizens, and when, exactly, did this start to take over our lives?

And it has taken over. If you work for a medium to large-size company, chances are that you don't just wander in and out of work. You probably carry some kind of access card, electronic or otherwise, that allows you in and out of your place of work. Maybe the security guard at the front desk knows your face and will wave you in most days, but the fact remains that the business you work for feels threatened enough to keep outsiders away via these "keys".

It wasn't always like this. Even a decade ago, most private businesses had a policy of free access. It simply didn't occur to managers that the proper thing to do was to distrust people.

Look at the airports. Parents used to take children out to departure gates to watch planes land and take off. That's all gone. Airports are no longer a place of education and fun; they are the most sophisticated of security encampments.

With electronic X-ray equipment, we seem finally to have figured out a way to hold the terrorists, real and imagined, at bay; it was such a relief to solve this problem that we did not think much about what such a state of affairs says about the quality of our lives. We now pass through these electronic friskers without so much as a sideways glance; the machines, and what they stand for, have won.

Businessmen, in increasing numbers, are purchasing new machines that hook up to the telephone and analyze a caller's voice. The machines are supposed to tell the businessman, with a small margin of error, whether his friend or client is telling lies.

All this is being done in the name of "security"; that is what we tell ourselves. We are fearful, and so we devise ways to lock the fear out, and that, we decide, is what security means.

But no, with all this "security", we are perhaps the most insecure nation in the history of civilized man. What better word to describe the way in which we have been forced to live? What better indictment of all that we have become in this new and puzzling time?

We trust no one. We have become so smart about self-protection that, in the end, we all outsmarted ourselves. We may have locked the evils out, but in doing so we have locked ourselves in.

That may be the legacy we remember best when we look back on this age: In dealing with the unseen horrors among us, we became prisoners of ourselves. All of us are prisoners, in this time of our troubles.

NEW WORDS

feature/ˈfiːtʃə/ v. display, represent prominently 展示,特写
 n. prominent article in a newspaper 特写;特别报道
resort/riˈzɔːt/ v. make use of for help or to gain one's purpose 求助,付诸
elaborate/iˈlæbərit/ a. carefully prepared and finished; complicated 精心完成的;复杂的
reinforce/ˌriːinˈfɔːs/ v. make stronger by adding or supplying more men or material 增援,加强

Unit 7

latch /lætʃ/ *n.*		门闩
patrol /pə'trəul/ *v.*		巡逻；巡查
dramatically /drə'mætikli/ *ad.*	in a dramatic manner	紧张地；戏剧性地
allege /ə'ledʒ/ *v.*	declare; state	宣称；提出
tranquil /'træŋkwil/ *a.*	calm, quiet	安静的，平静的
pry /prai/ *v.*	get sth. open, lift sth. up	撬开，举起
paste /peist/ *v.*	stick with paste	粘贴
decal /di'kæl/ *n.*	a design on specially prepared paper for transfer to wood, metal, or glass	贴花纸，贴花转成的图案
premise /'premis/ *n. pl.*	house or building with its outbuildings, land, etc.	房屋连同附属建筑、土地等，房产
surveillance /sə'veiləns/ *n.*	close watch kept over someone or something	监视；盯梢
actuarial /ˌæktju'ɛəriəl/ *a.*	of an actuary or his work	保险核计的；理赔员的
padlock /'pædlɔk/ *n.*		挂锁；扣锁
psychic /'saikik/ *a.*	of the soul or mind	灵魂的，心灵的
transformation /ˌtrænsfə'meiʃən/ *n.*	changing or being changed	变化，转变
barrier /'bæriə/ *n.*	sth. that prevents, hinders or controls progress or movement 阻碍物，障碍物；hindrance	阻碍，障碍
barricade /ˌbæri'keid/ *v.*	block with a barricade	以阻绝障碍物堵塞
access /'ækses/ *n.*	way to a place	通路
via /'vaiə/ *prep.*	by way of	（拉）经由
sophisticated /sə'fistikeitid/ *a.*	complex; with the latest improvements and refinements	复杂的；最新式且最先进的
encampment /in'kæmpmənt/ *n.*	place where troops, etc. are encamped	宿营地，露营地
frisker /'friskə/ *n.*		搜查仪
sideways /'saidweiz/ *a.*	moving, directed or tending toward one side	斜着，斜向一边
indictment /in'daitmənt/ *n.*	accusation	控告，起诉，谴责
outsmart /aut'smɑːt/ *v.*	be smarter, clever, more cunning than	比……更聪明，以机智胜过
legacy /'legəsi/ *n.*	property or money given by a last will and testament	遗产，祖先或先辈传留下来的东西

PHRASES

resort to: make use of for help or to gain one's purpose, etc.　求助;依赖;诉诸

on the latch: 上着门闩(并非锁着)

the premises are under surveillance: (police term) the property is being watched　本房产在监护之下

chances are that: probably, in all probability　很可能

in the name of: with the authority of　以……的名义

at any rate: in any case; whatever happens　总之,无论如何

attach to: go with, be joined to　附有,附属

hook up: connect sth. to　安装

stand for: represent　代表,象征

take over: assume control or possession　接管,接收

hold/keep (sb. or sth.) at bay: to keep (sb. or sth.) some distance away　不使……接近,遏制

NOTE

Bob Greene is a feature writer whose column is published in many newspapers throughout the United States. His articles explore particular aspects of contemporary life—news events, political issues, and social problems.

EXERCISES

I. *Reading Comprehension*:

Choose the best answer to each question.

1. The new atmosphere of American life refers to _____.

    A. feeling satisfied when we think we are well-protected

    B. distrust and fear

    C. relying on the insurance company

    D. doing everything in the name of security

Unit 7

2. What does "we have outsmarted ourselves" mean?
   A. We are not so smart as we think.
   B. Many people are smarter than us.
   C. You can never be too smart.
   D. We are victims of our own cleverness.
3. People are buying machines that hook up to telephones to _____.
   A. analyze a caller's voice
   B. know the caller's phone number before answering it
   C. answer the phone when they are out
   D. narrow the margin of error
4. From the passage, we can infer that _____.
   A. country areas are much more safer than cities
   B. with all the security, the US is the most secure country in the world
   C. Americans take many precautions to protect themselves because they do not trust the insurance company
   D. airports used to be a place for learning and enjoyment
5. Which statement is NOT true according to the passage?
   A. Managers a decade ago thought it was natural they should trust people.
   B. Modern people have taken the security facilities for granted.
   C. People nowadays don't believe in strangers, but they take neighbours as their friends.
   D. We are all prisoners of ourselves.

II. *Getting Information*:

Answer the following questions in English.

1. What was the custom in the author's childhood?
   _____
2. Do people there keep the custom till now?
   _____
3. Are the suburbs less likely to suffer from crime than the cities?
   _____
4. What does the "lock" stand for?
   _____
5. What kinds of safeguards do people use in addition to regular keyed locks?
   _____

6. Since insurance companies pay for loss of personal property, what else does the author worry about?

7. What does the "psychic payment" refer to in the author's opinion?

8. Do people ask themselves why they have to defend themselves against others?

9. What might people do when they took their children to the airport in the past?

10. What will we remember best when we look back on this age?

III. *Vocabulary and Structure*:

A. Choose the correct word to fit into each sentence, using the proper form.

access	allege	barrier	indictment	sophisticated
feature	vulnerable	devise	legacy	via
transformation	outsmart	patrol	trip	

1. _____ in the color of sea water from blue to green seems to be caused by high and low concentration of salt.
2. Students must have _____ to good books.
3. Poor health and lack of money may both be _____ to educational progress.
4. It was so kind of you to send that message _____ Jim.
5. It has been necessary to _____ a system of universal schooling.
6. The report _____ that the motive was financial.
7. These characteristics of British industry are a(n) _____ of pre-war unemployment.
8. These planes are among the most _____ aircraft now being manufactured.
9. It is a striking _____ of our educational system that so many children cannot read or write.
10. Lack of employment tends to make women _____ to depression.

Unit 7

B. Choose from Column (B) words which are close in meaning to those in Column (A).

(A)	(B)
buy	purchase
accusation	surveillance
complex	transformation
safe	barricade
social environment	indictment
watch	complicated
change	atmosphere
barrier	secure

C. Complete the following sentences with the missing prepositions or adverbs.
1. If other means fail, we shall resort _____ force.
2. Ray went out, leaving the door _____ the latch.
3. Police are keeping the area _____ constant surveillance.
4. Cruel experiments on animals are carried out _____ the name of science.
5. They've had technical problems _____ any rate that's what they told me.
6. The web was only attached _____ the leaf by one thread.
7. Is the video hooked _____ to the TV?
8. "My name is Dean E. Beller." "What does the E stand _____?"
9. Will you take _____ the driving when we reach Madison.
10. The growling of dogs held the strangers _____ bay.

IV. *Translation*:

A. Translate the following into English.
1. 如果你卷入别人的问题，你很可能会以陷入不愉快的境况而告终。(chances are that)
2. 他认为保卫祖国抵御敌人是自己的职责。(defend against)
3. 不要太重视他的话。(attach to)
4. 住宅逐渐消失，慢慢变成了办公室。(take over)
5. 他应该已经在工作，但是他却在忙别的事情。(otherwise)
6. 他从来没有想过她也许是在撒谎。(occur to)
7. 他还没想好将来要干什么。(figure out)
8. 他们以五个坐席的微弱优势获胜。(margin)

9. 回想起我们在那里度过的一个月,我们心中充满了感激之情。(look back on)
10. 这辆汽车很旧,但不管怎样,花费的钱不多。(at any rate)
11. 他们不能使用煤气炉,因为还没安装好。(hook up)
12. 他忘记自己应该维持秩序了。(be supposed to)

B. Translate the following into Chinese.

1. In this essay, Greene regrets that people can no longer trust each other and have to resort to elaborate security systems to protect themselves and their valuables.
2. Statistics show the crime rate is rising more dramatically in those allegedly tranquil areas than in cities.
3. The ad pointed out that, yes, it is the insurance companies that pay for stolen goods, but who is going to pay for what the new atmosphere of distrust and fear is doing to our way of life?
4. It simply didn't occur to managers that the proper thing to do was to distrust people.
5. It was such a relief to solve this problem that we did not think much about what such a state of affairs says about the quality of our lives.

V. *Writing Task*:

Write a short passage on "Trust". Your writing should include the following information. (about 120 words)

1. 相互信任是人与人交往的基础。
2. 现代社会更需要信任。
3. 没有信任的社会是不存在的。

VI. *Oral Practice*:

1. Advances in technology have made it possible to develop very clever and sophisticated security devices. Although a person is physically safe, what is his or her psychological state like? What happens to people when trust is lost? What should they do?
2. Define the word "trust" as it applies to this article. Then give and discuss examples of trust or the lack of it in specific situations around you. What conclusions can you reach about trust in contemporary society?
3. What is the main idea, or theme, of this article?

Unit 7

Part B Grammar

定语从句（Attributive Clauses）

定语从句是以从句的形式修饰某一名词，一般用关系代词或关系副词引导。如：
- I've read all the books that you lent me. （关系代词）
- She knows that man who came to see us yesterday. （关系代词）
- This is the school where he studied ten years ago. （关系副词）
- That is the reason why he was late for the class. （关系副词）
- The tool with which he is working is called a spanner. （介词+which 的定语从句）

常用的关系代词还有 whom, whose, which；常用的关系副词还有 when, why 和 how。

练 习

1. 将下面的中文句子翻译成英语并注意定语从句的翻译及表达。
   （1）你去过九寨沟吗？那可是个好地方。
   （2）汤姆向老师解释了他迟到的原因。
   （3）这是小王最爱去的餐馆之一。
   （4）她就是昨天给我们做报告的教授。
   （5）北京是全国人民向往的首都。
   （6）我们班有 33 名同学，其中 10 人来自上海。
   （7）图书馆是学生自习的好地方。
   （8）这就是多年前毛主席用过的书桌。
   （9）他向我们详细介绍了研究的过程，这对我们来说非常重要。
   （10）他们还没有决定他们去上海的时间。

2. 选择适当的词语填空。
   （1）He often visited the grain mill of Peter, _____ to experiment with new things.
       A. that likes   B. whom liked
       C. who liked   D. which liked
   （2）She found a place in the building _____ she used as her first laboratory.
       A. which   B. where   C. in which   D. when

(3) Do you know the exact time _____ the meeting will begin?

　　A. which　　　B. when　　　C. why　　　D. as

(4) She wanted to join the group of men _____ was to explore the mysteries of the mountains.

　　A. their work　　B. who work　　C. who　　D. whose work

(5) This is the reason _____ an airplane can't fly in space.

　　A. for that　　B. which　　C. why　　D. where

(6) More and more people are beginning to learn English, _____ is becoming popular here.

　　A. that　　B. it　　C. which　　D. what

(7) The factory _____ last year was equipped with the latest machinery.

　　A. which I worked　　　　　B. in which I worked

　　C. for which I worked in　　D. where I worked in

(8) This is the house _____ last year when I was in this city.

　　A. about that I wrote to you

　　B. that I wrote to you

　　C. about which I wrote to you

　　D. which I wrote to you

(9) He is the very man _____ we have been looking for.

　　A. who　　B. whom　　C. which　　D. that

(10) It's the best film _____ I've ever seen.

　　A. it　　B. which　　C. that　　D. what

(11) This is Peter _____ you met last week.

　　A. his sister　　　　　B. whose sister

　　C. that sister　　　　D. the sister whom

(12) These were the graduate assistants _____ to do the research work in the lab.

　　A. to whom it was their responsibility

　　B. whose responsibility there was

　　C. whose responsibility it was

　　D. of whom with the responsibility

(13) He will never forget the days _____ he spent with his grandma.

　　A. that　　B. when　　C. where　　D. on which

(14) The tree, the branches _____ are almost bare, is a very old one.

　　A. whose　　B. in which　　C. of which　　D. which

(15) An old friend from abroad, _____ I was expecting to stay with me, telephoned from the airport.

A. which B. from which C. whom D. that

3. 将下面每组中的两个英语句子以定语的方式转换成一个复合句。

(1) This is my classmate. I share a room with him.
(2) He has signed the contract. Under this contract he has to work here for three years.
(3) The teacher advised me to read this book. This book may help me to pass the test.
(4) This is one of those things. We have to put up with such things.
(5) The fire started on the first floor of the building. Many of its rooms are offices.

Part C Supplementary Reading

Beyond the *Right* to Die, Will It Become a *Duty* to Die?

By Arthur D. Silk

Here is a physician's view of who should decide whether a terminally ill person should live or die. In his argument, Dr. Silk examines the problems of prolonged suffering, extended medical treatment, financial drain, guilt, and decision making.

It is morally terrifying to me to consider legislating "the right to die".

No one has the right or desire to extend life simply to prolong suffering, but economic pressures are beginning to erode humanitarian considerations. Medical economists have calculated that 60% or more of an individual's entire lifetime medical expense is generated in the last year of life. It follows, then, that if we could predict that terminal period (and eliminate or ignore it) we could find the long-sought magic that would immediately and drastically cut soaring medical expenses.

Since it is not given to the best of our medical prognosticators to predict with certainty and finality just when that last 12 months will begin or end, and because our Judeo-Christian ethic is dedicated to the sanctity of life, we physicians, with the endorsement of society, keep trying to extend, as well as to improve, life. But, as several sociologists familiar with the British hospice movement have asked, if the right to die is legitimized by statute, how long will it be before the *right* to die becomes the *duty* to die?

Committees of physicians are already legally required to decide what medical and surgical procedures should be done, whether they may be done in a hospital, and how long the hospital convalescence may take. Is it too much to imagine that, empowered by right-to-die laws, the duties of these committees will extend to the judgment of who shall live and who shall die?

The moral precedent for such decisions is already taken for granted by triage physicians in war and disaster—those who assign the priorities for medical treatment on the basis of urgency or chance of survival. It would be such a little step, and with such big potential for massive financial savings, to allow a committee to decide that a patient beyond a certain stage of colon or breast cancer could not be treated. Would we apply a different standard to those whom we choose to condemn by benevolent neglect if they were over 70 or under 35, if they were rich and famous or poor and unknown?

Indeed, how long would it take before the stricken individual, feeling comfortable and functional but sensing the emotional and financial drain of his loved ones, became sufficiently guilt-ridden to request the right to die prematurely?

Prematurely! Ah, there's the rub. We're all going to die—some gracefully and without suffering, some after protracted, painful and debilitating treatment. In retrospect, it is easy to make decisions when we have seen the quality of a life deteriorate. But who among us can sufficiently codify the stages of the quality of life to make the decision in advance to extinguish it? Would we be successfully transplanting kidneys, hearts and livers today if we had legislated the right to die 20 years ago?

What is the answer? How do we let go of our relatives and friends without guilt or sin or unnecessarily prolonged suffering? We do it in the same way in which we have done it over the years. First a caring physician establishes rapport with the patient and his family. Together they make a compassionate, *unwritten* decision to stop trying. Lawyers and legislators have no part in life's final drama.

NEW WORDS

beyond/bi'jɔnd/*prep.* surpassing, exceeding 超出；出乎
legislate/'ledʒisleit/*vt.* to make or pass laws approving or disapproving certain actions 通过立法以使……产生或成立

Unit 7

prolong/prə'lɔŋ/*vt.*	lengthen or extend 延长;拖延
erode/i'rəud/*vt.*	wear away, weaken, disintegrate 腐蚀;削弱
terminal/'tə:minl/*a.*	of the point at the end 末期的,尽头的
eliminate/i'limineit/*vt.*	remove, get rid of 除去,剔除
long-sought/ˌlɔŋ'sɔ:t/*a.*	long searched for or looked for 长期以来一直寻找的
drastically/'dræstikli/*ad.*	severely; harshly 激烈地,猛烈地
soaring/'sɔ:riŋ/*a.*	elevated or rapidly rising above usual and ordinary levels 崇高的,高涨的
prognosticator/prəgnɔsti'keitə/*n.*	person who can foretell or predict 预言家
sanctity/'sæŋktiti/*n.*	sacredness; holiness 圣洁,神圣
endorsement/in'dɔ:smənt/*n.*	written approval or support; sanction 认可,赞同,背书
hospice/'hɔspis/*n.*	an institution devoted to the care of the terminally ill 临终护理所
statute/'stætju:t/*n.*	law 法律,法令
convalescence/kɔnvə'lesns/*n.*	gradual recovery period after illness 逐渐恢复健康,恢复期
empower/im'pauə/*vt.*	to give power or authority 授权,准许
precedent/'president/*n.*	an action that may serve as an example or reason for a later action 先例
triage/'traieidʒ/*n.*	a system of assigning priorities of medical treatment based on urgency, chance for survival, etc. and used on battlefields and in hospital emergency wards 根据紧急程度、生存可能性而决定优先治疗的制度
urgency/'ə:dʒənsi/*n.*	need for action; necessity; importance 紧急,迫切
colon/'kəulən/*n.*	part of the large intestine extending to the rectum 结肠
benevolent/bi'nevələnt/*a.*	charitable, suggestive of good will 仁慈的,慈善的,好心好意的
condemn/kən'dem/*vt.*	denounce; declare incurable 谴责;宣告(患者)无法治疗

stricken /ˈstrikən/ *a.*　　afflicted (by wounds or illness)　患病的
guilt-ridden /ˈgiltridn/ *a.*　　dominated by guilty in thoughts　自责,内疚
prematurely /prəˈmætjuəli/ *ad.*　　before the proper or usual time　过早地,不到期地
protracted /prəˈtræktid/ *a.*　　lengthened; prolonged　延长的,拖延的
retrospect /ˈretrəuspekt/ *n.*　　view of past events　回顾,回溯
debilitating /diˈbiliteitiŋ/ *a.*　　weakening; enfeebling　衰弱的
deteriorate /diˈtiəriəreit/ *vi.*　　worsen; lower in quality　变坏,恶化,变质
codify /ˈkɔdifai/ *vt.*　　systematize, classify　系统整理,分类
extinguish /iksˈtiŋgwiʃ/ *vt.*　　put an end to; destroy　消灭
caring /ˈkɛəriŋ/ *a.*　　affectionate, helpful and sympathetic　有爱心的,助人为乐的,富有同情心的
rapport /ræˈpɔ:t/ *n.*　　close or sympathetic relationship　(尤指和睦、亲善的)关系,联系

PHRASES

in retrospect: looking at past events, etc.　回顾
in advance to: before　事前,在前
let go of sb. or sth.: release one's hold of　放开,放手,松手

NOTES

There's the rub.: difficulty; point at which doubt or difficulty arise　困难,引起疑虑或困难之点
Judeo-Christian: common to Judaism and Christianity　犹太教和基督教所共有的

EXERCISES

I. Reading Comprehension:

Choose the correct answers among the four choices below. There is only one correct answer.

1. Legislating "the right to die" is good in many respects EXCEPT _____.
   A. cutting down the medical expense in a great amount

B. lessening the suffering of the terminally ill
   C. unnecessary suffering
   D. advancing medical treatment
2. From the passage, physicians are ready to extend or improve life because _____.
   A. it is their responsibility
   B. they are kind enough to help their patients
   C. they don't want to break the law
   D. they are guided by the Judeo-Christian ethic
3. The concern of several sociologists who are familiar with the hospice movement is _____.
   A. to make it a law to decide who shall live and who shall die
   B. how long it will take for us to take up the duty to die
   C. to strengthen the hospice movement
   D. to ask the law-making body to pass a law of right to die as soon as possible
4. The long-sought magic refers to _____.
   A. lightening economic pressures in medical care
   B. extending life by some newly developed medicine
   C. immediate fulfillment of dying without pain
   D. an increasing number of qualified physicians
5. The author holds that "the duty to die" can be decided by _____.
   A. legislators and lawyers   B. physicians
   C. relatives   D. both B and C

II. *Getting Information*:

Answer the following questions in English.

1. How does Silk feel about legislating "the right to die"?

_____

2. What is the relationship between economic pressures and humanitarian considerations?

_____

3. What is the way Silk mentions to cut the medical expenses "immediately and drastically"?

_____

4. Why shouldn't all physicians do as the triage physicians have done?

_____

5. What moral problems does Silk foresee with legislating the right to "premature" death?
_____

III. *Vocabulary*:
Choose the correct word to fill into each sentence, using the proper form.

| beyond | soaring | endorsement | empower | precedent |
| prematurely | protracted | debilitating | codify | rapport |

1. This meeting is _____ unexpectedly.
2. We want to _____ the procedures.
3. The police are _____ to arrest suspected criminals.
4. It's _____ me why she stole the money.
5. The lung cancer he suffered _____ him.
6. She is capable of making a close _____ between herself and her students.
7. The housing price in this city is getting higher and higher at a(n) _____ speed.
8. He promised full _____ of the plan.
9. The lawyer found a(n) _____ from a court case in the 19th century.
10. He made an announcement that he had won the election _____.

114

Part A   Text (Perfume)
Part B   Grammar (状语从句)
Part C   Supplementary Reading
         (Travelling Pamphlet)

Part A   Text

Warm-up Questions:

1. *Do you still remember your school teachers?*
2. *Can you tell about one teacher who gave you a deep impression?*
3. *What do you think is the function of a teacher?*

Perfume

Anonymous

As she stood in front of her 5th grade class on the very first day of school, she told the children an untruth. Like most teachers, she looked at her students and said that she loved them all the same. But that was impossible, because there in the front row, slumped in his seat, was a little boy named Teddy Stoddard. Mrs. Thompson had watched Teddy the year before and noticed that he didn't play well with the other children, that his clothes were messy and that he constantly needed a bath. And Teddy could be unpleasant. It got to the point where Mrs. Thompson would actually take delight marking his papers with a broad red pen, making bold

X's and then putting a big "F" at the top of his papers.

However, when she reviewed his file, she was in for a surprise. Teddy's first grade teacher wrote, "Teddy is a bright child with a ready laugh. He does his work neatly and has good manners... he is a joy to be around." His second grade teacher wrote, "Teddy is an excellent student, well liked by his classmates, but he is troubled because his mother has a terminal illness and life at home must be a struggle." His third grade teacher wrote, "His mother's death has been hard on him. He tries to do his best, but his father doesn't show much interest and his home life will soon affect him if some steps aren't taken." Teddy's fourth grade teacher wrote, "Teddy is withdrawn and doesn't show much interest in school. He doesn't have many friends and he sometimes sleeps in class."

By now, Mrs. Thompson realized the problem and she was ashamed of herself. She felt even worse when her students brought her Christmas presents, wrapped in beautiful ribbons and bright paper, except for Teddy's. His present was clumsily wrapped in the heavy, brown paper that he got from a grocery bag. Mrs. Thompson took pains to open it in the middle of the other presents. Some of the children started to laugh when she found a rhinestone bracelet with some of the stones missing, and a bottle that was one-quarter full of perfume. But she stifled the children's laughter when she exclaimed how pretty the bracelet was, putting it on, and dabbing some of the perfume on her wrist. Teddy Stoddard stayed after school that day just long to say, "Mrs. Thompson today you smelled just like my Mom used to." After the children left she cried for at least an hour. On that very day, she quit teaching reading, writing, and arithmetic. Instead, she began to teach children.

Mrs. Thompson paid particular attention to Teddy. As she worked with him, his mind seemed to come alive. The more she encouraged him, the faster he responded. By the end of the year Teddy had become one of the smartest children in the class and, despite her lie that she would love all the children the same, Teddy became one of her "teacher's pets." A year later, she found a note under her door, from Teddy, telling her that she was still the best teacher he ever had in his whole life. Six years went by before she got another note from Teddy. He then wrote that he had finished high school, third in his class, and she was still the best teacher he ever had in his whole life. Four years after that, she got another letter, saying that while things had been tough at times, he'd stayed in school, had stuck with it, and would soon graduate from college with the highest of honors. He assured Mrs. Thompson that she was still the best and favorite teacher he'd ever had in his whole life. Then four more years passed and yet another letter came. This time he explained that after he got his bachelor's degree, he decided to go a little further. The letter explained that she was still the best and favorite teacher he ever had. But now his name was a little longer... the letter was signed, Theodore F. Stoddard, MD.

The story doesn't end there. You see, there was yet another letter that spring. Teddy said he'd met this girl and was going to be married. He explained that his father had died a couple of years ago and he was wondering if Mrs. Thompson might agree to sit at the wedding in the place that was usually reserved for the mother of the groom. Of course, Mrs. Thompson did. And guess what? She wore that bracelet, the one with several rhinestones missing. And she made sure she was wearing the perfume that Teddy remembered his mother wearing on their last Christmas together.

They hugged each other, and Dr. Stoddard whispered in Mrs. Thompson's ear, "Thank you Mrs. Thompson for believing in me. Thank you so much for making me feel important and showing me that I could make a difference". Mrs. Thompson, with tears in her eyes, whispered back. She said, "Teddy, you have it all wrong. You were the one who taught me that I could make a difference. I didn't know how to teach until I met you."

NEW WORDS

anonymous /əˈnɒniməs/ a.	having an unknown or unacknowledged name 匿名的
untruth /ˈʌnˈtruːθ/ n.	something untrue; a lie 不真实的某件事物；谎言
slump /slʌmp/ v.	to droop, as in sitting or standing 懒散地坐着
messy /ˈmesi/ a.	disorderly and dirty 凌乱的，肮脏的
constantly /ˈkɒnstəntli/ ad.	all the time, very often 不变地；经常地
mark /mɑːk/ v.	to make a visible trace or impression on 根据字母或数字的级别来打分数
bold /bəuld/ a.	clear and distinct 醒目的；清晰的；易见的
review /riˈvjuː/ v.	to look over, study, or examine again 复习；重新仔细察看
terminal /ˈtəːminəl/ a.	causing, ending in, or approaching death 晚期的；引起、导致或接近死亡的；致命的
withdrawn /wiðˈdrɔːn/ a.	not friendly or sociable 孤独的；性格内向的
ashamed /əˈʃeimd/ a.	feelings shame or guilt 羞愧的；感到害臊或有罪的
wrap /ræp/ v.	to enclose, especially in paper, and fasten 包裹

ribbon/ˈribən/ n.　　　　　　　　a narrow strip or band of fine fabric　缎带;窄条带或条饰
clumsily/ˈklʌmzili/ ad.　　　　　awkwardly constructed　制作粗陋的
rhinestone/ˈrainstəun/ n.　　　a colorless artificial gem　莱茵石;人造宝石
bracelet/ˈbreislit/ n.　　　　　an ornamental band or chain encircling the wrist or arm　手镯
stifle/ˈstaifl/ v.　　　　　　　hold back; repress　打断或切断(如声音)
dab/dæb/ v.　　　　　　　　　to apply with short, poking strokes　轻拍;轻触;很快地涂抹
tough/tʌf/ a.　　　　　　　　bad, difficult　麻烦的;困难的
stick/stik/ v.　　　　　　　　to persist or endure　坚持或保持
assure/əˈʃuə/ v.　　　　　　　to cause to feel sure　向……保证
reserve/riˈzəːv/ v.　　　　　　to keep back, as for future use or for a special purpose　保留
groom/gruːm/ n.　　　　　　　bridegroom　新郎
hug/hʌg/ v.　　　　　　　　　to clasp or hold closely　拥抱
whisper/ˈ(h)wispə/ v.　　　　 to say or tell privately or secretly　暗中秘密地及私下里说

PHRASES

be in for a surprise: be very much surprised　大吃一惊
a joy to be around: a person who makes people around him happy　让周围的人开心的人
take delight doing sth.: enjoy doing sth.　高兴做某事
take steps: take action　采取措施
be ashamed of: feel shame　感到羞愧
take pains to do sth.: make an effort to do sth. or to be careful in doing sth.　费尽力气,小心翼翼地做
quit doing sth.: stop doing sth.　停止做某事
stick with: continue with sth. and not turn away　[口]坚持做(某事)
make a difference: have an important effect on sth. or a situation　有影响;起重要作用

Unit 8

NOTES

an untruth: (formal) a word meaning a lie, used because one wants to avoid saying it directly 讲不实在的话(以避免直接用"谎言"一词)

a big "F": 学业中的不及格(美国学校一般都使用字母等级来表示学生的学业表现: A 表示优秀, B 表示优良, C 表示平均水平, D 表示低于平均水平, F 表示不及格)

bachelor's degree: 学士学位

MD: 医学博士

EXERCISES

I. Reading Comprehension:

Choose the best answer to each question.

1. When Mrs. Thompson met Teddy Stoddard, she felt all the following EXCEPT that _____.
    A. he was not active in class
    B. his clothes were not clean
    C. he should take a bath
    D. he needed a mother to take care of him

2. From the comments of Teddy's previous teachers it can be implied that _____.
    A. Teddy used to be a smart boy
    B. Teddy had been liked by his classmates
    C. Teddy's father had neglected his duty towards Teddy
    D. Family changes had a huge effect on little kids

3. Mrs. Thompson tried the perfume given by Teddy because _____.
    A. she liked the smell of the perfume
    B. she did not want Teddy to be embarrassed
    C. she did not want other children to give her any gift
    D. she was moved by the gift given by Teddy

4. According to Paragraph 4 all the following statements are correct EXCEPT _____.
    A. Teddy turned into a smart student again after getting attention from Mrs. Thompson
    B. Mrs. Thompson has become the most important teacher in Teddy's life
    C. Teddy finished his high shool with the highest of honors
    D. Teddy continued to study for a higher degree after getting his bachelor's degree

5. We can infer from the last paragraph that _____.
   A. teaching has changed Teddy's life
   B. teaching has changed Mrs. Thompson's life
   C. so long as love is put into teaching, both teachers and students can learn things through it
   D. teaching can change a person's life

II. *Getting Information*:

Answer the following questions in English.

1. When Mrs. Thompson said that she loved all the students, why was it an untruth?
   _____

2. Why did Mrs. Thompton feel happy giving "F" to Teddy's papers?
   _____

3. What did Mrs. Thompton learn from Teddy's previous file?
   _____

4. When it says "…, she quit teaching reading, writing, and arithmetic. Instead, she began to teach children", what does it mean?
   _____

5. At the wedding, why did Teddy have that place for the mother of the groom reserved for Mrs. Thompson?
   _____

III. *Vocabulary and Structure*:

A. Choose the correct word/phrase to fill into each sentence, using the proper form.

| mark | reserve | review | ashamed | wrap |
| stifle | stick | withdraw | assure | hug |

1. The shop assistant _____ it up for her as quickly as possible.
2. I behaved badly yesterday and I am _____ of myself now.
3. _____ have a long tradition here, just to show friendliness to each other.
4. Don't forget to _____ your calendar for The 50th Annual CSI Show & Convention in Las Vegas, March 29 ~ April 1.
5. I am _____ in this close room.

6. We _____ all rights to allow or terminate a membership without any prior notification.
7. Nothing in history _____ the success of our civilization.
8. The passengers _____ against the wall as the car passed by.
9. The wheels of the car _____ in the mud and we could not go on.
10. If you wish to _____ a book that you already own or have access to for *Social Thought and Research*, feel free to submit it.

B. Find the proper forms of the following words according to the given word class.

1. withdraw   (*a.*) _____
2. hug   (*n.*) _____
3. reserve   (*n.*) _____
4. assure   (*n.*) _____
5. clumsily   (*a.*) _____
6. realize   (*n.*) _____
7. ashamed   (*n.*) _____
8. wed   (*n.*) _____
9. terminate   (*a.*) _____
10. encourage   (*n.*) _____

C. Complete the following sentences with the missing prepositions or adverbs.

1. As she stood in front of her 5th grade class _____ the very first day of school, she told the children an untruth.
2. Mrs. Thompson had watched Teddy the year _____ and noticed that he didn't play well with the other children, that his clothes were messy and that he constantly needed a bath.
3. However, when she reviewed his file, she was _____ for a surprise.
4. His mother's death has been hard _____ him.
5. By now, Mrs. Thompson realized the problem and she was ashamed _____ herself.
6. Some of the children started to laugh when she found a rhinestone bracelet _____ some of the stones missing, and a bottle that was one-quarter full of perfume.
7. Teddy Stoddard stayed _____ school that day just long to say, "Mrs. Thompson today you smelled just like my Mom used to."
8. Six years went by _____ she got another note from Teddy.
9. This time he explained that after he got his bachelor's degree, he decided to go a

little _____.

10. He explained that his father had died a couple of years ago and he was wondering if Mrs. Thompson might agree to sit _____ the wedding in the place that was usually reserved for the mother of the groom.

IV. *Translation*:

A. Translate the following into Chinese.

1. As she stood in front of her 5th grade class on the very first day of school, she told the children an untruth.

2. Mrs. Thompson had watched Teddy the year before and noticed that he didn't play well with the other children, that his clothes were messy and that he constantly needed a bath.

3. Teddy is an excellent student, well liked by his classmates, but he is troubled because his mother has a terminal illness and life at home must be a struggle.

4. But she stifled the children's laughter when she exclaimed how pretty the bracelet was, putting it on, and dabbing some of the perfume on her wrist.

5. Four years after that, she got another letter, saying that while things had been tough at times, he'd stayed in school, had stuck with it, and would soon graduate from college with the highest of honors.

B. Translate the following into English.

1. 最近,我有一个朋友辞去了他公司里的那份工资高但要求也高的工作。(quit)

2. 她以烹饪美食为乐。[take delight (in) doing sth.]

3. 她要查寻是否给她预定了房间。(reserve for)

4. 当你打开立体图书,你肯定会大吃一惊。(be in for)

5. 他一生中的两大爱好是音乐和绘画。(interest)

6. 婚礼以后,我们就回到中国去,因为我们在那里工作,并且打算在那里生活。(wedding)

7. 他们都饿了,因而感到饭菜喷香。(smell)

8. 树越高,风越大。(the... the...)

9. 他的妻子开玩笑说跟他结婚的是他的工作。(marry)

10. 这本书还到图书馆时,缺了12页。(missing)

V. *Writing Task*:

In your life, there should have been some teachers who left you a deep impression. Write a 120-word article about "**An Unforgettable Teacher**".

VI. *Oral Practice*:

Form a pair, and then talk about the following questions:
1. What do you think about Mrs. Thompson?
2. Do you think that love from a teacher makes a difference in teaching?
3. Do you think that love is the most important factor in education? Why or why not?

Part B　Grammar

状语从句 (Adverbial Clauses)

在复合句中,修饰主句中的动词、副词或整个句子等的从句叫状语从句。状语从句根据其表达的意思可分为时间、地点、原因、目的、结果、让步、比较和条件,分别由不同的连接词引出这些从句。

1) 时间状语从句的连词有: before、after、when、while、as soon as、once、since、the

moment 等:
- After he had completed the experiment, he got the results published in a journal.
- He has been experimenting on the new material since he came back from the United Sates.
- When he was ten, he started to compose music.

2) 原因状语从句的连词有: as、because、since、now that 等:
- Now that you are all here, let's begin our discussion.
- As we are all in favor of the plan, we can carry it out soon.

3) 条件状语从句的连词有: if、in case、on condition that、provided that、suppose、so（as）long as、unless 等:
- As long as you rely on yourself, you will succeed.
- Take the dictionary with you in case you need it for the test.

4) 目的状语从句的连词有: in order that、in case、so that、for fear that 等:
- We must set off now so that we can reach there before 5.
- I have to send an air mail to him in order that he may know the results soon.

5) 结果状语从句的连词有: so that、so…that、such…that 等:
- Bring it nearer so that we see it clearly.
- He studies so hard that he always gets the highest score in the class.

6) 让步状语从句的连词有: though、although、even though、whether、no matter why、as、while 等:
- He is modest even though he has achieved great successes.
- No matter how difficult it is, we have to complete the work on time.

7) 比较状语从句的连词有: as、than、not so…as、as…as 等:
- She is not as tall as her sister.
- He can play football as well as his brother.

练 习

1. 选择适当的形式填入空内。

 (1) He walked into the restaurant _____ it had belonged to him.

   A. like   B. as if   C. so that   D. if

 (2) Don't eat that fruit _____ it is ripe.

   A. unless   B. in case   C. if   D. so that

(3) I don't think it'll rain, but I'll take an umbrella _____ it does.

    A. before   B. in case   C. unless   D. as if

(4) She felt very silly _____ everyone laughed at her question.

    A. after   B. before   C. when   D. as soon as

(5) He insured his car _____ he had an accident.

    A. unless   B. if   C. in case   D. since

(6) Put your luggage in the van quickly _____ the train will be off in a minute.

    A. when   B. now that   C. so that   D. unless

(7) That's a good suggestion! Let's finish our work now _____ we can be free this evening.

    A. after   B. because   C. than   D. so that

(8) _____ we can make laws to protect certain animals, we are frequently incapable of controlling the environment.

    A. Even if   B. Whatever   C. After   D. However

(9) Rare animals are still hunted, _____ we can now imitate their skins with other materials.

    A. when   B. ever since   C. so that   D. even though

(10) _____ you understand this rule, you'll have difficulty.

    A. While   B. Once   C. Though   D. Unless

(11) The doctor urges that he should have an operation on his back _____ his health will improve quickly.

    A. though   B. before   C. so that   D. as soon as

(12) They went _____ they could find a good job.

    A. where   B. wherever   C. when   D. unless

(13) _____ inspected this radio, he should have put his identification number on the box.

    A. That   B. No matter who   C. Whatever   D. Whomever

(14) Although _____ happened in that developed country sounds like science fiction, it could occur elsewhere in the world.

    A. what   B. which   C. how   D. it

(15) _____ woke me up last night was a big noise.

    A. How   B. What   C. That   D. Why

2. 将下面的句子翻译成英语。

    (1) 由于我离开得太匆忙,忘记带课本了。(leave in a big hurry)

    (2) 如果你能保持整洁的话,我们可以让你使用这个房间。(keep... clean and tidy)

（3）虽然不想参加宴会，她还是接受了邀请。

（4）只要我们不灰心，我们一定能够找到解决问题的办法。(lose heart)

（5）这项工程完成得比我们预计的要早。

（6）我不知道在会议上采取了什么决定，因为我们的代表还没有向我汇报。

（7）今天早上他起床晚了，所以没有赶上汽车。

（8）假如我们弄不到设备的话，我们将怎么办？

（9）他感到失望，因为工作没有达到预期的水平。(come up to what was expected)

（10）当他到家的时候，他发现房子已经起火了。

Part C Supplementary Reading

Travelling Pamphlet

旅游指南是旅游文化的一个重要组成部分。各种旅游指南，归纳起来，一般包括如下内容：

1. 有关旅游景点的介绍

2. 介绍有关旅游辅助设施情况

3. 介绍各种服务收费标准

4. 介绍日程安排

下面就是一份具体的旅游指南范例。

Traveling Information in Melbourne, Australia

Tour Name: Phillip Island, Penguins, Koalas and Kangaroos

Price: Starting from AUD ＄115 per person

Duration: 9-10 hours

Commences: Melbourne, Australia

I. Introduction

Get close to the remarkable penguins and wildlife of Australia...

The little penguins provide a wonderful spectacle as they break free of the surf and waddle home across the sand at dusk at Phillip Island. Nature is on stage and we are the audience to these fishermen of the sea as they feed their families. Phillip Island is home to an astounding array of wildlife, including Australia's largest fur seal colony, the Little Penguins and cuddly koalas.

Tour Highlights:
- The Melbourne bayside suburbs of St. Kilda and Brighton.
- Visit Warrook, a working cattle farm. Enjoy the opportunity to pat and feed kangaroos, wallabies and a host of farm animals.
- Encounter koalas in their natural habitat at the Koala Conservation Centre. Stroll along elevated boardwalks and spot koalas in the trees.
- View spectacular coastal scenery at Nobbies. From the walkway, see Australia's largest population of fur seals living along the rugged southern coastline.
- Browse through the educational and interesting Phillip Island Visitors Information Centre.
- Visit the popular seaside town of Cowes—the main town on Phillip Island and a holiday retreat for fishermen and beach lovers.
- Viewing Platform Penguin Plus (Tour Option V)—More personalized wildlife viewing limited to 130 people with ranger interpretation providing closer viewing of the penguin arrival than the main viewing stands. Includes a complimentary drink.

II. Schedule Details

Dates: Daily

Location:
Australian Pacific Touring office
180 Swanston Street
*Located between Bourke and Little Bourke Streets

If you do not indicate your hotel for pick up at the time of booking, please call Australian Pacific Touring and advise them of this information directly. The contact details will be on your voucher once you have a confirmed booking.

Time: 1:30 p.m. (Hotel pick ups start prior to this time.)

Hotel Pickup:
- Please advise your hotel details at time of booking in the "hotel pickup" field.

- If your hotel is not on the pick up list, please include the details at the time of booking. You must then call the tour operator at least 24 hours prior to tour commencement to obtain the closest pick up location. The contact details for the tour operator will be written on your voucher.

Return Details:
Tour concludes in Melbourne between 10:30 p.m. and 11:30 p.m.

III. Additional
Inclusions:
- Coach travel to Phillip Island
- Visit Warrook Cattle Farm
- The Koala Conservation Centre
- Penguin Parade
- Viewing Platform Penguin Plus (If Tour Option V is selected at time of booking)
- Complimentary hotel pick up and drop off
- Commentary by driver
- Australia's Goods and Services Tax (GST)

Exclusions:
- Food and beverages not specified in the tour itinerary

Additional Info.:
- This tour must be booked at least 24 hours in advance of your travel date.
- Confirmation for this product will be received within 24 hours, subject to availability.
- Please remember to bring warm, waterproof clothing on this tour. You may also wish to bring a towel or a rug to sit on at the Penguin Parade viewing platform.

Penguin Parade:
Please note: Photography and video cameras are NOT permitted.
- The Park did not take lightly the decision not to allow cameras. After many years of consideration the cameras were banned to keep the disturbance down to a minimum. The whole evening is more peaceful for people and penguins.

Wheelchair Accessibility:
- All passengers with limited mobility will require a companion to assist with boarding and alighting from the touring vehicle, pushing a collapsible wheelchair and all other assistance required. The driver is not permitted to lift or push wheelchairs due to health and safety regulations.

Pricing Policy:
- Children aged between 3 and 14 years inclusive qualify for child rate
- Infants aged 2 years and under travel free of charge, providing they are not utilizing a coach seat

IV. *Pricing*

Phillip Island, Penguins, Koalas and Kangaroos			per person
Season		Aug 1, 2005 to Mar 31, 2006	
Tour Code	Days of Week	Adult	Child
Tour only	Mon... Sun	$115.00	$58.00
Tour inc Viewing Platform Penguin Plus	Mon... Sun	$140.00	$83.00

Prices are in AUD and are listed as a guide only.

Travel Voucher:

For every confirmed booking you will be required to print a voucher which is presented at the destination. You will receive a link to your voucher via email once your booking is confirmed.

Local Operator Information:

Complete Operator information, including local telephone numbers at your destination, are included on your Confirmation Voucher. Our Product Managers select only the most experienced and reliable operators in each destination, removing the guesswork for you, and ensuring your peace of mind.

Product Code: 2230M10

NEW WORDS

ridiculous /ri'dikjuləs/ *a.*   absurd 可笑的；荒谬的
koala /kəu'ɑ:lə/ *n.*   树袋熊（澳洲产，树栖无尾动物）
kangaroo /ˌkæŋgə'ru:/ *n.*   袋鼠
remarkable /ri'mɑ:kəbl/ *a.*   worthy of notice, unusual 值得注意的
surf /sə:f/ *n.*   the swell of the waves of the sea breaking on the shore 海浪
waddle /'wɔdl/ *v.*   to walk with short steps, swaying from side to side in the manner of a duck 蹒跚而行
cuddly /'kʌdli/ *a.*   sth. or sb. that makes you want to embrace fondly and closely 令人想拥抱的
encounter /in'kauntə/ *v.*   meet face to face, come across 遇到；相遇
habitat /'hæbitæt/ *n.*   the place where an animal or plant naturally live or grows （动植物的）生活环境
rugged /'rʌgid/ *a.*   rough and uneven 高低不平的；崎岖的
ranger /'reindʒə/ *n.*   one of a body of guards who patrol a region 护林员
complimentary /ˌkɔmpli'ment(ə)ri/ *a.*   given free as a gift or courtesy 免费赠送的
voucher /'vautʃə(r)/ *n.*   a written record of an expenditure 凭证；凭单
pickup /'pikʌp/ *n.*   letting sb. into a vehicle, taking on as a passenger 让人搭车
coach /kəutʃ/ *n.*   a bus used for long journey 长途汽车
itinerary /ai'tinərəri, i't-/ *n.*   a plan of travel, a way followed in traveling 路线
availability /əˌveilə'biliti/ *n.*   being available, being at hand, being ready 可用性
alight /ə'lait/ *v.*   get down/off 下车
inclusive /in'klu:siv/ *a.*   including, containing 包含的
utilize /'ju:tilaiz/ *v.*   use, put to use 利用

Unit 8

PHRASES

break free of: escape from a place or a situation 摆脱
conservation center: an area where animals and plants are protected 保护中心
holiday retreat: a quiet place where people go for their holiday 度假地

NOTES

Melbourne：墨尔本（澳大利亚东南部港市）
Phillip Island：菲利普岛

EXERCISES

I. *Reading Comprehension*：

1. Which of the following statement is true about the tour?
   A. The price of Phillip Island, Penguins, Koalas and Kangaroos tour starts from USD $115 per person.
   B. The tour usually takes half of the day.
   C. During the tour visitors can view bayside suburbs of St. Kilda and Brighton.
   D. The tour can be booked at any time.

2. Which of the following is NOT the place that the visitors will go to?
   A. Warrook cattle farm
   B. Koala Conservation Center
   C. Australian Eastern coastline
   D. Phillip Island Visitors Information Centre

3. The charge of the tour includes all the following EXCEPT _____.
   A. visit of Warrook Cattle Farm
   B. coach to and back from Phillip Island
   C. hotel pickups
   D. viewing Platform Penguin Plus

4. The booking of the tour _____.
   A. is available to everyone
   B. can be made anytime

131

C. can be confirmed anytime

   D. should be made 24 hours before the starting of the travel

5. Which of the following is NOT true about the Penguin parade?

   A. No photo should be taken.

   B. No video should be taken.

   C. The park lay down the rule to forbid the using of cameras.

   D. Visitors can be taken photos with penguins.

6. If a person is handicapped,_____.

   A. he can also join the tour by himself

   B. he should be in company with somebody else

   C. the driver may help him

   D. the tourist guide will help him

7. Which of the following group need only pay $58 per person?

   A. adults   B. infants

   C. kids between 3 and 14   D. 2-year-old kids

8. On the travel voucher, tourists can find _____.

   A. contact information of the local operator

   B. price of the tour

   C. the contents of the tour

   D. ending time of the tour

9. The tourist agency guarantees that the local operators are _____.

   A. warmhearted   B. most experienced

   C. knowledgeable   D. affable

10. Why should tourists bring a towel or a rug?

    A. Because they may want to sit on the platform.

    B. Because it makes them warm.

    C. Because they will take a spa.

    D. Because they will swim during the tour.

II. *Vocabulary and Structure*:

Choose the correct word/phrase to fill into each sentence, using the proper form.

book	advance	permit	companion	rate
provide	utilize	inclusive	charge	reliable

Unit 8

1. The Allied troops are _____ on the camp of the enemy.
2. The secretary has _____ the manager in at the Hilton Hotel.
3. It is _____ in the contract that the work should be accomplished within a year.
4. The wording of the note _____ of several interpretations.
5. It's not _____ to judge a man only by his looks.
6. The monthly rent is ＄20 _____ of everything.
7. He was my only Chinese _____ during my stay in Australia.
8. We hope that many commuters will continue to _____ mass transit after the bridge has reopened.
9. That seaside hotel _____ exorbitant prices during the summer holidays.
10. Many film critics _____ the latest movie of Harry Portter excellent.

Part A　Text (Managers for the Twenty-first Century)
Part B　Grammar (名词性从句)
Part C　Supplementary Reading
　　　　(Announcement Letters)

Part A　Text

Warm-up Questions:
1. *What do you suppose to be a good manager's central role?*
2. *How do you think managers for the 21st century will be different from managers of the past?*
3. *What do you think will cause the differences?*

Managers for the Twenty-first Century

By Lester Thurow

　　Historical developments of the past half century and the invention of modern telecommunication and transportation technologies have created a world economy. Effectively the American economy has died and been replaced by a world economy.

5　　In the future there is no such thing as being an American manager. Even someone who spends an entire management career in Kansas City is in international management. He or she will compete with foreign firms, buy from foreign firms, sell to foreign firms, or acquire financing from foreign banks.

The globalization of the world's capital markets that has occurred in the past 10 years will be replicated right across the economy in the next decade. An international perspective has become central to management. Without it managers are operating in ignorance and cannot understand what is happening to them and their firms.

Partly because of globalization and partly because of demography, the work forces of the next century are going to be very different from those of the last century. Most firms will be employing more foreign nationals. More likely than not, you and your boss will not be of the same nationality. Demography and changing social mores mean that white males will become a smaller fraction of the work force as women and minorities grow in importance. All of these factors will require changes in the traditional methods of managing the work force.

In addition, the need to produce goods and services at quality levels previously thought impossible to obtain in mass production and the spreading use of participatory management techniques will require a work force with much higher levels of education and skills. Production workers must be able to do statistical quality control; production workers must be able to do just-in-time inventories. Managers are increasingly shifting from a "don't think, do what you are told" to a "think, I am not going to tell you what to do" style of management.

This shift is occurring not because today's managers are more enlightened than yesterday's managers but because the evidence is rapidly mounting that the second style of management is more productive than the first style of management. But this means that problems of training and motivating the work force both become more central and require different modes of behavior.

To be on top of this situation, tomorrow's managers will have to have a strong background in organizational psychology, human relations, and labor economics. The MIT Sloan School of Management attempts to advance our understanding in these areas through research and then quickly bring the fruits of this new research to our students so that they can be leading-edge managers when it comes to the human side of the equation.

The first three decades after World War II were unusual in that the United States had a huge technological lead over all of the rest in the world. In a very real sense the world was not technologically competitive. American firms did not have to worry about their technological competitiveness because they were superior.

But that world has disappeared. Today we live in a world where American firms no longer have automatic technological superiority. In some areas they are still ahead, in some areas they are average, and in some areas they are behind, but on average they are average.

What this means is that American managers have to understand the forces of technical change in ways that were not necessary in the past. Conversely, managers from the rest of the world know that it is now possible for them to dominate their American competitors if they understand the forces of technical change better than their American competitors do.

45　　In the world of tomorrow managers cannot be technologically illiterate regardless of their functional tasks within the firm. They don't have to be scientists or engineers inventing new technologies, but they have to be managers who understand when to bet and when not to bet on new technologies. If they don't understand what is going on and technology effectively becomes a black box, they will fail to make the changes. They will be losers, not winners.

NEW WORDS

effectively /iˈfektivli/ *ad.*　　for practical purposes; in effect　事实上,实际上; in an effective way　有效地

finance /faiˈnæns/ *vt.*　　provide money for　为……提供资金

replicate /ˈreplikeit/ *vt.*　　be or make a copy of; reproduce　复制;复现

perspective /pəsˈpektiv/ *n.*　　particular way of considering sth.　考虑某事的独特方法;观点,视角

ignorance /ˈignərəns/ *n.*　　lack of knowledge or information　无知

demography /diˈmɔgrəfi/ *n.*　　statistical study of populations　人口统计学,人口学

mores /ˈmɔreiz, ˈmɔriz/ *n.*　　customs with the force of law　传统,习俗

fraction /ˈfrækʃən/ *n.*　　small part, bit, amount or proportion　小部分,少许,片段

statistic /stəˈtistik/ *n.*　　item of information expressed in numbers　数据,统计数字

statistical /stəˈtistikl/ *a.*　　统计(上)的

inventory /ˈinvəntri/ *n.*　　complete list or stock of goods　详细目录,清单;库存

enlightened /inˈlaitənd/ *a.*　　free from prejudice, ignorance, superstition, etc.　摆脱偏见、无知、迷信等的;开明的;有知识的

mount /maunt/ *vi.*　　increase in amount or intensity　增加,上升

motivate /ˈməutiveit/ *vt.*　　stimulate the interest of; cause to want to do sth.　激发……的兴趣,激励,诱导

mode /məud/ *n.*　　way or manner in which sth. is done　方式,方法

leading-edge /ˈliːdiŋedʒ/ *a.*　　the most modern and advanced　前卫的;前锋的

equation /iˈkweiʒn/ *n.*　　statement that two expressions are equal　等式,方程式

Unit 9

superior /sjuːˈpiəriə/ a.　　　better than average 优秀的, 优等的 better, stronger, etc. than sb./sth. else （比某人/物）好的、强的等
superiority /sjuːˌpiəriˈɔriti/ n.　优越, 优胜
illiterate /iˈlitərət/ a.　　　unable to read or write 不识字的; ignorant in a particular field （对某一领域）无知的
bet /bet/ v.　　　　　　　risk (money) on the result of a future event 以……打赌,（与……）打赌
　　　　n.　　　　　　　an arrangement to risk money on the result of a future event 打赌 a sum of money so risked 赌金, 赌注

PHRASES

more likely than not: (very) probably （很）可能
on top of: having control of 控制
when it comes to: when it is a case, matter or question of 当涉及……的情况、事情或问题时
in that: for the reason that; because 因为, 基于……的理由
in a sense: if the statement, etc. is understood in a particular way 在某种意义上
on (the) average: 平均, 按平均数计算
regardless of: paying no attention to 不理会, 不顾
black box: small machine that records information about an aircraft during its flight 黑盒, 黑匣子

NOTES

Lester Thurow: 莱斯特·瑟罗, 美国麻省理工学院斯隆管理学院前院长 (1987—1993), 管理学与经济学教授, 著名电视评论家及经济问题演说家
participatory management technique: （民主）参与型管理技术
just-in-time inventory: 最低存货, 刚好能维持生产的存货
MIT Sloan School of Management: 麻省理工学院斯隆管理学院, 全球最著名的商学院之一

EXERCISES

I. Reading Comprehension:

1. In which of the following fields has globalization occurred in the past decade?
   A. International management.　　B. Marketing.
   C. Capital markets.　　D. Financing.

2. What was/were "previously thought impossible" (Para. 5)?
   A. The need.　　B. Goods and services.
   C. Quality levels.　　D. Mass production.

3. Which of the following can be inferred from the passage?
   A. The whole economy will be globalized in the next 10 years.
   B. White males will form a smaller fraction of the work force than women and minorities.
   C. The world was technologically inferior in the first 30 years after World War II.
   D. Today American firms are no longer superior in automatic technology.

4. What is "a black box" (Para. 11) likely to mean in the passage?
   A. An automatic device for recording details of the flight of a plane.
   B. A sigh of failure.
   C. Something on which people are not sure whether to bet or not.
   D. Something inside which what is going on is unknown.

5. According to the passage, Sloan expects its students to do all of the following EXCEPT _____.
   A. making changes in their organizations
   B. working with international companies
   C. being better managers of the work force
   D. understanding the forces of technical change

II. Getting Information:

Complete the following diagram with information from the text.

Three central driving forces underlying change:

1. Paras. 1–3 the growth of _____
   (1) causes:
   _____
   _____

(2) what is required of a manager: _____
2. Paras. 4-7 the changing nature of _____
   (1) differences:
       a. difference in the make-up:
          more _____
          more _____ and _____
       b. difference in the quality
          higher levels of _____
   (2) what is required of a manager: a strong background in _____,
       _____ and _____
3. Paras. 8-11 the arrival of _____
   (1) situation in the past and situation today
   (2) what is required of a manager: a good understanding of _____

III. Vocabulary and Structure:

A. Choose the correct word/phrase to fill into each sentence, using the proper form.

average	dominate	perspective	effectively	motivate
in a sense	enlighten	mount	operate	regardless of
advance	lead	replicate	participatory	more likely than not

1. His wife left him when the children were small, so he _____ brought up the family himself.
2. _____, she'll end up in court over this problem.
3. We're looking for someone who will be able to _____ the staff to work hard.
4. She is right, _____, because we did agree to wait, but only until June.
5. Listen to both sides and you will be _____.
6. He tends to view most issues from a philosophical _____.
7. They work as a group—no one person is allowed to _____.
8. The plan for a new office tower went ahead _____ local opposition.
9. The _____ people are a lot better off than they were forty years ago.
10. Harlem has been _____ to a higher position.
11. As the organizer of the team, he took the _____ in setting the pace of the project.
12. Scientists successfully found that some kinds of bacteria grow very fast because they

can _____ by themselves.
13. Managers of this generation are more likely to exercise _____ management in their own companies.
14. Without strong background of education and skills, it is very hard for anyone to _____ a business successfully.
15. Rapid _____ of daily expenses is a threat to social stability.

B. Complete the following sentences with the missing prepositions or adverbs.
1. The developing countries have to compete _____ the developed for world market.
2. It is always very difficult to have this group of people to be _____ the same mind.
3. At that time, the United States had a huge technological lead _____ all of the rest in the world.
4. Finally, _____ the graduate level, James recognized his own value.
5. It is not right to shift the blame _____ anyone else.
6. The girls bet the boys a big fancy cake _____ their winning the game.
7. Health is above wealth _____ the latter cannot give so much happiness as the former.
8. Some sparrows are six inches long, but _____ average they are still smaller than magpies.
9. They've finally got _____ the situation.
10. Such things _____ silver and gold are incomparable with love.

C. Guess the meaning of the following words.
1. participatory   2. competitiveness   3. superiority   4. statistical
5. globalization   6. telecommunication   7. productive   8. demography

IV. *Translation*:
A. Translate the following into Chinese.
1. The globalization of the world's capital markets that has occurred in the past 10 years will be replicated right across the economy in the next decade.

2. Demography and changing social mores mean that white males will become a smaller fraction of the work force as women and minorities grow in importance.

3. In addition, the need to produce goods and services at quality levels previously thought

impossible to obtain in mass production and the spreading use of participatory management techniques will require a work force with much higher levels of education and skills.

4. In a very real sense the world was not technologically competitive.

5. Today we live in a world where American firms no longer have automatic technological superiority.

B. Translate the following into English.
1. 很可能她把这事全忘了。(more likely than not)

2. 这意味着我们实际上没有可能按时完成。(effectively)

3. 他的第一部小说不算太好也不算太糟,就是一般水平。(average)

4. 谈到现代爵士乐,没几个人比汤姆知道得更多。(when it comes to)

5. 这项研究的重要性在于它证实了 A 与 B 之间存在联系。(in that)

6. 尽管以前我们失败过,但仍要坚持下去。(regardless of)

7. 考试不能促使学生去追求更多的知识。(motivate)

8. 成功的领导者是事先控制事件而不是事后才做出反应。(dominate)

9. 他必须将重担从一肩移至另一肩上。(shift)

10. 科技力量上的优势帮助这家公司战胜所有对手。(superiority)

V. Writing Task:
Write about 120 words on the topic "**My Ideal of a Great Manager for the 21st Century**".

VI. *Oral Practice*：

How can Chinese universities produce leading-edge managers for the 21st century?

Part B　Grammar

名词性从句（Substantive Clauses）

在句子中起名词作用的句子叫名词性从句（Noun Clauses）。名词性从句的功能相当于名词词组，它在复合句中能担任主语、宾语、表语、同位语、介词宾语等，因此根据它在句中不同的语法功能，名词从句又可分别称为主语从句、宾语从句、表语从句和同位语从句。名词性从句多由连词 that、wh- 疑问词或由 what、whatever 等关系代词引导。

1. 主语从句
1）主语从句在句子中充当主语，句子的谓语动词用第三人称单数。如：
   · Why he refused to work with you is still a mystery.
   · Whoever comes is welcome.
2）主语从句前的 that 不能省略，仅起连接作用。有时为了保持句子平衡，将 that 从句后置，由 it 作形式主语。如：
   · That he became a lawyer may have been due to his mother's influence.
   · It is not true that he has moved to New York.
2. 宾语从句在句子中充当宾语，如：
   · I don't know where the sound came from.
   · Don't be satisfied with what you have achieved.
3. 当从句放在系动词 be、look、remain、seem 等后即构成表语从句。如：
   · The trouble is that I have lost his address.
   · It seemed that the night would never end.
4. 同位语从句
1）同位语从句是对与之同位的名词中心词作进一步解释。能接名词性从句的常见名词有：idea、fact、news、belief、hope、evidence、opinion、problem、truth、answer、proposal、theory、decision、discovery、problem、thought、understanding 等。如：
   · The news that he has passed the examination is exciting.

Unit 9

2）同位语从句与定语从句的区别在于：定语从句是对先行词加以修饰、限制，而同位语从句是说明名词中心词的具体内容；that 在定语从句中充当成分，为关系代词，而在同位语从句中不做任何成分，仅起连词作用。如：

- The fact <u>that we talked about</u> is very important.（定语从句）
- The fact that he succeeded in the experiment pleased everybody.（同位语从句）

练 习

1. 找出下列句中的名词性从句，并分析其在句中的作用。

   （1）Of even more importance, of course, is that you follow your schedule regularly.
   （2）I will tell you when you will come for the meeting.
   （3）It was proved that the coins had been in the ground for thousands of years.
   （4）Anyhow, what they would do has to be decided by the committee.
   （5）That things will improve is obvious.
   （6）He admitted to us that he had done it without permission.
   （7）The fact that she was a few minutes late is no reason for discharging her.
   （8）The problem is where we should put our invest.
   （9）In spite of the fact that he is in very poor health, he is still very cheerful.
   （10）That's why he is late.

2. 选择适当的名词性从句填空。

   （1）Last week he promised _____ today, but he hasn't arrived yet.
   　　A. that he would come　　　　　B. what would he come
   　　C. which he came　　　　　　　D. that he would have come
   （2）He is trying all kinds of materials to learn _____ used.
   　　A. what of them can be　　　　B. that they can be
   　　C. which of them can be　　　　D. which of them be
   （3）His family had almost forgotten _____ like.
   　　A. how his face was　　　　　　B. which was his face
   　　C. what his face was　　　　　　D. that his face was
   （4）It is obvious _____ on more important things.
   　　A. which the money should we spend
   　　B. what the money should we spend

C. that the money should we spend

D. that we should spend the money

(5) We were greatly amused by _____.
 A. that you told us   B. which you told us
 C. what you told us   D. what did you tell us

(6) That is _____ now. I would like you to know I can finish it by myself.
 A. that I'm doing   B. which I'm doing
 C. what am I doing   D. what I'm doing

(7) At about the same time, doctors began to understand _____ together.
 A. which went dirt and disease   B. what went dirt and disease
 C. that dirt and disease went   D. that did dirt and disease go

(8) The problem is _____.
 A. why the cheapest way is   B. that is the cheapest way
 C. whichever is the cheapest way   D. which is the cheapest way

(9) These exercises are different from _____.
 A. that you expect   B. what do you expect
 C. what you expect   D. which you expect

(10) _____ was to return to school.
 A. That really interested him   B. What really interested him
 C. Which really interested him   D. That interested him really

(11) _____ will be known tomorrow.
 A. If the flower will be black   B. When will the flower be
 C. Whether the flower is black   D. Whether is the flower black

(12) Not one of us has a clear idea about _____ to do.
 A. that the others want   B. what the others want
 C. which do the others want   D. what do the others want

(13) I will let you know _____ the meeting will be held.
 A. which   B. where
 C. what   D. that

(14) The question is _____ to land men there.
 A. if safe it will   B. if will be it safe
 C. whether it will be safe   D. whether safe it will be

(15) He was afraid of _____ would happen to his child.
 A. which   B. when   C. why   D. what

Unit 9

Part C Supplementary Reading

Announcement Letters

通告信函是商业往来信函中的一部分,虽然并非直接与买卖交易相关,但对于加强与客户的联系、保持良好的合作关系,有着相当重要的意义。通告的内容很广,一般包括:开业通知、改组通知、成立分公司、扩大营业、合并通告、解散合伙关系,等等。

此类信函的基本行文结构是:首先开门见山提出通告的要旨,然后给出解释性说明,最后礼貌地表示愿意竭诚为对方提供服务,继续和扩大合作。

能够正确理解此类贸易往来信件,并在此基础上撰写此类信件是一些同学工作中的必要环节。请阅读下面两封信件,然后完成文后练习。

Passage I

THE ORIENTAL TRADING CO.
No. 24 Nanjing Road
Shanghai, P. R. China

10th April, 2003

New Era Technology Company
No. 37, Xinhua Road
Beijing, P. R. China

Ladies and Gentlemen:

We have the pleasure to inform you that on 1st May, we have established ourselves as Commission Agents for the sale of Motorola electric products at the above address.

You will be interested to find that our extensive connections with Motorola Corporation Ltd. and the possession of large capital will enable us to execute orders at the lowest possible prices, and we, therefore, hope to receive your orders.

References: Bank of China
　　　　　　China Bank of Industry and Commerce, Beijing

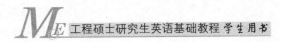

We hope to receive your inquiries.

  Yours sincerely,

  Zhang Qunfang

  General Manager

Passage II

XINHUA TRADING CO., Ltd
33 Renmin Road
Changchun, Jilin

Sept. 15, 2004

  Brothers Company
  116 Qianjin Road
  Changchun, Jilin

Dear Sir or Madam:

We are pleased to announce that as from 1st October our firm, with whom you have had dealings over many years, will amalgamate with Baiqiang Trading Co. Ltd. of this city to form the new firm of Yuanda Trading Co., Ltd.

The new firm will carry on business in larger premises at 45 Chongqing Road, Changchun, to which address you should send all communications after 1st October.

We appreciate the confidence you have placed in us in the past and look forward to continuing dealings with you. There will be no falling off in the standards of service we have always tried to maintain—and we believe in it.

  Your faithfully,

  Zhen Li

  General Manager

NEW WORDS

commission/kəˈmiʃən/ n. act of committing to the change of another 代办；经纪
agent/ˈeidʒənt/ n. one who has power to act for a company, etc. 代理人，

Unit 9

	代办人
extensive/iks'tensiv/*a*.	Large in area, broad in scope 大量的,范围广泛的
capital/'kæpitəl/*n*.	wealth available for the production of more wealth 资本,本钱
execute/'eksikju:t/*vt*.	carry out 执行;实行
reference/'refərəns/*n*.	statement of qualification of a person; person to whom inquiries can be made (身份、能力等的)证明书,服务经历;证明人
inquiry/in'kwaiəri/*n*.	act of inquiring or seeking 询问
dealing/'di:liŋ/*n*.	transaction 行为,交易;(*pl.*)生意,交易;交际
amalgamate/ə'mælgəmeit/*v*.	unit or combine portion of real estate 合并;联合
premise/'premis/*n*.	land and the buildings on it (*pl.*) 房屋(及其附属基地、建筑等);院内,屋内

PHRASES

commission agent: person who has power to act for a company, ect. 代办人,代办商
carry on: continue to do 继续开展
fall off: decline 下降,衰退

NOTES

Motorola Corporation Ltd：摩托罗拉有限公司
Bank of China：中国银行
China Bank of Industry and Commerce：中国工商银行

EXERCISES

I. *Reading Comprehension*：

1. The purpose of the first passage is _____.

   A. to inform the extension of the company
   B. to ask for more inquiries
   C. to inform the opening of the agency
   D. to bargain for a better price for the orders

147

2. In the first passage, what advantage(s) does this agent have to attract more inquiries?
   A. Close relation with Motorola Corporation.
   B. The powerful financial ability.
   C. Reasonable prices.
   D. Both A and B.
3. Which of the following statement is NOT true?
   A. Connections between the involved companies are important in doing business.
   B. It is common that people judge the company by its financial power.
   C. The lowest prices are always more attractive.
   D. Whether the order will be signed at last largely depends on the relationship among all the companies involved.
4. What is "reference" for in the first passage?
   A. To tell the readers the information of the bank account.
   B. To inform receivers of the letter where to deposit money in order to make a deal.
   C. To tell the readers the person or the unit where they can get all information confirmed.
   D. To make known the partnership the company has.
5. The writer of the second letter is to _____.
   A. inform the receivers its relation with Baiqiang company
   B. make known that the two companies are going to come together
   C. bid for more dealings
   D. confirm that his company is as reliable as ever
6. Which of the following part is optional to this kind of letter?
   A. Compliments for the receivers.
   B. Purpose of writing this letter.
   C. Expectations for the future cooperation.
   D. Address of the new company.

II. *Vocabulary and Structure*:

Choose the correct word/phrase to fill into each sentence, using the proper form.

| commission | inquiry | execute | establish | look forward to |
| carry on | fall off | announce | extensive | enable |

Unit 9

1. We wish to _____ the cooperation to the advantage of both our firms.
2. Some salesmen in big shops receive a _____ of 10% on everything they sell, as well as a salary.
3. The rights protection law for the consumers _____ any impaired consumer to claim money from the company.
4. The school has _____ playing fields.
5. The government _____ that they would build a new highway to the mountain.
6. I _____ seeing you this summer vacation.
7. The number of staff meetings _____ after a few months.
8. A new office was set up to file the _____ about the lost shipment.
9. We must _____ till success in spite of the extremely difficult conditions.
10. The manager assistant came here to _____ a few small commissions for the manager.

III. Translate the following into English:

1. 感谢您对本公司的信任。(appreciate)

2. 政府执行执政党的决定。(execute)

3. 今后我们将以"永葆青春化妆品公司"之名义,继续营业,特此奉告。(carry on)

4. 兹定于下月1日,于本市开设蓝宝石百货公司。(establish)

5. 因公司业务增大,原办公地点已不能满足需要,因而迁址至北京立汤路15号。(premises)

Part A   Text (How the Rich Got Rich—and You Could Too)
Part B   Grammar(强调句)
Part C   Supplementary Reading
         (The Irresponsibility That Spreads AIDS)

Part A   Text

Warm-up Questions:

1. *Do you have any idea on how to get rich?*
2. *Have you heard of Bill Gates or any other famous rich persons? Can you give some examples to illustrate how they get rich?*
3. *What does wealth stand for in your mind?*

How the Rich Got Rich—and You Could Too

Condensed from "LEARN TO EARN"
By Peter Lynch and John Rothchild

　　Every year *Forbes* magazine prints The Forbes Four Hundred, a list of the richest individuals in the United States. This issue makes for interesting reading because it tells how these people made their money and, indirectly, how the country has changed over the years.

　　When *Forbes* published its first list in 1982, five of the top ten were in the Hunt family that drilled Texas full of holes and hit a lot of gushers, which reminds us of advice attributed to billionaire J. Paul Getty on how to get ahead in the world: rise early, work hard, strike oil. Getty got his big start the old-fashioned way—from his father's money.

The original list 14 years ago was crawling with Rockefellers, and Du Ponts, a Frick, a Whitney, Mellon or two—all great family fortunes that stretched back to the 19th century. The word "inheritance" appeared in the biographies 75 times.

There weren't as many old-money fortunes on last year's list—which leads to some conclusions about wealth in America. First, it's not easy to hold on to money, even for billionaires. Taxes put a big dent in family fortunes, and unless the heirs are careful and invest wisely, they can lose their millions as fast as their ancestors made them.

Second, the old ways to riches aren't as dependable as they used to be. Besides the three Du Pont entries, only 43 of the 400 entries on the most recent Forbes list represent people who got there through inheritance. And only 18 in the latest 400 made their fortunes from oil, so Getty's quote no longer rings as true as it once did.

Third, America is still the land of opportunity where smart young people like Bill Gates of Microsoft can end up on top of the list of richest Americans ahead of the Rockefellers, Mellons, Gettys and Carnegies.

Today's Horatio Alger heroes often come from a modest background and rise to the top on pluck, luck and a clear idea of what they want. Just behind Gates on the 1995 list is Warren Buffett, who made over $12 billion picking stocks. Buffett could be considered the greatest stocks picker in history. Most of his gains come from stocks in familiar companies you could buy for yourself, such as Coca-Cola, Gillette and the Washington Post Co.

A surprising number of dropouts have made it into the 400. Bill Gates, the Microsoft whiz, left Harvard to tinker with software and developed the operating brain that is installed in nearly every personal computer. Kirk Kerkorian, a junior-high dropout and son of an Armenian (亚美尼亚) immigrant fruit farmer, made millions from Hollywood deals and Las Vegas properties and is now a major Chrysler stockholder. Ted Turner of Turner Broadcasting was booted from Brown University, although he later went back to graduate.

Harry Wayne Huizenga, another college dropout, started a trash-hauling business with a beat-up old truck. By the time he was 31, he and his partner, Dean L. Buntrock, had built the business into the world's largest waste-services company, Waste Management, Inc. Later he turned his attention to a Dallas video-rental store that he built into Blockbuster Video.

However, don't drop out of school because these people did. When they got started in business, it was still possible to land a decent job without a college education. Today it's nearly impossible. Also, every one of them had mastered the basic skills they needed to succeed in business. They didn't drop out to avoid work—they dropped out to start a company or devote themselves to an interest.

In fact, the latest Forbes list is ample proof that there's no end to the ways to make millions these days: disposable cups (Styrofoam), golf clubs (Ping), pizza franchises (Domino's and little Caesar's), rental cars (Enterprise).

Several of these billion-dollar ideas were hatched in basements or garages on shoestring budgets. Hewlett-Packard, the computer giant, came out of $538 worth of electronic parts in David Packard's garage. Wal-Mart came out of a five-and-dime store in Newport, Ark. Richard De Vos and Jay Van Andel started Amway Corp. in their basements, from which they distributed a biodegradable cleaner they bought from a Detroit chemist.

You may remember F. Scott Fitzgerald's famous line about the very rich: "They are different from you and me." But you couldn't prove it by the Forbes list. It turns out there are all kinds of rich people: short, tall, fat, skinny, good-looking, homely, high IQ, not-so-high IQ, generous and tightfisted.

What's more, it's amazing how many of these people keep their frugal habits after they've made it big. Sam Walton, the Wal-Mart billionaire who died in 1992, continued to drive around in a beat-up Chevy with dog-teeth marks on the steering wheel.

Among The Forbes Four hundred, there are many such stories of self-made millionaires living modestly, avoiding publicity and working long hours even though they can pay the bills without lifting a finger. These people are still doing whatever it was that led to their success.

There is a good lesson in this. Find something you enjoy doing, give it everything you've got, and the money will take care of itself.

Eventually, you may reach the point where you can afford to spend the rest of your life at the side of a swimming pool with a drink in your hand, but you probably won't. You'll be having too much fun at the office to stop working.

NEW WORDS

gusher /'gʌʃə/ n.　　oil well emitting unpumped oil　喷油井,自喷井

dent /dent/ n.　　depression　缩减;a weakening effect　削弱的作用

heir /ɛə/ n.　　person with the legal right to receive a title, property when the owner dies　后嗣,继承人

ring /riŋ/ v.　　produce a certain effect when heard　听起来

Unit 10

pluck /plʌk/ *n.* courage; spirit 勇气,精神
dropout /ˈdrɔpaut/ *n.* 退学者
whiz /wiz/ *n.* a person notably qualified or able usu. in a specified field of interest 能手,极出色的人
boot /buːt/ *v.* get rid of, dismiss, expel 解雇,开除
haul /hɔːl/ *v.* pull with effort or force 拖运
beat-up /ˈbiːt ʌp/ *a.* worn or damaged by use, shabby 年久失修的;残破的,褴褛的
ample /ˈæmpl/ *a.* sufficient, quite enough 充分的,足够的
hatch /hætʃ/ *v.* think out and produce (a plot, etc.); contrive and develop 策划(计谋等)
franchise /ˈfræntʃaiz/ *n.* special right given by public authorities to a person or company 特权,特许,专营
shoestring /ˈʃuːˌstriŋ/ *a.* consisting of a small sum of money 小额金钱的,钱数不多的
biodegradable /ˌbaiəudiˈgreidəbl/ *a.* 可生物降解的
frugal /ˈfruːgəl/ *a.* careful, economical 节俭的

PHRASES

make for: contribute to, tend towards 有利于,有助于
attribute to: consider as coming from 把……归因于,归咎于
get ahead: go forward and pass sb. 领先;make progress 取得成功
crawl with: be full of, covered with 爬满,充斥着
stretch back to: 回忆;回想
hold on to: keep one's grip on 抓住,掌握;not give up the ownership of 不放弃拥有
tinker with: work with sth. in an experimental manner 钻研
on a shoestring: to do sth. on a very small amount of capital 花很少的钱,节约
make it: be successful 成功
lead to: have as a result 导致
five-and-dime store: 出售低价小商品的杂货商店

NOTES

Peter Lynch: Former manager of the Fidelity Magellan Fund, and John Rothchild, financial columnist of *Time*, are also co-authors of *Beating the Street* and *One Up on Wall Street*.

Forbes: Published fortnightly since 1917, Forbes magazines is a business-oriented publication that profiles leaders in industry, seeking to define the qualities and impact of management policies. Founded by Bertie Charles Forbes (1880—1954), the magazine attempts to raise the standards of corporate responsibility to investors.

Horatio Alger: After Horatio Alger, an American clergyman, and author of juvenile fiction: of, relating to, or resembling the works of Horatio Alger in which success is achieved through self-reliance and hard work.

Wal-Mart: 沃尔玛，全美最大的百货连锁店

F. Scott Fitzgerald: 菲茨·杰拉尔德，美国小说家，属于"迷惘的一代作家"。其作品有《尘事乐园》《了不起的盖茨比》《最后一个巨头》等。

Hewlett Packard: 惠普公司创始人

EXERCISES

I. Reading Comprehension:

Choose the best answer to each question.

1. What can we infer from J. Paul Getty's advice (Para. 2)?

    A. J. Paul Getty gave the advice when striking oil was popular.

    B. J. Paul Getty's advice is still useful even today.

    C. J. Paul Getty's own success proved his advice.

    D. Many people had taken his advice and got rich by striking oil.

2. According to the passage, which statement is NOT true?

    A. Not so many people got rich through inheritance as they did in the past.

    B. Bill Gates and others dropped out of school because they did not like working.

    C. Today it is impossible to get a good job without university education.

    D. There are many ways to make fortune these days.

3. Can you guess what does "shoestring budget" mean?

    A. A very small amount of capital.

B. A flexible economics.

C. A very difficult situation.

D. A very large sum of money.

4. The author gives the example of Sam Walton in order to show _____.

   A. it is not easy to hold on to money

   B. there are numerous ways to make fortunes

   C. the rich is different from you and me

   D. some rich people still keep their frugal habits

5. What does "self-made millionaires" mean in this passage?

   A. It means those who work for themselves without an employer.

   B. It means those who are proud of their own efforts.

   C. It means those who succeed by their own efforts.

   D. It means those who are over-confident that their opinions are correct.

II. *Getting Information*:

Answer the following questions in English.

1. Why is the list of the richest individuals interesting?

   _____

2. What is the biggest difference between the first list in 1982 and last year's list?

   _____

3. What is the characteristic of today's rich people?

   _____

4. Why did these people drop out of school?

   _____

5. What can we infer from the latest Forbes list?

   _____

III. *Vocabulary and Structure*:

A. Fill in the blanks, using the following words properly.

1. Jane used to be slow in class, but now she is _____.

   A. getting along   B. getting ahead   C. getting by   D. getting above

2. Nobody is able to explain the _____ of this commonly-used expression.

   A. beginning   B. starting-point   C. foundation   D. origin

3. Paul _____ me very much of a schoolmate I used to know at university.

A. remembers   B. reminds   C. recalls   D. recollects

4. Don't count your chickens before they are _____.

A. harvested   B. hatched   C. hurried   D. hastened

5. They _____ the boat up onto the shore.

A. hauled   B. handed   C. held   D. heightened

B. Choose one of the following words which is closest in meaning to the underlined word.

1. He was wearing a decent suit in the party last week.

A. suitable   B. tight   c. loose   d. tidy

2. Several car manufactures will boot half of their workers because of the economic difficulty.

A. discount   B. dispose   C. dismiss   D. disclose

3. A(n) frugal buyer purchases fruit and vegetables in season.

A. careful   B. clever   C. ignorant   D. economical

4. They had ample funds to cover the cost of the trip.

A. luxious   B. sample   C. sufficient   D. superb

5. Eventually, the case proved to have nothing to do with him.

A. Remarkably   B. Naturally   C. Noticeably   D. Ultimately

6. All living things have certain attributes that are passed on from one generation to the next.

A. cells   B. viruses   C. traits   D. flaws

7. Traffic was moving at a crawl.

A. at a slow pace   B. at an instant moment
C. within a certain distance   D. with a rapid speed

8. That story rings true.

A. tells   B. speaks   C. sounds   D. recounts

9. There has been a modest decrease in house prices this year.

A. little   B. humble   C. simple   D. quiet

10. The country made social and political gains under the new government.

A. rewards   B. progress   C. victories   D. increase

C. Choose from Column (B) words which are close in meaning to those in Column (A).

(A)　　　　　　　　　　　(B)

descent　　　　　　　　　tightfisted

Unit 10

forefather	heir
drag	haul
extend	ample
frugal	ancestor
plentiful	stretch
finally	eventually

IV. *Translation*:

A. Translate the following into Chinese.

1. Taxes put a big dent in family fortunes, and unless the heirs are careful and invest wisely, they can lose their millions as fast as their ancestors made them.
2. Today's Horatio Alger heroes often come from modest backgrounds and rise to the top on pluck, luck and a clear idea of what they want.
3. Bill Gates, the Microsoft whiz, left Harvard to tinker with software and developed the operating brain that is installed in nearly every personal computer.
4. They didn't drop out to avoid work—they dropped out to start a company or devote themselves to an interest.
5. Eventually, you may reach the point where you can afford to spend the rest of your life at the side of a swimming pool with a drink in your hand, but you probably won't.

B. Translate the following into English.

1. 排行榜前 10 名
2. 一辆破旧的卡车
3. 追溯到 19 世纪
4. 转移注意力
5. 保持节俭的习惯
6. 小本经营

C. Translate the following into English.

1. 文化交往有助于相互理解。(make for)
2. 当三家公司都决定要她的时候，她知道自己已经成功了。(make it)
3. 这个男孩抓住那矮树，直到有人爬下悬崖去救他。(hold on to)
4. 经济学家认为没有进步的原因是合作不好。(attribute to)
5. 在那时，没有受过大学教育就能找到一个体面的工作还是可能的。(decent)
6. 前院布满了保安人员。(crawl with)
7. 我已经听说了你们两个正在策划的那个大阴谋。(hatch)

8. 他的回答听起来总是很正确。(ring)

9. 令人吃惊的是他炒股发了财。(pick stock)

10. 这些人仍然在做着使他们成功的各种事情。(lead to)

V. Writing Task：

Some people tend to work only for money, while others believe people should enjoy what they do. Which opinion do you prefer? Why? (120 words)

VI. Oral Practice：

There is a popular saying "Money is not everything, but without money you can do nothing." Do you agree with this saying? Use some examples to illustrate your point of view.

Part B Grammar

强调句(Emphatic Sentence)

强调句型的结构为：It is (was)… that…。它可以用来强调句子中的某些成分，如：主语、宾语、状语等。强调主语时，可以用 that；指人时可用 who 或 whom；which 指物。在强调状语时，不能使用 when、where、why 等连接词，只能用 that。强调句型不能用于强调谓语和表语。

- It is in this building that we held the first preparatory meeting.
- It is our teacher that (who) told us about the change in the timetable.

在强调谓语动词时，可以在动词的前面加入 do、does、did，以表示"的确""一定"等。

- She does like the film.
- They did say that.

另外一种强调形式是加入 on earth、in the world、the hell、the devil 等词语，一般用于疑问和否定。

- Where on earth can he be?
- What the hell did she want?

Unit 10

练 习

1. 选择适当的词语填入空内。

   (1) Was it he _____ broke the glass yesterday?

   A. who   B. and   C. but   D. has

   (2) It is for this reason _____ he refused to take the job.

   A. why   B. when   C. that   D. so

   (3) _____ be careful in making such experiments.

   A. Do   B. Does   C. Did   D. Will

   (4) It was not until 11 last night _____ the meeting came to an end.

   A. when   B. and   C. before   D. that

   (5) _____ was in 1990 that the economy started to be revived.

   A. That   B. Which   C. It   D. What

   (6) Who _____ that spoke first at yesterday's meeting?

   A. was it   B. was   C. it was   D. did

   (7) No force _____ can hold back the wheel of history.

   A. on the world B. on earth   C. does   D. did

   (8) George _____ tell me yesterday that he put the dictionary on the table before he left.

   A. does   B. will   C. would   D. did

   (9) It wasn't _____ personal interests that they did all this.

   A. because   B. only   C. just   D. for

   (10) Where _____ did you go yesterday afternoon?

   A. was it   B. devil   C. until   D. in the world

2. 将下面的英文句子翻译成汉语。

   (1) It was not until long afterwards that she wondered if she had made a mistake.

   (2) It was only by an exercise of self-control that he allowed himself to raise his eyes as they came in.

   (3) It is what the committee has decided that should be given priority to.

   (4) Her uncle told her that it was by a retired old professor that she was brought up after

her mother's death.

(5) It is because he is modest and thoughtful that he is respected by his colleagues.

(6) It is earth's heat that scientists have developed a sensitive instrument to measure.

(7) It is on April 15 every year that income taxes are due, which all people who receive an income must pay.

(8) It was Einstein who wrote and published his famous theory of relativity in 1916.

(9) It was only last year that I made her acquaintance.

(10) Who was it that called this morning?

Part C Supplementary Reading

The Irresponsibility That Spreads AIDS

From "*NEW YORK TIMES*"
By Alan J. Mayer

The Centers for Disease Control and Prevention (CDC) estimates that more than 650,000 people in the United States are HIV positive, with at least 40,000 people newly infected every year. In a recent study, 40 percent of HIV patients did not inform a sex partner about their condition.

Despite the new drug therapies being developed, the end of the AIDS epidemic is not in sight. Prevention is as important as ever. In the following essay, the author, who is HIV positive, sheds provocative yet necessary light on an important way to slow the spread of this deadly virus.

Nearly three years ago, I tested positive for HIV. Since then I have discovered a support system that steadfastly refuses to encourage responsible behavior, and a society whose silence ensures the continued spread of this disease.

Most HIV-positive people I have encountered do not voluntarily disclose their status to potential partners. Indeed, even people in long-term relationships lie about their status. These are the realities of HIV transmission today.

The people I am talking about are nothing like Nushawn William, the drug dealer who is believed to have infected numerous people in New York State. They did not grow up in ghettos surrounded by street gangs. They come from stable homes in safe neighborhoods. They went to high school and college and graduate school.

They remain silent because it is difficult to tell the truth, and because their friends and community support them in their silence. Their doctors, psychiatrists, even the AIDS organizations they call for help, offer comfort and sympathy but don't necessarily encourage them to tell the truth.

We are more than 15 years into the AIDS epidemic, and I have been asked my status by prospective partners only twice. Since testing positive, I've made a point of disclosing my status to any potential partner; all but one told me I was the first person to do so. Each believed that if he practiced safe sex, there would be no need to know. There is no such thing as safe sex, only levels of risk that one must choose. In making that choice, a partner's HIV status is the critical piece of information.

Leading advocacy groups have perpetuated the culture of irresponsibility. Last year when I called the hot line for the Gay Men's health Crisis, one of the nation's leading AIDS service agencies, I was advised to "experiment"—informing some partners of my HIV status while remaining silent with others. In this way I could decide which was more comfortable for me.

The CDC will only "suggest that you might want to consider informing your partner", a hot-line counselor told me. Counselors at the San Francisco AIDS Foundation said it was their job to dispense information, not moral or ethical recommendations, and, again, that I must do what makes me feel comfortable.

We are not talking about being comfortable here. We are talking about life and death.

The emphasis on the individual's right, without an equally strong emphasis on the individual's responsibility, is wrong and is a direct cause of the spread of this disease.

Groups such as the Gay Men's Health Crisis claim they cannot dictate behavior. Granted. But that is all the more reason that AIDS organizations have a responsibility to encourage people who are HIV positive to do what is right.

35   For years the AIDS community has rallied around the battle cry "Silence = Death". What it has failed to realize is that silence comes in many forms and that all are lethal.

NEW WORDS

therapy /ˈθerəpi/ *n.*	curative treatment	治疗,疗法
epidemic /epiˈdemik/ *n.*	(disease) spreading rapidly	流行病,传染病
a.		流行性的
provocative /prəˈvɔkətiv/ *a.*	causing anger, argument, interest, etc.	激怒的,引起争论的
steadfastly /ˈstedfəstli/ *ad.*	firm and unchanging	坚定地,不移地
ensure /inˈʃuə/ *v.*	make sure, guarantee	确定,保证
voluntarily /ˈvɔləntərili/ *ad.*	willingly, without being compelled	自愿地,自动地
disclose /disˈkləuz/ *v.*	uncover, make known	揭露,透露
potential /pəˈtenʃəl/ *a.*	that can or may come into existence or action	可能的,潜在的
transmission /trænzˈmiʃən/ *n.*	passing, spread	传送,传播
ghetto /ˈgetəu/ *n.*		城市中未享受正当权利阶级或受歧视的人民居住的地区,贫民窟
psychiatrist /saiˈkaiətrist/ *n.*	expert in psychiatry	精神病专家,精神病医师
critical /ˈkritikəl/ *a.*	of or at a crisis	紧要关头的,转折点的
advocacy /ˈædvəkəsi/ *n.*	pleading in support	主张;支持;提倡
perpetuate /pəˈpetjueit/ *v.*	preserve from being forgotten or from going out of use	使永存;使不被遗忘,使不朽
dispense /diˈspens/ *v.*	deal out; distribute; administer	分配;施给
moral /ˈmɔrəl/ *a.*	concerning principles of right and wrong	有关是非原则的;道德的
ethical /ˈeθikəl/ *a.*	of morals or moral questions	道德的;伦理的
dictate /dikˈteit/ *v.*	state with force of authority	指定,指令;order 命令
battle cry /ˈbætl krai/ *n.*	war cry	斗争口号,战斗号召
lethal /ˈli:θəl/ *a.*	causing, designed to cause, death	致命的

Unit 10

PHRASES

shed light on: make sth. clearer, provide new information　阐明,说清楚

make a point of: regard or treat it as important or necessary　认为某事是重要的,坚持做某事

rally around: (of a group) come to someone's help　支持,支援

life and death: 生死攸关的事

EXERCISES

I. *Reading Comprehension*:

Choose the best answer to each question.

1. As far as the author knows, most HIV-positive people _____.
    A. voluntarily tell their condition to their partners
    B. lie about their status
    C. come from the poor quarters of the city
    D. have got necessary help from the AIDS agency

2. Most HIV-positive people remain silent because _____.
    A. society supports them in their silence
    B. they feel it is their own business
    C. they don't have long-term relationship with each other.
    D. they intend to infect other people

3. What is right for the HIV-positive people to do?
    A. To do whatever makes them feel comfortable.
    B. To put emphasis on the individual's right.
    C. To call the AIDS service agencies for advice.
    D. To inform others of their HIV status.

4. What is NOT the job for the AIDS foundation?
    A. To offer sympathy and comfort to the HIV-positive people.
    B. To distribute information to people.
    C. To give moral or ethical suggestion.
    D. To advise people to do what is comfortable for them.

5. According to the passage, which statement is true?

A. Some of the HIV-positive people even have college education.

B. AIDS community has realized "Silence = Death", so they encourage people to tell the truth about their status.

C. If you practice safe sex, you will have nothing to worry about.

D. Many people ask about their prospective partner's HIV status.

II. *Getting Information*:

Answer the following questions in English.

1. What did the author find out after he tested positive for HIV?

2. What is the most important factor in choosing safe sex?

3. What was he told to do when the author called the hot line for help?

4. What is the direct cause of the spread of AIDS?

5. What didn't the AIDS community realize?

III. *Fill in the blanks, using the following words properly*:

1. Many people have been attracted to the _____ speech.
   A. provocative   B. difficult   C. boring   D. accidental
2. We can _____ that the work shall be done in the right way.
   A. agree   B. ensure   C. argue   D. maintain
3. The new library will _____ its founder's great love of learning.
   A. include   B. give   C. perpetuate   D. grow
4. He is a man with a _____ eye.
   A. given   B. colorful   C. critical   D. few
5. I oughtn't to do that, it's not _____.
   A. bad   B. ethical   C. pure   D. sharp

UNIT 11

Part A Text (Kicking the Big-Car Habit)
Part B Grammar (倒装句及反意问句)
Part C Supplementary Reading (An Impression of Zhu Diwen—A Nobel Physics Prize Winner of Chinese Descent)

Part A Text

Warm-up Questions:

1. *Have you got a plan to buy a car?*
2. *What kind of car do you want to buy? Big car or small car?*
3. *Have you got some ideas about increasing fuel efficiency?*

Kicking the Big-car Habit

The commercial exploitation of crude oil has been among the most liberating technologies the world has ever known. When pumped through an internal combustion engine stuck in a metal box, refined oil has given freedom of movement to billions. Before the automobile, the life experience of most of those who lived in the rich world were limited—as in much of the poor world they remain—to neighborhood and family. When shot through gas turbines on wings, oil has shrunk the planet in a way that was once the stuff of science fiction. Neither of my parents ever flew; both my children had flown 30,000 miles before they were 2 years old.

But on Sept. 11, 2001, the world was reminded that oil is also a dangerous drug. The cheapest, most easily accessible oil reserves are in the Middle East, the most volatile region on earth. Future supplies of oil will be costly not simply in terms of dollars and cents but also in their effect on the environment. As those in poor countries dream of the same freedom of movement that the wealthy have enjoyed for a century, oil's polluting effects will only get worse. The number of cars in Beijing, for example, is growing 15% a year, contributing to the yellow-gray haze that often envelops the city.

For all these reasons, it makes sense to dream of a world that is far, far less dependent on oil than it is now. *Winning the Oil Endgame: American Innovation for Profits, Jobs and Security*, written by a team led by Amory Lovins of the Rocky Mountain Institute in Snowmass, Colo., is one of the best analyses of energy policy yet produced. Lovins, who has been preaching the need for fuel efficiency for some 30 years, thinks big. His aim is to promote a set of policies that over the next two decades would save half the oil the US uses, before moving to a hydrogen-based economy that dispenses with oil altogether (save for possible use as a fuel to produce hydrogen). If that seems hopelessly Utopian, Lovins reminds us that we have done something very like it before. Spurred by the oil price shocks of the 1970s, the United States between 1977 and 1985 increased efficiency and cut oil consumption 17% (and net oil imports 50%) while the economy grew 27%. The key to that revolution was a huge increase in average miles-per-gallon of the US automobile fleet. If we had continued to increase energy efficiency at the same rate, the stability of Iraq and Saudi Arabia would by now be of minor concern to the US policy-makers. Instead, we bought SUVS and wasted two decades.

Those SUVS are no joke. In the United States, where 70% of oil is used for transportation, any energy policy is necessarily also and automobile policy. The single key insight of Lovins' report is to focus on the need to reduce the weight of cars (without sacrificing safety) by using advanced materials like carbon fiber and composites instead of heavy steel. When powered by hybrid technologies that combine electricity with the internal-combustion engine, such light vehicles will produce enormous oil savings. Lovins proposes a nifty scheme, which would reduce the consumer price of such energy-efficient cars while increasing the price of gas guzzlers.

So far, Japanese firms, especially Toyota and Honda, have taken the lead in advanced automobile technology. The Japanese car industry, Lovins said to me last week, has "uninhibited visionary leaders in a country which has no oil and is acutely aware of its oil dependence". If the US automobile industry waits for years to see if lightweight fuel-efficient cars are more than a niche business, Lovins argues, it will one day discover that it has lost another market to overseas firms. There is a need too for political leadership. Lovins insists the study's recommendations require "no major federal legislation". But at the very least, they need a Federal

Government prepared to encourage states and localities to experiment with policies that increase energy efficiency.

All reports that promise an easy solution to a complex problem need to be taken with a degree of skepticism, and *Winning the Oil Endgame* is no exception. The usual pork-barrel politics could quickly bog down some of the policy prescriptions in the book, like loan guarantees for the development of new energy-saving technologies. But in a sensible presidential election, the recommendations of *Winning the Oil Endgame* would be discussed and debated from now through November. Don't hold your breath.

NEW WORDS

exploit/iks'plɔit/ v.	to use or develop to a good purpose 开发; exploitation n.
stuck/stʌk/ v.	(past participle of stick) unable to continue 卡住,不能动
turbine/'tə:bin/ n.	a machine or motor driven by a wheel which is turned by a current of water, steam, air or gas 涡轮机,透平机
shrunk/ʃrʌŋk/ v.	(past participle of shrink) to make or become smaller 收缩,变小
stuff/stʌf/	a general word for unnamed or unknown things （泛指）物品,东西
accessible/ək'sesəbl/ a.	able to be entered or reached 可接近或进入的
volatile/'vɔlətail/ a.	unstable, likely to produce change or harm 易变的,不稳定的
envelop/in'veləp/ v.	to surround, enclose, cover completely 包围;封闭;覆盖
innovation/ˌinəu'veiʃən/ n.	something new made or improved with creativity 革新;创新
dispense/di'spens/ v.	to do or manage without (同 eliminate) 不用;不用……也行
spur/spə:/ v.	to cause action 促使,激励,鞭策
insight/'insait/ n.	ability to see or know the truth, intelligence about something 洞察力;洞悉
composite/kəm'pɔzit/ n.	something made up of different parts or materials 合成品
nifty/'nifti:/ a.	very good, smart, or effective 极好的;做得精巧的;机灵的

guzzler/ˈgʌzlə/ *n.*　　　　a person who eats or drinks a lot of something, eagerly and quickly　暴饮暴食者
uninhibited/ˌʌninˈhibitid/ *a.*　free, spontaneous　不受抑制的;思想解放的
acutely/əˈkjuːtli/ *ad.*　　very strongly or painfully　剧烈地;敏锐地;敏感地
niche/nitʃ/ *n.*　　　　　a suitable or comfortable position, place, job, etc.　适合的、舒适的位置、地方、职业等
skepticism/ˈskeptisizəm/ *n.*　a doubting state or habit of mind　怀疑
(= scepticism)
prescription/priˈskripʃən/ *n.*　a written direction by a physician; an idea or suggestion about how to make a situation, activity, etc. successful　(医生的)处方;建议,方案,解决办法

PHRASES

kick a habit: stop doing sth. that is a harmful habit　改掉/抛弃/停止不良习惯
in terms of: as regards　在某方面
dream of: think about something that would like to happen　梦想
contribute to: help to cause something　有助于,促进
be dependent on: change according to what else happens or whether something else changes　依赖,取决于
think big: plan to do things that are difficult, but will be very impressive, make a lot of profit, etc.　雄心勃勃,宏图大略,一显身手
dispense with: not to use or do something that you usually use or do, because it is no longer necessary　免除
at the same rate: at the speed of　以……速度
be of minor (great) concern to sb.: be not important (important) to sb.　对……来说不重要(重要)
bog down: become too involved in thinking about or dealing with one particular thing　陷于困境
hold one's breath: stop breathing for a short time (e.g. during a medical examination or from fear or excitement)　暂时屏住呼吸(如体检时或因恐惧、激动)

NOTES

Colo.：Colorado 的缩写，科罗拉多州（位于美国西部）
SUV：sport-utility vehicle　多用途汽车
Toyota：日本丰田公司
Honda：日本本田公司
pork-barrel：［US slang］government money spent on local projects in order to win votes
　　［美口］政府为争取选票而花费在地方项目上的款项

EXERCISES

I. *Reading Comprehension*：

Choose the best answer to each question.

1. Which of the following is not mentioned as one of the reasons of less dependence on oil?
   A. Future supplies of oil will be more expensive.
   B. Oil reserves will be hardly accessible.
   C. Oil consumption will do harm to the environment.
   D. Regional stability will be affected on earth.

2. The book *Winning the Oil Endgame* mainly talks about _____.
   A. future hydrogen-based economy
   B. the promotion of energy efficiency policies
   C. the instability of Iraq and the Middle East
   D. US policymakers' big concern of energy consumption

3. It can be inferred from Paras. 3 & 4, that the instability of the Middle East is partly because, in this area, _____.
   A. people are so rich
   B. people have different religions from those of the western people
   C. the oil reserves are rich
   D. people enjoy greater freedom of movement

4. Amory Lovins suggested reducing _____ to save energy consumption.
   A. the function of cars　　　　　B. the size of cars
   C. the decoration of cars　　　　D. the weight of cars

5. According to this text, Japanese firms have advanced automobile technology partly

because Japan _____.

A. has a long automobile history

B. has so many automobiles

C. has no oil and entirely depends on oil import

D. always takes the lead in advanced technology

II. *Getting Information*:

Answer the following questions in English.

1. What has helped the planet become "smaller" than before?

2. Which area on earth reserves the biggest amount of oil?

3. If people in poor countries enjoy the same freedom of movement as those in rich countries, what will happen?

4. What is the cause of the yellow-gray haze frequently enveloping Beijing?

5. What has Amory Lovins been doing over the past 30 years?

6. What did the US government do between 1977 and 1985, because of the oil price shocks in the 1970s?

7. If the United States had continued to increase energy efficiency from 1977, what would be the US government official's consideration about Iraq and Saudi Arabia?

8. What will happen to automobiles when they are powered by hybrid technologies?

9. What should the US political leadership do to increase energy efficiency?

10. What does the writer expect the government to do during the presidential election?

III. *Vocabulary and Structure*:

A. Choose the correct word/phrase to fill into each sentence, using the proper form.

Unit 11

| exploit | stuff | envelop | endgame | composite |
| nifty | guzzle | uninhibited | skepticism | hold one's breath |

1. The _____ is quite difficult to deal with.
2. Her _____ laughter surprised everybody.
3. The country _____ its natural resources in coal and timber.
4. The audience _____ as the acrobat walked along the tightrope.
5. The citizens had some _____ about the government's policy.
6. Fog _____ the airport that morning.
7. Behavior is a(n) _____ of individual and group influences.
8. They've been _____ beer all evening.
9. There is some old, smelly _____ in the back of the refrigerator.
10. He has got a(n) _____ little gadget for squeezing oranges.

B. Find the proper forms of the following words according to the given word class.

1. exploit   (*n.*)   _____
2. access   (*a.*)   _____
3. volatilize   (*a.*)   _____
4. contribution   (*v.*)   _____
5. depend   (*a.*)   _____
6. innovate   (*n.*)   _____
7. insightful   (*n.*)   _____
8. guzzle   (*n.*)   _____
9. acute   (*ad.*) _____
10. skeptical   (*n.*)   _____

C. Complete the following sentences with the missing prepositions or adverbs.

1. _____ terms of customer satisfaction, the policy cannot be criticized.
2. We dreamed _____ buying our own house.
3. Various factors contributed _____ his downfall.
4. How much you get paid is dependent _____ how much you produce.
5. They dispense _____ the formalities.
6. _____ this rate we won't even be able to afford a holiday.

7. The rise in unemployment is _____ great concern to the government.
8. Don't let yourself get bogged _____ in minor details.
9. I'm skeptical _____ the team's chances of winning.
10. It seemed extremely difficult to find a solution _____ that problem.

IV. *Translation*:
A. Translate the following into Chinese.
1. Future-supplies of oil will be costly not simply in terms of dollars and cents but also in their effect on the environment.

2. If we had continued to increase energy efficiency at the same rate, the stability of Iraq and Saudi Arabia would by now be of minor concern to the US policymakers.

3. When powered by hybrid technologies that combine electricity with the internal-combustion engine, such light vehicles will produce enormous oil saving.

4. If the US automobile industry waits for years to see if lightweight fuel-efficient cars are more than a niche business, Lovins argues, it will one day discover that it has lost another market to overseas firms.

5. All reports that promise an easy solution to a complex problem need to be taken with a degree of skepticism, and *Winning the Oil Endgame* is no exception.

B. Translate the following into English.
1. 我被这个问题卡住了,算不出结果。(stuck)

2. 我的毛衣洗过之后缩水了。(shrink)

3. 乘公共汽车、坐地铁或驾车都可以到达歌剧院。(accessible)

4. 局势很不稳定,暴乱者有可能试图推翻政府。(volatile)

5. 汽车电话是20世纪80年代的创新,但是现在它们已经很普遍了。(innovation)

6. 与会者免去通常的礼节,立即开始谈判。(dispense with)

7. 乌云促使我们在下雨之前更快地工作。(spur)

8. 到华盛顿后,那个参议员对政治运作的真正规律有了深刻的了解。(insight)

9. 院长深知需要更多医生和护士的急迫性。(acutely)

10. 在伊文斯先生念成绩报告单时,我们都屏住了呼吸。(hold one's breath)

V. *Writing Task*:

Write about Energy Reform in some 120 words. Try to cover the following points.
1. What is the present energy consumption situation in our country?
2. What kind of measures should Chinese government take to increase the energy efficiency?
3. What should we do personally?

VI. *Oral Practice*:

Form a pair, and then talk about the energy crisis in our country. Present your opinions to each other.

Part B Grammar

倒装句及反意问句 (Inverted Sentences and Disjunctive Questions)

1. 倒装句可分为两类:全部倒装和部分倒装。全部倒装指谓语动词全部提到主语之前;部分倒装指谓语的一部分提到主语之前。如:
   · Here comes the bus. (全部倒装)
   · How did you pass the test? (部分倒装)

倒装句经常出现在以下几种情况当中：
(1) 疑问句：
　　·Did you have lunch?
(2) 句首是以下副词开始：out、up、here、there、now、in、down、off、only、often、many a time
　　·Here is the book for you.
　　·Down came the car.
　　·Out ran the boy.
　　·Only when I finished the work, did I go to the movie.
(3) 句首含有否定副词和否定短语：hardly、little、scarcely、seldom、never、rarely、at no time、not until…、no sooner…than、hardly (scarcely) …when…、not only…but also…
　　·Seldom did she come here.
　　·Not until 11 o'clock does the dinning hall open.
　　·No sooner had they got to the station than the train left.
(4) 以 so、neither 和 nor 构成的倒装句：
　　·She cannot speak English, nor do I.
　　·He likes this film, so do I.
(5) 让步状语从句：
　　·Old as he is, he still works in the field.
　　·No matter who told you about it, we had to confirm it.
(6) 虚拟语气：
　　·Were I asked, I would help him.
　　·Had it rained yesterday, we would have stayed at home.
2. 反意问句位于句子的结尾，其反意部分需根据主句的谓语形式而变化。如：
　　·They are not in the room, are they?（需用 are）
　　·They came to the meeting, didn't they?（需用 didn't）
　　·He dare not travel alone in the evening, dare he?（需用 dare）
　　·Let's go home, shall we?（let's 句型需用 shall we）
　　·Close the door, will you?（祈使句需用 will you）
　　·Everything is going on smoothly, isn't it?（需用 isn't it）
　　·He seldom writes home, does he?（seldom、little、scarcely、hardly 等表示否定）

Unit 11

练 习

I. 倒装句

1. 选择适当的词语填空。

(1) So fast _____ that it is difficult for us to imagine its speed.

　　A. light travels　　　　　　B. travels the light

　　C. do light travels　　　　　D. does light travel

(2) Hardly _____ the people ran toward it.

　　A. had the plane landed when　　B. had the plane landed than

　　C. the plane landed before　　　D. the plane was landing that

(3) _____ a certain doubt among the students as to the necessity of the work.

　　A. It existed　　　　B. There existed

　　C. Here had　　　　 D. There had

(4) _____ that the pilot couldn't fly through it.

　　A. The storm so severe was　　B. So severe was the storm

　　C. So the storm was severe　　D. Such was the storm severe

(5) Seldom _____ any mistakes during my past five years of service here.

　　A. would I made　　　B. should I make

　　C. I would make　　　D. did I make

(6) No sooner _____ than he realized that he should have remained silent.

　　A. had the words been spoken　　B. the words had spoken

　　C. the words had been spoken　　D. had the words spoken

(7) Only when you have obtained sufficient data _____ come to a sound conclusion.

　　A. can you　　　　B. would you

　　C. you will　　　　D. you can

(8) Scarcely had he gone out _____.

　　A. that it started to snow　　　B. than it started to snow

　　C. when it started to snow　　 D. and it started to snow

(9) Many a time _____ that test.

　　A. we have tried　　　B. did we have tried

　　C. did we tried　　　　D. have we tried

(10) Wood does not conduct electricity, _____.

    A. so doesn't rubber   B. also doesn't rubber
    C. nor does rubber   D. nor rubber does

(11) Not until Mr. Smith came to China _____ what kind of a country it is.
    A. did he know   B. he knew
    C. didn't he know   D. he could know

(12) Nancy works in a huge shop which opened not long ago, and _____.
    A. so does Alan   B. so Alan too does
    C. that does Alan too D. that Alan too does

(13) She is not fond of cooking, shopping and cleaning, _____ I.
    A. so am   B. nor am
    C. neither   D. nor do

(14) Rarely _____ such a silly thing.
    A. have I heard of   B. did I heard of
    C. have I been heard of D. I have heard of

(15) Here _____ you want to see.
    A. comes the girl   B. come does the girl
    C. the girl comes   D. coming the girl is

2. 把下列句子译为英语。
(1) 只有这样,我们才能不辜负人们的期望。
(2) 他一到车站,火车就开了。
(3) 汤姆上学迟到了,约翰也迟到了。
(4) 我虽然很小,可是我知道我家里的一些秘密。
(5) 要是我当时在现场,我就帮你了。

II. 反意问句

1. 选择适当的词语填入空内。
(1) He scarcely (seldom, rarely, hardly) comes here, _____ he?
    A. did   B. didn't   C. does   D. doesn't
(2) You'd rather not do it, _____ ?
    A. shouldn't you   B. wouldn't you   C. would you   D. ought you
(3) Let's talk about the book, _____ ?
    A. shall we   B. can we   C. will we   D. ought we

(4) Come here a moment,_____?

　　A. will you　　　B. shall you　　　C. do you　　　D. don't you

(5) No one is interested in that,_____?

　　A. is she　　　B. isn't he　　　C. aren't they　　　D. are they

(6) Everything seems all right,_____?

　　A. doesn't it　　　B. didn't they　　　C. won't it　　　D. hasn't it

(7) We never dared to ask him a question,_____?

　　A. did we　　　B. doesn't it　　　C. dared we　　　D. daredn't we

(8) A fence needs the support of three stakes,_____?

　　A. does it　　　B. doesn't it　　　C. needn't it　　　D. needs not

(9) Give me that recorder,_____?

　　A. can't you　　　B. will you　　　C. don't you　　　D. shan't you

(10) Dennis said no one was qualified for the job,_____?

　　A. did he　　　B. didn't he　　　C. weren't they　　　D. wasn't he

(11) What a lovely day,_____?

　　A. is it　　　B. shan't it　　　C. isn't it　　　D. won't it

(12) You never told us why you were one hour late for the meeting,_____?

　　A. weren't you　　　B. didn't you　　　C. have you　　　D. did you

(13) She had enough money for dinner,_____?

　　A. doesn't she　　　B. hasn't she　　　C. haven't she　　　D. didn't she

(14) We had to wait a long time to get our visas,_____?

　　A. don't we　　　B. didn't we　　　C. couldn't we　　　D. shouldn't we

(15) He never used to swim in winter,_____?

　　A. did he　　　B. didn't he　　　C. was he　　　D. wasn't he

2. 把下列句子译为英语。

(1) 她已经辞职了,不是吗?

(2) 他敢于说出自己的想法,不是吗?

(3) 让我们马上开始干,好吗?

(4) 把那杯茶递给我,好吗?

(5) 他几乎不怎么回家,是吗?

Part C Supplementary Reading

An Impression of Zhu Diwen
—A Nobel Physics Prize Winner of Chinese Descent

In October, big news rocked Stanford University, the Harvard of the West Coast. Zhu Diwen, a professor of Chinese descent in Stanford's Department of Physics, along with two other scientists, an American and a Frenchman, won the Nobel Physics prize this year for their invention of a technique to cool atoms with a laser.

The day after winning the prize, Zhu Diwen held a press conference at the invitation of the all-American and overseas Chinese media. American born, Zhu Diwen is of course an American, but at the press conference he noted that, scientifically and genetically, he is one hundred percent Chinese. Having lived in America since his youth, Zhu Diwen is of course a very "Americanized" scientist. He impresses others with his self-confident, humorous and witty conversation, while remaining refined and cultivated. During the many press conferences and congratulatory gatherings, his peerless wit and humor overwhelmed participants, including members of the Chinese and foreign media, and the Stanford co-eds.

On the day the prize was announced, among a series of press conferences with the departments and faculty, celebration with champagne, visiting, and tours of his laboratory, Zhu gave a lecture to a class. Zhu said, "Winning an award is of course a kind of affirmation, but it doesn't affect me much. I am still who I was yesterday." Asked how he planned to dispose of the prize money, he said, "Uncle Sam will likely lop off 40% in taxes, which won't leave much. But at least I can pay off part of my unpaid loans."

A divorcee, Zhu is the sole provider in a typical "single parent" family. The two sons take turns at each parent's home, and Zhu treasures his regular reunion with his children. At an evening celebration party, the host begged Zhu to stay longer, but Zhu insisted that nothing could infringe on his "family time"—a 100% American outlook. He carried himself naturally, with good poise, when he introduced his new girl friend Jane to the media. Jane, like Zhu, is also a physicist. The two even embraced for the newsmen to take photographs. But in response to those who sought to get to the bottom of the matter with blunt questions like "When shall we attend your wedding feast", Zhu smiled and said, "This is not a public matter."

Stanford University students' respect for this newest Nobel Prize winner has broken office and departmental barriers. For a fortnight following the event, students from various departments made the pilgrimage to the Physics building, invariably pausing to peep into Professor Zhu's office. The present writer also visited the professor's office one evening at 8 p. m. , and found Zhu with his eyes glued to the computer, fingers flying on the keyboard. His two doctoral students in an adjacent room said that Professor Zhu keeps his own hours, and had not yet had his supper. Some newly enrolled Chinese students from Xi'an and Beijing were quite excited. They thought themselves fortunate in being able upon arrival to meet a Nobel Prize winner, and a professor of Chinese descent.

Polls revealed that the respect and warmth shown to Professor Zhu by people inside and outside the university surpassed that shown President Clinton's daughter on her enrollment a month ago.

In a cocktail celebration held in honor of Professor Zhu, as many as one hundred Chinese visiting scholars and students studying abroad experienced first-hand the charm and amiability of the graceful master of physics in his smart academic speeches. With his informal attire and satchel clasped behind his back, Zhu looks no different from other young men. His amiable and witty style of conversation has closed the gap between master and students. With plain but witty language, he explained a slide show presentation of the content and future of the scientific research subjects that landed him the prize. A number of doctoral students sighed with feeling after the event, saying they would benefit the rest of their life from listening to this esoteric lecture by a world-level master of physics.

On November 2, Zhu Diwen met Chinese President Jiang Zemin in Los Angeles. "Can you speak Chinese?" "A little bit," Professor Zhu replied humorously to the President's opening remarks. He said, "My parents are to blame for this. They regret it deeply now!" Jiang Zemin invited Zhu Diwen to visit Beijing again. Jiang said that China has a valuable export—scientists and engineers. Zhu Diwen responded that China can be a great nation which has not only economic power but also wisdom. He expressed delight at the opportunity to assist China in scientific and technological spheres, and promised to visit China very soon.

However, Zhu Diwen also put forward a small request to Jiang Zemin: he will teach Chinese experimental physics if they in turn teach him Chinese.

Throughout the past half month of media events, Zhu Diwen was seen dressed in Western-style clothes only when he met Jiang Zemin. The young scientist certainly looked smart and elegant, and his demeanor was natural and unrestrained in his Chinese-style jacket and trousers. Nobody would have thought that with a 60 hours plus workweek, he would have maintained his vim, vigor, and humorous outlook. His students revealed that Professor Zhu peppers his classes with a steady stream of witticisms, to their immense delight. But Zhu frankly confides that it is time for him to relax a bit. He plans to have a really nice vacation when he visits Sweden next spring to receive his award. All who have seen him have exclaimed, "What a humorous Nobel Prize winner!"

NEW WORDS

descent /di'sent/ *n.*　　ancestry　祖先;祖籍

rock /rɔk/ *v.*　　(cause to) sway or swing backwards and forwards, or from side to side　使摆动,摇动

genetical /dʒi'netikl/ *a.*　　of genes　遗传因子的

peerless /'piəlis/ *a.*　　without equal　无匹敌的,无双的

overwhelm /ˌəuvə'ʰwelm/ *v.*　　affect sb. strongly and suddenly　制伏,压倒;使不知所措

co-ed /ˌkəu'ed/ *n.*　　(Am E) coeducational student; a student and esp. a female student in a coeducational institution　男女同学同校的学生,尤指女生

faculty /'fækəlti/ *n.*　　department or grouping of related departments　(大学的)系,学院

affirmation /ˌæfə'meiʃən/ *n.*　　declaration　肯定,断言

infringe /in'frindʒ/ *v.*　　break (a rule), violate, encroach　侵占;侵害

poise /pɔiz/ *n.*　　way in which one carries oneself　姿势,姿态

blunt /blʌnt/ *a.*　　plain, not troubling to be polite　直率的,不客气的

feast /fi:st/ *n.*　　splendid meal with many good things to eat and drink　宴会,盛宴

fortnight /'fɔ:tnait/ *n.*　　period of two weeks　两星期

pilgrimage /'pilgrimidʒ/ *n.*　　journey of a pilgrim　朝圣者的旅程

invariable /in'vɛəriəbl/ *a.*　　unchangeable, constant　不变的,恒久的

peep /pi:p/ *v.*　　take a short, quick or inquisitive look　偷看,瞥见,窥视

adjacent /ə'dʒeisənt/ *a.*　　next to, lying near but not necessary touching　毗邻的,邻近的

enroll /in'rəul/ *v.*　　become a member of　登记,注册

poll /pəul/ *n.*　　survey of public opinion by putting questions to a representative selection of persons　民意调查

Unit 11

reveal/ri'vi:l/ *v.*	display; make shown 显示;透露
surpass/sə'pɑ:s/ *v.*	do or be better than, exceed, 超越,凌驾,胜过
attire/ə'taiə/ *n.*	dress 服装
satchel/'sætʃəl/ *n.*	small bag for carrying light articles, esp. school books 书包
clasp/klɑ:sp/ *v.*	fasten with a clasp 用钩环扣住
amiable/'eimjəbl/ *a.*	good-tempered; easy and pleasant to talk to 友善的;和蔼的
esoteric/,esəu'terik/ *a.*	intended for those who have special knowledge of it 秘密的,密传的
sphere/sfiə/ *n.*	range, extent 领域,范围
demeanor/di'mi:nə/ *n.*	way of behaving 行为,举止,风度
vim/vim/ *n.*	energy 精力,活力
vigor/'vigə/ *n.*	mental or physical strength; energy 智力;体力;活力
pepper/'pepə/ *v.*	(像撒胡椒般地)密布
immense/i'mens/ *a.*	very large 极大的
confide/kən'faid/ *v.*	tell to sb. 倾诉

PHRASES

along with: in company with; together with 伴随
a series of: 一系列
dispose of: get rid of, deal with 处理,处置
lop off: cut off 砍掉,砍去
infringe on: interfere with or take over (the right of another) 侵占,侵害……的权利
in response to: answer 回答,应答
seek to: look for 寻找
get to the bottom of the matter: discover the truth about it or the real cause of it 弄清……的真相
be glued to: give all one's attention to, watching 注意,盯着
keep one's own hours: 有自己的时间安排
in honor of: 为庆祝……,为纪念……
be to blame: deserve to be blamed 该受到责备

put forward: advance 提出

NOTES

Nobel Prizes：以瑞典科学家（Alfred Bernard Nobel, 1833—1896）的遗产设立的奖项，分物理、化学、生理或医学、文学、和平五项奖金。

EXERCISES

I. *Reading Comprehension*：

1. Which statement is true of Zhu Diwen?
    A. He was born in America and had spent a long time in China.
    B. His parents are Chinese.
    C. He was born in China and received education in America.
    D. He is 100% Chinese so he can speak Chinese well.

2. On the day the prize was announced, _____.
    A. he worked late into night
    B. he gave students a lecture
    C. he held a press conference only to Chinese media
    D. he celebrated with his two sons

3. After he won the prize, _____.
    A. he had to wear western-style suit every day to meet the media
    B. he had to change his working habit
    C. people from different departments went to visit him
    D. he told the reporters when to get married

4. What can we infer from this passage?
    A. He put on the airs of a great scientist after he won the prize.
    B. He will not receive the award until next summer.
    C. He divorced his wife after he won the prize.
    D. Clinton's daughter is in the same university.

5. From the conversation between Zhu and Jiang Zemin, we know that _____.
    A. he has never been to China before
    B. Zhu believes that China will be a great nation

C. his parents taught him Chinese when he was young, but he failed to learn

D. he wore a Chinese-style jacket at that time

II. *Getting Information*:

1. What is the main feature of his lectures?

2. How is Zhu Diwen going to spend the prize money?

3. How does Zhu dress himself usually?

4. What did doctoral students think after they heard Zhu's explanation in the celebration?

5. What does the "valuable export" refer to?

III. *Vocabulary*:

Choose the correct word to fit into each sentence, using the proper form.

| demeanor | peerless | faculty | infringe | adjacent |
| enroll | surpass | amiable | sphere | confide |

1. The beauty of the scenery _____ my expectations.
2. Be careful not to _____ the rights of other people.
3. He _____ his troubles to a friend.
4. I dislike his supercilious _____.
5. Go and make yourself _____ to the guests.
6. He has got himself _____ as a member of that society.
7. There are 25 _____ in this university.
8. His outstanding achievement made him _____.
9. She is a woman who is distinguished in many _____.
10. The house _____ to the church is beautiful.

Part A Text (The Advertising of a Product)
Part B Grammar (虚拟语气)
Part C Supplementary Reading
        (Dividing a Kingdom)

Part A Text

Warm-up Questions:
1. *What influences us when we dicide to buy one product instead of another?*
2. *What kind of information do we get from advertising?*
3. *What methods do advertisers use to sell products?*
4. *Who is not affected by advertising?*

The Advertising of a Product

    A consumer walks into a store. He stands in front of hundreds of boxes of laundry detergent. He chooses one brand, pays for it, and leaves. Why does he pick that specific kind of soap? Is it truly better than the others? Probably not. These days, many products are nearly identical to one another in quality and price. If products are almost the same, what makes consumers buy one brand instead of another? Although we might not like to admit it, commercials on television and advertisements in magazines probably influence us much more than we think they do.

    Advertising informs consumers about new products available on the market. It gives us information about everything from shampoo to toothpaste to computers and cars. But there is one serious problem with us. The "information" is actually very often misinformation. It tells us the products' benefits but hides their disadvantages. Advertising not only leads us to buy things that we don't need and can't afford, but also confuses our sense of reality. "Zoom toothpaste prevents cavities and gives you white teeth!" the advertisement tells us. But it doesn't tell us the complete truth: that a healthy diet and a good toothbrush will have the same effect.

Advertisers use many methods to get us to buy their products. One of their most successful methods is to make us feel dissatisfied with ourselves and our imperfect lives. Advertisements show us who we aren't and what we don't have. Our teeth aren't white enough. Our hair isn't shiny enough. Our clothes aren't clean enough. Advertisements make us afraid that people won't like us if we don't use the advertised products. "Why don't I have any dates?" an attractive young woman sadly asks in a commercial. "Here," replies her roommate, "try Zoom toothpaste!" Of course she tries it, and immediately the whole football team falls in love with her. "That's a stupid commercial," we might say. But we still buy Zoom toothpaste out of fear of being unpopular and having no friends. If fear is the negative motive for buying a product, then wanting a good image is the positive reason for choosing it. Each of us has a mental picture of the kind of person we would like to be. For example, a modern young woman might like to think that she looks like a beautiful movie star. A middle-aged man might want to see himself as a strong attractive athlete. Advertisers know this. They write specific ads to make certain groups of people choose their product. Two people may choose different brands of toothpaste with the identical price, amount, and quality; each person believes that he or she is expressing his personality by choosing that brand.

Advertisers get psychologists to study the way consumers think and their reasons for choosing one brand instead of another. These experts tell advertisers about the motives of fear and self-image. They also inform them about recent studies with colors and words. Psychologists have found that certain colors on the package of an attractive product will cause people to reach out and take that package instead of buying an identical product with different colors. Also, certain words attract our attention. For example, the words "new" "improved" "natural" and "giant size" are very popular and seem to draw our eyes and hands toward the package.

Many people believe that advertising does not affect them. They feel that they have freedom of choice, and they like to think they make wise choices. Unfortunately, they probably don't realize the powerful effect of advertising. They may not clearly understand that advertisers spend billions of dollars each year in aggressive competition for our money, and they are extremely successful. Do you believe that ads don't influence your choice of products? Just look at the brands in your kitchen and bathroom.

NEW WORDS

laundry/ˈlɔːndri/ *n.*	clothes, etc. that need to be washed 要洗的衣服；a place where clothes are washed and ironed 洗衣店
detergent/diˈtəːdʒənt/ *n.*	a liquid or powder used for washing clothes, dishes, etc. 清洁剂，去垢剂
identical/aiˈdentikəl/ *a.*	exactly the same 同一的，同样的
commercial/kəˈməːʃəl/ *n.*	an advertisement on television or the radio 广告
shampoo/ʃæmˈpuː/ *n.*	a liquid soap for washing your hair 洗发精，洗发香波
cavity/ˈkæviti/ *n.*	a hold in a tooth made by decay 洞，空穴；[解剖]腔
negative/ˈnegətiv/ *a.*	having a bad or harmful effect 否定的，消极的；负的；阴性的
motive/ˈməutiv/ *n.*	the reason that makes someone do something 动机，目的
positive/ˈpɔzətiv/ *a.*	having a good or useful effect 肯定的，积极的
athlete/ˈæθliːt/ *n.*	someone who is good at sports or who often does sports 运动员，运动选手
psychologist/saiˈkɔlədʒist/ *n.*	someone who is trained in psychology 心理学者
aggressive/əˈgresiv/ *a.*	intended to achieve the right result 好斗的，有闯劲的；侵略性的

EXERCISES

I. *Reading Comprehension*:

Choose the best answer to each question.

1. Advertising _____.
    A. informs us everything about some products
    B. doesn't influence us very much
    C. is always stupid
    D. doesn't always tell us everything about a product

2. Which of the following is NOT the reason for a person to buy a product?
    A. He or she is satisfied with himself or herself.
    B. He or she has the need for a good self-image.
    C. The colors on the package.
    D. Certain words on the package.

3. Advertisers _____ to make us buy products.

   A. employ very low prices

   B. get information from psychologists

   C. try to make us feel good

   D. need to use better package

4. Psychologists tell advertisers _____.

   A. which brands of toothpaste to produce

   B. to stop influencing shoppers

   C. about people's motives for buying

   D. how much money to spend on television commercials

5. Which of the following is true according to the passage?

   A. Advertising influences us to buy one kind of product instead of another.

   B. "The Psychology of Selling" is an important course in many business colleges.

   C. If you use Zoom toothpaste, there will be no more problems in your life.

   D. Advertisements always provides us with important information about products.

II. *Getting Information*:

An outline that gives a picture of the organization of reading material can contain topics, statements of ideas, or a combination of the two. Fill in the outline of the passage with complete sentences, using the expressions in the brackets as clues. The first two have been done for you as an example.

The Advertising of a Product

1. (Introduction) Commercials and advertising influence consumers.

   A. (Choice of brands) Consumers choose certain brands.

   B. (Sameness of brands) _____

2. _____

   A. (Benefits of products) _____

   B. (Disadvantages) _____

   C. (Reality) _____

3. (Methods of advertisers) _____

   A. (Fear) _____

   B. (Self-image) _____

   C. (Colors and words) _____

4. (Conclusion) _____

III. *Vocabulary and Structure*:

A. Choose words or phrases from Column B that are close in meaning to those in Column A. Note that there are some extra items in Column B.

Column A	Column B
1. specific	a. to produce an effect or change
2. identical	b. someone who is good at sports
3. commercial	c. someone who buys and uses products and services
4. consumer	d. extremely large
5. negative	e. likely to be successful
6. athlete	f. particular
7. giant	g. having a bad and harmful effect
8. affect	h. exactly the same
	i. an advertisement

B. Choose the correct word/phrase to fill into each sentence, using the proper form.

identical	motive	positive	specific
affect	aggressive	mental	brand

1. When I said no, she became rude and _____.
2. I think there is less _____ loyalty in computers than there was a few years ago.
3. Emergency relief will be sent to the areas most _____ by the hurricane.
4. My work hours are almost _____ to my daughters' school hours.
5. What was his _____ for committing the crime?
6. He was tested for brain damage and _____ disorders.
7. I'm not _____ of the address, but it's a round here somewhere.
8. Power plant employees must follow a very _____ safety guideline.

C. Complete the sentence with missing words.

1. Many products are identical _____ one another in quality.
2. Commercials _____ television influence us a lot.
3. Advertising informs consumers about new products available _____ the market.
4. Advertising leads us _____ buy things that we don't need.

5. We buy some products _____ fear of being unpopular.
6. Fear is the negative motive _____ buying a product.
7. There is one serious problem _____ it.
8. Certain colors will cause people to reach _____ and take that package.
9. People believe that they are expressing their personalities _____ choosing that brand.
10. A middle-aged man might want to see himself _____ a strong athlete.

IV. *Translation*:
A. Translate the following into Chinese.
  1. Advertising not only leads us to buy things that we don't need and can't afford, but also confuses our sense of reality.

  2. If fear is the negative motive for buying a product, then wanting a good image is the positive reason for choosing it.

  3. Two people may choose different brands of toothpaste with the identical price, amount, and quality; each person believes that he or she is expressing his personality by choosing that brand.

  4. Psychologists have found that certain colors on the package of an attractive product will cause people to reach out and take that package instead of buying an identical product with different colors.

  5. They feel that they have freedom of choice, and they like to think they make wise choices. Unfortunately, they probably don't realize the powerful effect of advertising.

B. Translate the following into English.
  1. 你需要积极的态度才能找到合适的工作。(positive)

  2. 这一事件的动机是种族歧视。(motive)

  3. 有时心理上的伤害比身体伤害更糟。(psychological)

4. 价格下调是由于供应商之间的竞争引起的。(competition)
_____

5. 这种洗发水自称能给头发带来光泽。(shine)
_____

V. Writing Task:

Write about advertisement in about 120 words. Try to cover the following points.

1. Advertisement is everywhere.
2. Advertisement brings advantages as well as disadvantages.
3. What is your opinion?

VI. Oral Practice:

In small groups, talk about your answers to the following questions.

1. What kinds of advertising attract your attention? Do you sometimes buy the products in the ads or commercials? For what reasons?
2. Do you think advertisements and commercials are similar or different in various cultures around the world. Give examples to support your answers.
3. What image would you like to have for yourself? Do you envy or want to be like any of the people you see in television commercials or magazine ads?
4. What famous brands of products do you have in your home or workplace now? Why did you buy them?

Part B Grammar

虚拟语气 (Subjunctive Mood)

虚拟语气常用于非真实条件句和表示命令、建议及祝愿等意义的句中。在非真实条件句用于表示假设或实现的可能性不大的概念；主要分为与现在事实相反、与过去事实相反和将来实现的可能性不大三种形式。

· If I had enough money, I would travel around the world. （与现在事实相反）

· If you had come yesterday, you would have met her. （与过去事实相反）

Unit 12

- If you were to go to the post office, I would ask you to buy some stamps. （实现的可能性很小）

在表达命令、建议及祝愿时常有以下的一些固定用法，如：

- I would rather he completed the work now.

（would rather、would sooner、would just as、soon 等词语的后面动词需用过去时或者是过去完成时）

- I wish I had learned English when I was a child.

（wish 后的宾语从句表示愿望，使用过去时表示与现在事实相反，使用过去完成时表示与过去事实相反，使用 could、would、might 或 were + doing 表示希望将来能实现的愿望）

- It is high time that we left for class.

（It is high time、about time 或 time 的句型，从句中的谓语动词需用过去时）

- It is imperative that he work hard.

（以 imperative、necessary、important、strange、desirable、natural、proper 等形容词为主句表语时，从句谓语动词需用虚拟语气；用 should + 动词原形或动词原形）

- She suggested that we (should) be there on time.

（以 suggest、insist、demand、propose、move、recommend、command、require、desire 等动词为主句谓语时，从句需用虚拟语气；使用 should + 动词原形或动词原形）

- His suggestion is that we (should) consider the plan again.

（主句中出现 suggestion、recommendation、advice、requirement、order、proposal 等名词时，从句需用虚拟语气，使用 should + 动词原形或动词原形。）

- But for the heavy traffic, we should have arrived earlier.

（通过介词引导的短语，如 but for、without 等，主句的谓语动词需用虚拟语气，使用 should + 现在完成时。）

- If only I had had time yesterday morning!

（if only 连词后面的谓语动词需用虚拟语气，使用过去完成时。）

练 习

1. 选择适当的词语填入空内。

(1) If I _____ in this uniform, I wouldn't feel so conspicuous.

    A. wasn't dressed   B. didn't dress

    C. weren't dressed   D. don't dress

(2) I would gladly have attended your wedding if you _____.
   A. would have invited me   B. invited me
   C. could have invited me   D. had invited me

(3) Jean would go to New York City, but she _____ money now.
   A. hadn't have   B. would not have
   C. has no   D. would have

(4) _____, he would help us without any hesitation.
   A. Were he here   B. Was he here
   C. If he is here   D. Is he here

(5) What would you do if war _____ out?
   A. is broken   B. were to break out
   C. will break out   D. are to break out

(6) He looks as if he _____ nothing about the news.
   A. would know   B. would have known
   C. knew   D. should know

(7) I would have invited her to the party, but I _____ her well.
   A. don't know   B. had not known
   C. didn't know   D. won't know

(8) But for the rain, we _____ our destination before 5 yesterday.
   A. would have reached   B. reached
   C. had reached   D. should reached

(9) But that he _____ it, he could not have believed it.
   A. had seen   B. had not seen
   C. didn't see   D. has seen

(10) Without water, there _____ no plants on the earth.
   A. would have   B. would be
   C. were to be   D. were

(11) I'd rather he _____ me tomorrow.
   A. visited   B. visit
   C. visiting   D. will visit

(12) Supposing the weather _____ bad, where would you go?
   A. is   B. will be
   C. were   D. be

(13) Mike hoped _____ his letter.

Unit 12

      A. her to answer   B. that she answer
      C. that she would answer   D. her answer

(14) I'd just as sooner _____ her about it.
      A. that you won't tell   B. you not tell
      C. you didn't tell   D. your not telling

(15) She studied very hard at the university for fear that she _____ fall behind.
      A. may   B. would
      C. should   D. did not

2．将下列短句翻译成英文。
  （1）如果有时间的话，我就会和你一起去看电影。
  （2）要不是你帮忙，他们是不可能取得成功的。
  （3）他坚持要求我们将实验报告在完成试验后第二天交上来。
  （4）希望他会原谅我。
  （5）他要是知道我们的电话号码该多好啊。
  （6）他早就该戒烟了。
  （7）我们需要马上出发。
  （8）如果你昨天没看电影的话，你现在就不会困了。
  （9）看起来他好像什么都知道。
  （10）我宁愿你明天走。

Part C   Supplementary Reading

Dividing a Kingdom

    The United Kingdom has been a union of four countries for hundreds of years. But for how much longer? Many fear that government plans to give independence to Scotland and Wales might ultimately cause Britain to break up.

    In the last century, Britain was the largest and most powerful nation on Earth. But, for much of this century, the British Empire has been shrinking. It finally came to an end a few months ago when Hong Kong was handed back to China.

Until recently, it was thought that the United Kingdom could not shrink any further, since all that is left are the small islands that make up the union itself. But now, Britain's Labour government plans to create new parliamentary assemblies in Scotland and Wales, raising fears that the union might one day disappear altogether.

Britain's prime Minister, Tony Blair, argues that his policy of devolution may be the only way to prevent the collapse of the UK. The granting of additional powers to Scotland and Wales will, he believes, put a stop to the ongoing demands for total independence for those countries.

The more important of the new governing bodies is the Scottish Parliament in Edinburgh, which is scheduled to take office at the start of the year 2000. The 129 members of the Parliament will set up an executive, which will have most of the powers of a full government over Scotland's five million citizens. The only functions of government that will still be determined in Westminster will be constitutional affairs, foreign and defence policy, national security and economic affairs (although the new Parliament will have the power to make income tax rates up to three per cent higher or lower than they are in the rest of Britain).

Nationalists argue that Scotland should be independent from the UK because it is so different from Britain as a whole. The most obvious differences are cultural-kilts, bag-pipes and certain sports and games are unique to Scotland. But the systems of law, education and religion also differ considerably to those of the rest of the Britain.

But even those who don't want Scotland to become a completely separate country agree that a parliament in Edinburgh may be necessary to ensure that the £ 14-billion the British government allocates to Scotland every year is spent properly.

The same argument applies to Wales, where the British government spends about £ 7-billion a year. However, the proposed Welsh Assembly will not have the same powers as Scotland's. It won't be able to raise or lower taxes, nor introduce any laws that have not already been approved by Westminster. In short, the Welsh Assembly will do little more than distribute money allocated by London. This, say critics, makes it little more than a large local authority.

Although Wales' three million inhabitants have a rich and distinct culture, as well as their own language—spoken by just under 20 per cent of the population—at present there is little popular support for a complete break with London. However, opponents of independence fear that the Welsh Assembly will make further independence seem more attractive, especially if the Scottish Parliament is successful.

More pressing though are the problems that the new assemblies could cause in London.

Scotland and Wales will continue to have MPs in Parliament at Westminster. This means they will be in the strange position of having a say over the affairs of England, with its far greater population of 48 million, but not over matters in their own countries. In England, there is already resentment about this, and there are fears that it could lead to calls for a separate Parliament for England itself. If that happens, there is little chance of the UK holding together in its current form.

Most British politicians agree that devolution will mark a step into unknown territory for the UK. But people like Alex Salmond, leader of the Scottish National Party, which wants total independence for Scotland, believe that history is on their side, "We see a pattern of big nations breaking up and separatist parties gaining ground throughout the world," says Mr. Salmond, "Within the European Union, there is clearly room for an independent Scotland to take its place alongside the new democracies of the former Soviet Union, eastern and central Europe."

Even those who disagree with Mr. Salmond believe that the end of the Cold War has encouraged moves towards independence by small nations, and not just in Europe but in countries as different as Canada and India. Indeed, some experts in government law believe that a federal system similar to that of the US or Germany may prove the best solution for Britain. This would include a new English Parliament which, like those of Scotland and Wales, would have major powers to negotiate international agreements.

In such a situation, the UK would stay as the overall sovereign power with the British Monarchy at its head. But many of its responsibilities would be handed over to regional parliaments. In the long run, this may be the best that those strongly in favour of a united Britain can hope for.

NEW WORDS

shrink/ʃriŋk/v.   become smaller 缩小
devolution/diːvəˈluːʃən/n. the giving of part of one's power, work, duties, etc. to another person or group 权利下放
ongoing/ˈɔngəuiŋ/a.   continuing 正在进行的
nationalist/ˈnæʃnəlist/n.   民族主义者
kilt/kilt/n.   苏格兰男子穿着的呢格裙
bagpipes/ˈbægpaips/n.   苏格兰风笛
pressing/ˈpresiŋ/a.   demanding or needing attention, action, etc., now 紧迫的

resentment/ri'zentmənt/*n.*   angry feeling   不满,愤恨
sovereign/'sɔvrin/*a.*   independent and self governing   有主权的;最高的,至尊的

PHRASES

break up：separate   分离,分开
come to an end：end   结束
take office：start one's job in his office   开始办公,上任
have a say over…：give one's opinion about sth.   对……有发言权
in the long run：later in the future   从长远来看
gain ground：improve or have more success   有进步,获得进展

NOTES

parliamentary assembly：议会机构(议会成员由民众选举,其任务是制定法律)
Westminster：威斯敏斯特,英国议院所在地,喻指英国议院或英国政府。
constitutional affairs：宪法规定的事务
income tax：个人收入所得税
Welsh Assembly：威尔士议会
MP：Member of Parliament：英国议院议员
federal system：联邦政府体系,联邦制
British Monarchy：英国皇室,英国的君主

EXERCISES

I. *Reading Comprehension*：
A. Based on the information presented in the passage, what would you say about the following statements? Write "Yes" "No" or "Maybe" in the space provided before each sentence.

    Yes   means it is true.
    No   means it is false.
    Maybe   means there is not enough information to decide whether it is true or false.

    _____ 1) The British Empire no longer exists.

_____ 2) The United Kingdom is going to shrink even further.
_____ 3) Scotland will have its own parliament.
_____ 4) Wales will have its own parliament.
_____ 5) Almost every Scottish citizen thinks a parliament of its own is necessary.
_____ 6) Both the Welsh and Scottish parliaments will have the same powers.
_____ 7) England will have its own parliament.
_____ 8) The United Kingdom is going to have a federal system.

B. Read the passage carefully again. Try to locate the information needed to fill in the following table. Write down the information in words and phrases.

Future Outlook in Scotland

	Responsible for
Scottish Parliament	
Westminster	

Future Outlook in Wales

	Responsible for
Welsh Parliament	
Westminster	

II. Vocabulary and Structure:

Choose the correct word/phrase to fill into each sentence, using the proper form.

| press | shrink | break up | in the long run |
| power | distinct | come to an end | have a say |

1. The _____ in our export trade is serious.
2. The state owned gas company was _____ into several smaller private companies.
3. It is important to remember the _____ between rights and laws.
4. Citizens should _____ in how their tax money is spent.
5. Ten of the world's _____ men met to discuss trade barriers.
6. Survival is the most _____ concern of any new company.
7. All our hard work will be worth it.
8. His soccer career _____ Friday after 18 seasons.

UNIT 13

Part A   Text (A Simple Truth About Happiness)
Part B   Grammar (直接引语和间接引语)
Part C   Supplementary Reading
         (To Win at Marriage, Learn to Lose)

Part A   Text

Warm-up Questions:
1. *What do you think makes a person happy?*
2. *Is it possible for us to do something to achieve happiness?*
3. *What may prevent us from feeling happy?*

A Simple Truth About Happiness

If you're waiting for it, you've missed the point.

By Dennis Prager

From "HAPPINESS IS A SERIOUS PROBLEM"

Each of us owes it to our spouses, our children, our friends to be as happy as we can be. Anyone can be unhappy; it takes no courage or effort. True achievement lies in struggling to be happy.

The concept that we have to work at happiness comes as news to many people. We assume it's a feeling that comes as a result of good things that just happen to us, things over which we have little or no control.

But the opposite is true: happiness is largely under our control. It is a battle to be waged and not a feeling to be awaited.

To achieve a happier life, it's necessary to overcome some obstacles, three of which are:

Comparison with Others

Most of us compare ourselves with anyone we think is happier—a relative, an acquaintance or, often, someone we barely know. I once met a young man who struck me as particularly successful and happy. He spoke of his love for his beautiful wife and their daughters, and of his joy at being a radio talk-show host in a city he loved. I remember thinking that he was one of those lucky few for whom everything goes effortlessly right.

Then we started talking about the Internet. He blessed its existence, he told me, because he could look up information on multiple sclerosis—the terrible disease torturing his wife. I felt like a fool for assuming nothing unhappy existed in his life.

Images of Perfection

Almost all of us have images of how life should be. The problem, of course, is that only rarely do people's jobs, spouses and children live up to these imagined ideals.

Here's a personal example: No one in my family had ever divorced. I assumed that marriage was for life. So when my wife and I divorced after five years of marriage and three years after the birth of our son, my world caved in. I was a failure in my own eyes.

I later remarried but confided to my wife, Fran, that I couldn't shake the feeling that my family life had failed. She asked me what was wrong with our family now (which included her daughter from a previous marriage and my son). I had to admit that, aside from the pain of being with my son only half the time (my ex-wife and I shared custody), our family life was wonderful.

"Then why don't you celebrate it?" she asked.

That's what I decided to do. But first I had to get rid of the image of a "perfect" family.

"Missing Tile" Syndrome

One effective way of damaging happiness is to look at something and fixate on even the smallest flaw. It's like looking up at a tiled ceiling and concentrating on the space where one tile is missing. As a bald man told me, "Whenever I enter a room, all I see is hair."

Once you've determined what your missing tile is, explore whether acquiring it will really make you happy. Then do one of three things: get it, replace it with a different tile, or forget about it and focus on the tiles in your life that are not missing.

I've spent years studying happiness, and one of the most significant conclusions I've drawn is this: there is little correlation between the circumstances of people's lives and how happy they are. A moment's reflection should make this obvious. We all know people who have had a relatively easy life yet are essentially unhappy. And we know people who have suffered a great deal but generally remain happy.

The first secret is gratitude. All happy people are grateful. Ungrateful people cannot be happy. We tend to think that being unhappy leads people to complain, but it's truer to say that complaining leads to people becoming unhappy.

The second secret is realizing that happiness is a byproduct of something else. The most obvious sources are those pursuits that give our lives purpose—anything from studying insects to playing baseball. The more passions we have, the more happiness we're likely to experience.

Finally, the belief that something permanent transcends us and that our existence has some larger meaning can help us be happier. We need a spiritual or religious faith, or a philosophy of life.

Whatever your philosophy, it should include this truism: if you choose to find the positive in almost every situation, you will be blessed, and if you choose to find the awful, you will be cursed. As with happiness itself, this is largely your decision to make.

NEW WORDS

spouse /spauz/ n. 配偶
concept /ˈkɔnsept/ n. idea, general notion 观念,概念
assume /əˈsjuːm/ vt. suppose, take for granted 假定,假设,以为; become responsible for, undertake, take on 承担,呈现
wage /weidʒ/ vt. begin and carry on, conduct 开始,进行
           n. income, payment 工资
overcome /ˌəuvəˈkʌm/ vt. conquer, defeat 战胜,克服
obstacle /ˈɔbstəkl/ n. barrier, block 障碍(物)
host /həust/ n. (电视节目等的)主持人;主人,东道主;(of) 大群,众多,许多
bless /bles/ vt. praise, glorify 颂扬,赞美; ask God's favor and protection

	for 求神赐福/保佑
multiple/ˈmʌltipl/*a.*	多重的,多样的
sclerosis/sklıəˈrəusis/*n.*	硬化(症);multiple sclerosis 多发性硬化(症)
torture/ˈtɔ:tʃə/*vt.*	cause great suffering to, torment 折磨
divorce/diˈvɔ:s/*vi. & n.*	离婚
confide/kənˈfaid/*vt.*	tell (a secret) to sb. 吐露,倾吐
custody/ˈkʌstədi/*n.*	监管、监护(的权利或责任)
tile/tail/*n.*	瓦;瓷砖;板
syndrome/ˈsindrəum/*n.*	综合病征,综合症状
fixate/ˈfikseit/(*on*) *vi.*	be attached to, be preoccupied with 异常依恋
bald/bɔ:ld/*a.*	having little or no hair 秃头的,无发或少发的
explore/iksˈplɔ:/*v.*	examine thoroughly, investigate 探索,仔细检查;travel into or through in order to learn about 探险,考察,勘探
correlation/ˌkɔriˈleiʃən/*n.*	相互关系
reflect/riˈflekt/(*on*) *v.*	think deeply, consider 沉思,思考;反映,反射; reflection *n.*
gratitude/ˈgrætitju:d/*n.*	being grateful, thankfulness 感激,感谢
byproduct/ˈbaiˌprɔdəkt/*n.*	副产品
pursuit/pəˈsju:t/*n.*	追求,寻求;从事;举行
passion/ˈpæʃən/*n.*	strong liking or enthusiasm 酷爱,热爱;strong feeling 强烈的情感;a thing for which sb. has a strong liking or enthusiasm 酷爱或热衷的事物
permanent/ˈpə;mənənt/*a.*	everlasting, perpetual 永久的,长久的,长期的
transcend/trænˈsend/*vt.*	be or go beyond the range of 超越,超出
philosophy/fiˈlɔsəfi/*n.*	哲学;人生哲学,生活的信念或原则
truism/ˈtru(:)izəm/*n.*	不言而喻的道理,起码的常识
awful/ˈɔ:ful/*a.*	extremely bad or unpleasant, terrible 极坏的,极讨厌的,极糟的,可怕的
curse/kə:s/*n.*	诅咒

PHRASES

live up to: behave according to 依照……行事,达到……的标准
cave in: (of sth. hollow) fall inwards 突然坍塌

aside from: apart from 除了

NOTE

talk-show: a radio or TV program in which usu. well-known persons engage in discussions or are interviewed 脱口秀,(广播或电视中的)答问节目

EXERCISES

I. *Reading Comprehension*:

Choose the best answer to each question.

1. Why did the author feel like a fool after his talk with the young talk-show host?

    A. Because he knew much less about the Internet than did the young man.

    B. Because the young man was much more successful than he was.

    C. Because he had assumed nothing unhappy existed in the young man's life.

    D. Because he didn't know how much fun the young man's job could be.

2. What can be said about the bald man?

    A. He liked to see other people's hair.

    B. There was something wrong with his eyes.

    C. He was jealous of other people's hair.

    D. He focused on what he did not have.

3. According to the passage, what's the relationship between complaining and being unhappy?

    A. Complaining leads to being unhappy.

    B. Being unhappy leads to complaining.

    C. There is little correlation between them.

    D. It depends.

4. What "can help us be happier" (the last but one paragraph)?

    A. A certain belief.   B. Something permanent.

    C. Our existence.   D. Some larger meaning.

5. Which of the following is true, according to the passage?

A. It's good to have images of how life should be.

B. You can decide whether to be happy or not.

C. Happiness is largely out of our control.

D. Some people are always luckier than we are.

II. *Getting Information*:

Complete the following outline in English.

A. We should try _____ instead of _____.

B. It's necessary to overcome three stumbling blocks:

    1. _____

        Implied advice: Realizing that _____.

    2. _____

        Advice: Getting _____.

    3. _____

        Advice: First, _____

                Then, _____.

C. Secrets to happiness:

    1. Being _____.

    2. Realizing _____.

    3. Believing _____.

D. Conclusion:

It is largely a personal decision whether to find _____ in almost every situation or to find _____, just as it is largely a personal decision whether to be _____ or to be _____.

III. *Vocabulary and Structure*:

A. Choose the correct word/phrase to fill into each sentence, using the proper form.

owe	torture	strike	significant	achieve
obstacle	pursuit	barely	circumstance	live up to

1. The union is on strike in _____ of a 10% pay increase.

2. He will do anything to _____ his aim.

Unit 13

3. His refusal to talk is the main _____ to peace.
4. The house _____ you as welcoming when you go in.
5. We _____ loyalty to our motherland.
6. All drivers suffer the _____ of traffic and bad weather.
7. He tried hard to _____ his parents' expectations.
8. Marriage is a(n) _____ commitment.
9. They have _____ enough to pay the rent this month.
10. The meeting has been cancelled due to _____ beyond our control.

B. Use words/phrases from the passage to replace the italicized words/phrases in the following sentences.

1. It is *possible* that she will call me tonight.
2. The conference *examined* the possibility of closer trade links.
3. He *defeated* a strong temptation to run away.
4. A moment's *consideration* will show you are wrong.
5. I *take it for granted* that you don't drink.
6. He is a *loser* in school because of inattention.
7. They had better *find* out exactly what happened as soon as possible.
8. *Basically* she's saying that she is not interested in seeing you again.
9. The disease can cause *lasting* damage to the brain.
10. I'm so *thankful* to you for all that you've done.

C. Complete the following sentences with the missing prepositions or adverbs.

1. Tonight's program focuses _____ homelessness.
2. His skill lies _____ his ability to communicate quite complex ideas very simply.
3. You need to work _____ improving your writing.
4. Happiness is largely _____ our control.
5. The concert was brilliant—it lived _____ all our expectations.
6. Money continues to be a problem but aside _____ that we're all well.
7. We got rid _____ our unwelcome guests by saying we had to go to bed.
8. As _____ happiness itself, this is large your decision to make.
9. She's got no control _____ that child—it's terrible.
10. I remember thinking that he was one of those lucky few _____ whom everything goes effortlessly right.

IV. *Translation*:

A. Translate the following into Chinese.

1. Each of us owes it to our spouses, our children, our friends to be as happy as we can be.
2. The concept that we have to work at happiness comes as news to many people.
3. I once met a young man who struck me as particularly successful and happy.
4. Only rarely do people's jobs, spouses and children live up to these imagined ideals.
5. The most obvious sources are those pursuits that give our lives purpose.

B. Translate the following into English.

1. 事实正好相反。(opposite)

2. 略加思索就很清楚了。(reflection)

3. 我认为你该给我一个解释。(owe)

4. 他们花了两个小时才控制住火势。(bring/get… under control)

5. 大部分夫妻都会同意,要想婚姻成功,双方都需努力。(work at)

6. 吸烟和肺癌之间关系很大。(high correlation)

7. 这家公司主攻欧洲市场。(concentrate on)

8. 你们今天早上的会议得出了什么结论吗?(draw a conclusion)

9. 他从不谈起家人,你不觉得奇怪吗?(strike… as)

10. 他越声称自己无辜,他们似乎越不相信他。(the more… the less)

V. *Writing Task*:

Write about 120 words on the topic "**Happiness**". Your writing should include the following information:

1. Whether one is happy or not is decided by _____.
2. To be happy, we should try to _____.

3. To be happy, we should avoid _____.

VI. *Oral Practice*:

Working in pairs, tell each other your ideal image of a spouse and what you think of the image now that you have read "A Simple Truth About Happiness".

Part B Grammar

直接引语和间接引语（Direct Speech and Indirect Speech）

当我们引用别人的原话,被引用部分称为直接引语;当用自己的话把别人的意思转述出来,这部分称为间接引语。如：

- He said, "I passed the English test last week."（直接引语）
- He said that he had passed the English test the week before.（间接引语）

在采用间接引语时,需注意时态、时间状语、地点状语、指示代词、疑问句的变化。

I 时态的变化

一般来说,直接引语变成间接引语时,时态要往后推一步（如果直接引语中是一般过去时表示过去特定的时间,间接引语的时态可以不变）,即,一般时要变成过去时,完成时变成过去完成时,现在进行时变成过去进行时等。如：

- He said, "I was late for the meeting."

  He said that he had been late for the meeting.
- He said, "I have worked here since 1980."

  He said that he had worked there since 1980.
- He said, "we are planting trees in the hill."

  He said that they were planting trees in the hill.

II 时间状语、地点状语和指示代词变化

在转化成间接引语时,时间状语、地点状语和指示代词也要做出相应的变化。如：

- He said, "I will visit the school tomorrow."（时间状语词、指示代词）

He said that he would visit that school the next day.

- He said, "I was here two days ago." (时间状语词、指示代词、地点状语词)

  He said that he was there two days before.

III 疑问句的变化

当直接引语是疑问句时，间接引语的语序要做适当的调整。直接引语中的疑问词保留，疑问句序变成陈述句式。如：

- "Does he like fish?" John asked.

  John asked him if he liked fish.

练 习

1. 将下面的直接引语句改写成间接引语句。

   (1) He said, "I am not your classmate."
   _____

   (2) "My parents are very well." said he.
   _____

   (3) "Is John going to learn Chinese?" Peter asked.
   _____

   (4) She said, "By 10 o'clock last night I'd finished my homework."
   _____

   (5) "I have given up smoking," said my father.
   _____

   (6) She asked, "Is it difficult to finish the homework within two hours?"
   _____

   (7) He said, "He will go to the party at 6 tomorrow."
   _____

   (8) Mary asked me, "When will we have a meeting?"
   _____

   (9) The old lady said, "I don't know where to go."
   _____

   (10) They asked, "Why is she crying?"
   _____

Unit 13

2. 将下面的中文句子翻译成英文。

（1）他说:"我是1970年出生,并于1990年参军。"

（2）他承认这的确是他的错。

（3）他问我们能否为他安排参观那所中学。

（4）他告诉我们:"去年我在5月份访问了美国。"

（5）她说上一年那里建立了一所新的医院。

（6）他问我明天什么时候开会。

（7）他问到:"你们是什么时间完成的这项工作?"

（8）他让我明天同他一道吃饭。

（9）他问道:"哪条路去机场最近?"

（10）他们告诉我,他们没有参加昨天的讲座。

Part C　Supplementary Reading

To Win at Marriage, Learn to Lose

Knowing how to argue with your spouse
is the cement of
a successful life partnership.
By Gerry Spence
From "HOW TO ARGUE AND WIN EVERY TIME"

　　Having been married for more than 40 years, I can prove the truth of the following statement: to excel in the art of domestic argument, one must master the art of losing.

Modern psychologists are taken with the "win-win" solution. But in marriage, success lies more in "lose-lose" solutions. Out of these, both parties can win. For in the love configuration, losing gives a gift that always returns.

The issues that people argue over most in marriage, such as how to spend money, often aren't the real ones. The key issue is: who is going to be in control? When I was younger, my need to control arose out of fear, a lack of trust, insecurity. Finally I realized I didn't need to control my wife—that, indeed, I ought not to control her, that I couldn't control her, and that if I tried to, I would destroy our marriage.

Giving up control is often confused with weakness. But the winner in a domestic argument is never really the winner. When you win a battle and your partner submits, you have, paradoxically, lost.

What is it we want most from a marriage? To love and be loved. To be happy and secure. To grow, to discover. A love relationship is the garden in which we plant, cultivate and harvest the most precious of crops, our own self, and in which our spouse is provided the same rich soil in which to bloom.

We cannot obtain what we want unless our partner also gets what he or she wants. A woman may, for instance, want to go to the symphony. Her husband might hate symphonies. But by spending a few hours listening to music he doesn't care for, he can bring joy to his partner. That's a pretty cheap price to pay for joy, isn't it?

But what if a husband wants to go on a fishing trip with friends?

Already you can hear the usual power strategies: "I'll spend my money any way I please," or "How come you're such a millstone? Jim's wife is happy that he gets to go."

Instead of such strategies, he might try empowering his partner: "Honey, I'd like to go on a fishing trip with the boys. What do you think?"

"I thought we were going away."

"How about this fall? I've always wanted to take a trip with you to see the fall foliage in New England."

"Good idea. I'll go to see my mother while you're fishing."

Such a dialogue, as idealistic as it sounds, is born of a marriage of mature adults.

But what if she says, "You always make promises you never keep. This fall there will be some excuse. I think you owe me a trip first?"

Now he must decide. Is she right? She could be, you know. When the couple arrives at this point, it's time for him to listen.

When anger is hurled at us, it hurts us. If it were a pistol, I would insist anger, like control, be checked at the door. But anger can also be a response to pain. So when your spouse responds in anger, you must terminate the argument. It's that simple: the argument must end because another person may be in pain.

Try this: Let a little space occur between you. Let the storm recede a little. Then tell your partner you understand that when a person is angry, it means she's been hurt, and that you want to do something about it because you love her.

Perhaps she'll tell you why she's hurt—angrily. Try not to be put off, but to hear the anger as sounds of hurt. When you discover the pain, you can address its cause, and the anger will begin to fade.

You're allowed to get angry too. But dumping anger on your partner is a poor way to comfort your hurt. When you talk of your hurt without anger, an unangry response usually comes.

So remember: If you want to overcome anger in your relationship, search for the hurt. If you want to feel loved and respected, give up control. And if you want to win arguments at home, learn to lose them.

NEW WORDS

cement /siˈment/ n.　　　　　水泥，粘合剂
excel /ikˈsel/ (in, at) v.　　　be exceptionally good　擅长
psychologist /saiˈkɔlədʒist/ n.　心理学家
configuration /kənˌfigjuˈreiʃən/ n.　arrangement of the parts of sth., shape or outline　某物的构造、布局；形状，外观
issue /ˈisjuː, ˈiʃjuː/ n.　　　problem, important topic for discussion, point of debate　问题，争论点；supply and distribution of items for use or sale　分发，发行
　　　　　　v.　　　　　　publish (books, articles, etc.) or put into circulation (stamps, banknotes, shares, etc.)　出版，发行；come, go or flow out　流出，出来；supply or distribute　供给，分配，发出
arise /əˈraiz/ v.　　　　　come into being, occur　形成，发生
submit /səbˈmit/ v.　　　　give in, surrender, yield　屈服，顺从；present　提交，呈送

paradoxical /ˌpærəˈdɔksikəl/ a.	似非而是的,看似矛盾而实际正确的; paradoxically ad.
symphony /ˈsimfəni/ n.	交响乐
strategy /ˈstrætidʒi/ n.	战略,策略
millstone /ˈmilstəun/ n.	磨盘,重担
empower /imˈpauə/ vt.	give lawful power or authority to 授权
foliage /ˈfəuliidʒ/ n.	植物的叶子(总称)
mature /məˈtjuə/ a.	fully developed, fully grown 成熟的,成年的
hurl /hə:l/ vt.	throw violently 用力扔、摔、砸
pistol /ˈpistl/ n.	手枪
check /tʃek/ v.	hold back, restrain 抑制,阻止; inspect, look at 检查,核对
terminate /ˈtə:mineit/ vt.	bring to an end, stop 结束
recede /ri(:)ˈsi:d/ vi.	move back 后退,退去
address /əˈdres/ vt.	direct one's attention to, tackle 把注意力集中于,致力于; make a speech to 对/向……讲话
fade /feid/ vi.	disappear gradually, become indistinct 逐渐消失,变弱; lose color, freshness or vigor 褪色,凋落,衰弱

PHRASES

be taken with: be pleased with or attracted to (sb. or sth.) 被……吸引,对……感兴趣

care for: like, be fond of 爱好,喜爱

put sb. off: discourage (sb.) from (sb. or sth.) 使某人不高兴,引起某人不悦、厌恶或反感

NOTE

New England: 新英格兰地区(美国东北部一些州的统称),包括 Maine、New Hampshire、Vermont、Massachusetts、Rhode Island 和 Connecticut 六个州。

Unit 13

EXERCISES

I. Reading Comprehension:

Answer the following questions in English.

1. What does losing give in love?

2. What are most arguments in marriage about?

3. What will happen if we try to control our spouse?

4. What does the author think is the most precious of crops in the marriage garden?

5. What is meant by "you're such a millstone"?

6. What is meant by "you owe me a trip first"?

7. What does the author compare to a pistol?

8. What does the author suggest we do with anger and control?

9. What may be true of angry people, according to the author?

10. What should we do to win arguments at home?

II. Vocabulary and Structure:

Choose the correct word/phrase to fill into each sentence, using the proper form.

arise	issue	confuse	care for	secure	dump
excel	submit	domestic	cultivate	address	born of

1. We have to _____ the problem before it gets worse.
2. Paula always _____ in languages at school.
3. When the opportunity _____, he decided to take it.

213

4. Children need to feel _____ in order to do well at school.
5. Isn't the need to hire more staff what's really at _____ here?
6. I have to say I don't much _____ modern music.
7. The tax was so unpopular that the government decided to _____ it.
8. _____ opinion had turned against the war.
9. We're trying to help these kids _____ an interest in science.
10. He had never been able to _____ himself to that sort of discipline.
11. With a courage _____ necessity, she seized the gun and ran at him.
12. You're _____ me with my sister—she's the one studying drama.

Part A Text (The Coming Age of Talking Computers)
Part B Grammar (倒装句)
Part C Supplementary Reading (Bill Gates' Speech to Tsinghua University)

Part A Text

Warm-up Questions:
1. *Do you think written language is important to humanity?*
2. *Have you ever thought of the idea that written language will disappear one day?*
3. *What do you know about the talking computers?*
4. *Do you really believe that talking computers will replace written language one day?*

The Coming Age of Talking Computers

By Elton John

The voice-in/voice-out (VIVO) computer will be the last nail in written language's coffin. By enabling us to access stored information orally-aurally, talking computers will finally make it possible for us to replace all written language with spoken language. With this giant step forward into the past, we're about to recreate oral culture on a more efficient and reliable technological foundation.

From a Darwinian perspective, written language is the bridge spanning humanity's first golden age of oral culture to the second. We undertook this journey to survive as a species. Six thousand to 10,000 years ago we lacked the ability to store and retrieve by memory the growing sum of survival information; we faced two options: develop new storage-retrieval technology or self-destruct. That's when and why we created the written language bridge.

Humans instinctively understand that any failure in our ability to store and retrieve information is a threat to our survival. Now, we are instinctively reacting to the fact that written language has hit its limits and is failing us.

It is failing us, first, because it is no longer able to do the tasks we created it to do: For most literate people, communicating, storing, and retrieving information by writing and reading is still far slower and more tedious than doing it by speaking.

Second, the great majority of the world's people—by conservative estimates 80% of humanity—still can't use written language effectively.

Located at the far end of the written-language bridge, the second golden age of oral culture has been visible to us since the invention of the phonograph in 1877. By mid-twenty-first century, we will finally reach the bridge's end and step off into the future. Once across, we will never look back.

The growing feelings of alienation from writing and reading, which schoolchildren and people of all ages are experiencing and expressing through their everyday behavior, are signs and symptoms of a profound historical, social, technological, and evolutionary change. They are symptomatic of a massive shift that is taking place away from the use of written language and back to the use of spoken language to communicate, store, and retrieve information in our daily lives.

The electronically developed countries are witnessing nothing less than the abandonment of reading and writing, of written language itself, and, in its place, the recreation of oral culture. The push to develop voice-recognition technology and VIVO computers that we can talk to and that can talk back to us is part of this evolutionary leap.

Before humans developed written language, they accessed stored information by speaking and listening, as well as by seeing, smelling, tasting, and touching. They relied on their memories to store information that they gathered through their senses and retrieved it for others by speaking and acting.

With the onset of the agricultural revolution 6,000 to 10,000 years ago, people's memories were no longer efficient and reliable enough to store and retrieve the increasing influx of new information. To transcend their memories' limits, our ancestors came up with a remarkable solution: written language.

I exaggerate this point somewhat to help lay the groundwork for a different view of written language. Throughout this article, I characterize written language as a technology, a technological solution to specific information storage and retrieval problems that people faced at a specific moment in history. Written language isn't an eternal verity. We can admire it, but we shouldn't worship it.

We developed written language to store and retrieve information, and we are developing talking computers to perform the very same function. Because talking computers will do it more easily, quickly, efficiently, universally, and cheaply, they will replace written language. Simple.

With written language about to make its exit, and its replacement already stepping through our front door, it is vital that we see written language clearly for what it is: a transitory technology. This reality check will help us prepare ourselves to say goodbye to it and to welcome back its replacement: our old friend, spoken language.

NEW WORDS

coffin /'kɔfin/ *n.*   large, strong box for a dead person to be buried in 棺材,柩

access /'ækses/ *vt.*   get at, gain freedom or ability to obtain or make use of information （电脑）取出(资料),存取

retrieve /ri'tri:v/ *v.*   get possession of again 再获得;检索

perspective /pə'spektiv/ *n.*   point of view 观点

span /spæn/ *vt.*   extend across (from side to side) 跨过,横跨(从一边到另一边)

instinct /'instiŋkt/ *n.*   natural tendency to behave in a certain way without reasoning or training 本能

instinctive /ins'tiŋktiv/ *a.*   based on instinct 凭本能的; **instinctively** *ad.*

tedious /'ti:djəs/ *a.*   tiresome; weary; uninteresting 沉闷的,乏味的

phonograph /'fəunəgra:f/ *n.*   gramophone 唱机,留声机

alienate /'eiljəneit/ *vt.*   turn away 转移

alienation /ˌeiljə'neiʃən/ *n.*   separation 疏远,脱离,摆脱

evolution /ˌi:və'lu:ʃən/ *n.*   process of opening out or developing 发展;演变,演进 (theory of the) development of more complicated forms of life from earlier and simpler forms 进化；进化论

evolutionary /ˌiːvəˈluːʃənəri/ *a.* of, being produced by, evolution; developing 演进的，渐进的；进化的；发展的

symptomatic /ˌsimptəˈmætik/ *a.* serving as a sign of the existence of sth. (of) 征兆的，征候的

onset /ˈɔnset/ *n.* vigorous start 有力的开始

influx /ˈinflʌks/ *n.* flowing in 流入，注入

transcend /trænˈsend/ *vt.* go or be beyond or outside the range of 超出，超越

remarkable /riˈmɑːkəbl/ *a.* out of the ordinary; deserving or attracting attention 不平常的，值得注意的

eternal /iˈtəːnl/ *a.* without beginning or end; lasting for ever 永恒的，永远的

verity /ˈveriti/ *n.* sth. that really exists; true statement 真正存在之事物，真实的陈述

universal /ˌjuːniˈvəːsəl/ *a.* of, belonging to, done by, all; affecting all 普遍的，一般的；影响全体的

vital /ˈvaitl/ *a.* supreme 极度的，非常的

transitory /ˈtrænsitəri/ *a.* lasting for a short time only; brief 仅持续片刻的，倏忽的，短暂的

PHRASES

hit one's limit: reach the limit 达到极限
nothing less than: 和……一模一样，完全是
make one's exit: (the act of) leaving a place/the stage 退出，退场

EXERCISES

I. *Reading Comprehension*：

A. Choose the best answer to each of the following questions.

1. This passage mainly discusses _____.
   A. talking computers will finally replace written language

B. nothing can replace written language

C. talking computers are transitory technology

D. people's memories are no longer efficient to store and retrieve new information

2. What does the first sentence of this article imply?

   A. The VIVO computer will make a coffin for written language.

   B. The VIVO computer will provide some nails for written language's coffin.

   C. Written language will be partly replaced by VIVO computer.

   D. Written language will be completely replaced by VIVO computer.

3. What do the expressions "Written language isn't an eternal verity. We can admire it, but we shouldn't worship it." in the last paragraph but two mean?

   A. Written language is destined to fail us.

   B. Written language is will not continue for ever; it will come to an end someday.

   C. Written language is a remarkable creation, it can not be replaced by any technology.

   D. Although written language is a remarkable creation, it can also be replaced by some better technology.

4. Written language is regarded as _____ by the author.

   A. a transitory technology

   B. an eternal technology

   C. a replacement of spoken language

   D. human's old friend

5. The author's attitude toward the existence of written language is that _____.

   A. it is one of the necessities of human existence

   B. without written language, humans could not store and retrieve information well

   C. without written language, humans could also store and retrieve information quite well

   D. without written language, humans could store and retrieve information better

B. Answer the following questions.

1. How long has written language existed?

_____

2. How could have humans stored information before they developed written language?

_____

3. Why did humans have to create written language thousands of years ago?

_____

4. Why does the author say that "written language is failing us"?

5. Compared with written language, what are the advantages of talking computers in storing and retrieving information?

II. *Vocabulary and Structure*:

A. Choose the correct word/phrase to fill into each sentence, using the proper forms.

access	undertake	instinctive	evolution	hit one's limit
witness	abandon	transcend	replace	nothing less than

1. Branch officials can _____ the central data bank.
2. The scientist _____ his research for lack of fund.
3. The climbers had _____ of their endurance.
4. The _____ act of a frightened person is to run away.
5. The origin of the universe _____ human understanding.
6. Who will _____ the job of decorating the classroom?
7. Only about a thousand people could be admitted to _____ the ceremony.
8. The space program is the _____ of years of research.
9. That is _____ a miracle.
10. John is ill and has been _____ in our team by Tom.

B. From the list, choose the word which is closest in meaning to the italicized word in each sentence, making any necessary changes.

tedious	alienate	symptomatic	efficient	remarkable
eternal	universal	vital	evolutionary	transitory

1. There were some *impressive* new flowers at the Flower Show.
2. New Orleans is filled with *transient* visitors during Mardi Gras.
3. A long talk that you cannot understand is *tiresome*.
4. War causes *widespread* misery.
5. His conduct *separated* him from his old friends.
6. The minister spoke of the soil's *endless* life.

7. Your support is *important* to the success of this project.
8. These quarrels *signal* the state of tension between them.
9. This new copy machine is more *productive* than the old one.
10. The gradual *developing* and changing process resulted in the formation of modern society.

C. Complete the following sentences with the missing prepositions or adverbs.
1. We will be able to store and retrieve information simply _____ talking, listening, and looking at the graphics.
2. You will not be lacking _____ support from me.
3. Teachers should help students develop the ability to see things _____ its right perspective.
4. He should not rely _____ them to tell him the truth.
5. Reasonable pressure from his parents helped lay him the groundwork _____ his future study.
6. As bird flu endangers the whole nation, it is the duty of committees of physicians to come _____ a cure for it in no time.
7. China is undoubtedly characterized _____ one of the ancient civilized countries.
8. VIVO computers refer to those that we can talk _____ and that can talk _____ to us.
9. The technicians prepared the ship _____ the artic expedition.
10. Located _____ the center of the community, this gym provides local residents with more accesses to different means of exercises.

III. *Translation*:
A. Translate the following into Chinese.
1. By enabling us to access stored information orally-aurally, talking computers will finally make it possible for humans to replace all written language with spoken language.

2. From a Darwinian perspective, written language is the bridge spanning humanity's first golden age of oral culture to the second.

3. The second golden age of oral culture has been visible to us since the invention of the phonograph in 1877.

4. Like most technologies, written language will serve its function until some better technology comes along to replace it.

5. This reality check will help us prepare ourselves to say goodbye to written language and to welcome back its replacement: our old friend, spoken language.

B. Translate the following into English.

1. 因特网使人们更方便地获取各种信息。(access to)

2. 话语电脑一旦出现,书面语言就面临被取代的危险。(risk, replace)

3. 这完全是胡说。(nothing less than)

4. 我们本应该在去年底完成那个项目。(completed, project)

5. 人类应该不断超越自己的极限。(transcend)

6. 在可怕的饥荒时代,我需要的是面包而从来不是时间。(lack for)

7. 偶尔回顾过去有助于展望未来。(perspective)

8. 这个律师免费承办那个案件。(undertake)

9. 这个古老的礼堂内举行过许多次典礼。(witness)

10. 你应永远履行你的诺言。(perform)

IV. Writing Task:

Write about 120 words on the topic "Computer—A Good Friend". You should write according to the three-point outline given below.

1. Nowadays computers are widely used in modern society.
2. They help people in different ways.

3. They also offer entertainment to people.

V. *Oral Practice*:

Work in groups of 3 or 4 to talk about the advantages of talking computers and disadvantages of written language. Then please predict the future trend of talking computers and written language.

Part B Grammar

倒装句（Converted Sentence）

倒装语序是英语中的一个比较重要的语法现象,分为部分倒装和全部倒装两种。全部倒装指谓语部分全部提到主语之前;部分倒装指谓语的一部分提到主语之前。倒装语序通常在以下情况中出现:

1. 当具有否定意义的词或短语置于句首时,句子一部分倒装。如:
   · <u>Never has</u> he been to London before.
   · <u>Seldom did</u> he come here.

   这类词或短语包括:hardly、rarely、scarcely、by no means、in no way 等。

2. 当 so、often、only 等表示程度或频率的副词位于句首时,句子一般倒装。如:
   · <u>So nice is</u> the classroom.
   · <u>Only in this way can</u> we finish the work on time.

3. 当 there、here、then、now 等副词置于句首,或动词为 come、go、be 等词时,句子一般倒装。如:
   · <u>Here comes</u> the bus.
   · <u>Here is</u> a letter for you.

4. 一些方位词或拟音词于句首时,句子一般全部倒装。这类词有 out、in、away、up、bang 等。如:
   · <u>Up went</u> the plane into the sky.
   · <u>Out came</u> the man.

5. 为避免句子部分内容重复,英语中常用倒装句。如:
   · He did a good job. <u>So did</u> I.

- He didn't attend the meeting, nor did I.

练 习

选择适当的词语填空。

1. Hardly _____ seen me when he ran away.
   A. he had   B. would he
   C. had he   D. he would

2. Never _____ any experience in teaching English.
   A. will he has   B. he has
   C. he will   D. has she had

3. The door opened and in _____ the important man.
   A. came   B. will come
   C. comes   D. to come

4. The bus driver said to them, "Here _____".
   A. are you   B. will you be
   C. you are   D. you will be

5. Not only _____ helpful, but also he is very kind.
   A. he is   B. is he
   C. will he   D. he will be

6. _____ in his situation, you would oppose the plan.
   A. Were you   B. You were
   C. Being you   D. To be

7. _____, he is still working in the factory.
   A. As is he old   B. Old as he is
   C. Is as he old   D. He is old as

8. He didn't finish the homework, _____ I.
   A. would not do   B. nor did
   C. did not   D. did not finish

9. Only when he got to school _____ realize what happened to his friend.
   A. he would   B. did he
   C. will he   D. does he

10. _____ much trouble with the job, you could come to her for help.
   A. Will you   B. You will have
   C. You had   D. Had you

Part C Supplementary Reading

Bill Gates' Speech to Tsinghua University

By Bill Gates

It's great to be here and have a chance to share some of my excitement with you.

I was 19 when I realized that if I wanted to be the first to do a software company for these new cheap computers, I needed to get my friends together and start right away, so Microsoft became the first company doing software for these new machines. Our vision was a computer on every desk and in every home. In the last 20 years, that vision is certainly becoming a reality. If we had to change it today, we would simply add that now we also want to have a computer in every pocket, every car—many other places that we had not thought about when we first started doing development. I believe software is the key element that really unlocks the power of all this technology, and the idea of making it easy to find information, easy to create information, easy to communicate with other people. Software is at the center of that, and so software will be the fastest growing industry in the world and one that will create lots and lots of great jobs. Certainly here in China the opportunity for hundreds of thousands of great jobs should be very exciting because there is a global shortage in terms of computer skills.

The personal computer revolution got started in 1975, that's when I left college and started Microsoft. These last 22 years have really been amazing, every prediction we've made about improvements have all come true. As we look ahead, that pace of innovation is not slowing down, in fact if anything it's speeding up. Very high speed processors like 300 MHz Pentiums, or new 64-bit processors that we're already developing Windows NT for; incredible storage capacity, which will let us store, not just data, but also digital video as well, treat screen technology to create a tablet-like device that would be good enough for reading and writing; advanced graphics and now the ability to connect computers together at very high speed.

The Internet is the way that all these machines can be connected together. And those standards, and the improvement of those standards, is very very important. Some people like to think about how the computer industry compares to other industries. I've shown before what the cost of the typical car was in 1980 in the US, and that rose up to be about from 8,000 to 19,000 today, and likewise cereal has increased in price. How does that compare to PCs? If the same model was followed for PCs, you can buy car for 27 cents and cereal for less than one cent, so there's no other area of the economy that has this rapid improvement, and people just aren't used to it. You almost have to tell people, "What would you do if Internet computing power was free", because that's what we'll be able to deliver with all these improvements.

Microsoft's vision of computing is global computing. We see PCs connected to the Internet making the world a smaller place, and that's positive in so many ways: to build understanding between people, to share research in key science areas, including medicine, to allow world commerce to work very well. And the Internet is driving this already. Microsoft has set up operations around the world, and we are very pleased with the success we're having here in China. We are doing significant software development on products here, and that will continue to increase, and key for us is having very very high quality software people, and we've been lucky to hire a great number of people from this university. Really I'd say that the core of the teams we've put together have come from here, and I've listed some of those employees here, and we certainly hope that in the future this list will increase dramatically, and the quality of our work continues to rise.

Microsoft believes in doing a lot of research because the software of today is not adequate for tomorrow. It's come a long way, such as the graphics interface, the application, and the way we deal with linguistics; it's much better than it was a year ago. Building the Internet into the software has come a long way. Some of the more ambitious things, like teaching the computer to speak or listen or see, still require a lot of software work that's not yet done, and so we've been investing in research, and building the number of research locations, which will be increasing in the years ahead. One advance is teaching the computer to pick up sentences and understand them, and not just think of them as a series of characters.

That just gives you a glimpse of one area that is expected to make the personal computer really disappear into the environment and connect up in a rich way. Tomorrow's PC will be quite different from what we have today, tomorrow's Internet will be much better than what we have today, but it will all evolve out of this technology that we have right now.

It's clear that the reason we refer to this as the information age is that the capabilities available in the information age will let people reach out and get what they need, whether it's business, learning, or for entertainment. Microsoft feels in a very lucky position to be helping to drive these things, and the key for us is working with other software companies so that they can build other applications on top of the system. Every industry needs a lot of software work there, and so I talk about the software industry creating so many great jobs in the years ahead. I think you picked a great field to be in, and we look forward to working with you.

Thank you.

NEW WORDS

vision/'viʒən/ n.　　power of seeing or imagining, looking ahead, grasping the truth that underlies facts　眼光;远见;想象力

global/'gləubəl/ a.　　worldwide; embracing the whole of a group of items, etc.　全球的;综合的

innovation/,inəu'veiʃən/ n.　　innovating; something new that is introduced　革新,创新,改革;新方法,新事物

processor/'prəusesə/ n.　　处理器

storage/'stɔridʒ/ n.　　存储器,存储

digital/'didʒitl/ a.　　relating or using data in the form of numerical digits　数字式,数字的

video/'vidiəu/ n.　　图像;电视图像

graphics/'græfiks/ n.　　图形学,制图学

cereal/'siəriəl/ n.　　the grain　谷类;谷类食物(如麦片)

interface/'intəfeis/ n.　　接口,界面;接口程序;联系装置

evolve/i'vɔlv/ v.　　(cause to) unfold; develop; be developed, naturally and (usually) gradually　进展;进化,演变

PHRASES

in terms of: with regard to　在……方面,从……方面(说来)

as well (as): in addition to (being)　也,又

be used to: be accustomed to　习惯于……的

set up: prepare (an instrument, machine, etc.) for use; establish (an organization, business, etc.)　开办,设立;创立;建立

come a long way: show much improvement, make great progress 改进很多,进步神速
refer to sb. (sth.) as: mention, speak about 称某人(某物)为

EXERCISES

I. *Reading Comprehension*:

Choose the best answer to each question.

1. When was Microsoft founded?
   A. 1997.　　　　B. 1975.　　　　C. 1977.　　　　D. 1995.
2. Which of the following do you think software can NOT do?
   A. To find information.　　　　B. To create information.
   C. To communicate with other people.　　D. To make appropriate inference.
3. What is the main idea of Para. 3?
   A. The personal computer results in people's revolution.
   B. The personal computer has been getting more and more advanced.
   C. The social reform leads to the innovation of computers.
   D. Development of software falls behind the innovation of hardware.
4. Why does the speaker make comparison between computers and cars (or cereal)?
   A. Cars and cereal are too expensive.
   B. Computers will be cheaper than cars and cereal.
   C. The price of computers has been going down amazingly with its rapid improvement.
   D. Cars and cereal should have been cheaper.
5. Which of the following is NOT the positive aspect of PCs connected to the Internet?
   A. To build understanding between people.
   B. To share research in key science areas.
   C. To allow world commerce to work very well.
   D. To make people suffer from information explosion.
6. What does Microsoft think of research on software?
   A. It is not wise to continue research on software since it is getting more and more challenging.
   B. Enough work has been done on software, so it is unnecessary to go on with the research.
   C. A lot of work has to be done in order to meet the increasing need.
   D. There will not be a new field for research on software.

7. Why does the speaker say we live in the information age?
   A. Without information, we cannot live now.
   B. All of us have to reach out for information now.
   C. Information is important only in business, learning and entertainment.
   D. We can get any information we need in the information age.
8. Which of the following is implied in Gates' speech?
   A. Microsoft ought to work with other software companies.
   B. Microsoft is proud of its position in the information age.
   C. The software industry has been creating many new jobs.
   D. Other software companies can build applications on top of the system.

II. *Vocabulary and Structure*:

Fill in the blanks with the appropriate form of the given phrases.

| get used to | speed up | set up | refer to sb. (sth.) as |
| in terms of | as well (as) | | |

1. He thought of everything _____ money.
2. Warmth _____ chemical reactions.
3. It brought him a good deal of local fame-money _____, obviously.
4. After a few days, I _____ it all.
5. The government _____ an inquiry into the affair.
6. Don't _____ your sister _____ a silly cow!

Part A Text (Mind Games)
Part B Grammar (插入语)
Part C Supplementary Reading
        (When to Say No to Your Kids)

Part A Text

Warm-up Questions:
1. *What do you think economics studies?*
2. *Do you think studying human brain has anything to do with economics?*
3. *Do you know what "neuroeconomics" is about?*

Mind Games

Can studying the human brain revolutionise economics?

Although Plato compared the human soul to a chariot pulled by the two horses of reason and emotion, modern economics has mostly been a one-horse show. It has been obsessed with reason. In decisions from how much to produce to whether to save and invest, humans have been assumed to be coolly rational calculators of their own self-interest. Over the past few years, however, evidence from psychology has persuaded many economists that reason does not always have its way. Now, judging from a series of presentations at the American Economic Association meetings in Philadelphia last weekend, a burgeoning new field dubbed "neuroeconomics" seems poised to provide fresh insights on how the two horses together produce economic behaviour.

The current bout of research is made possible by the arrival of new technologies such as functional magnetic-resonance imaging, which allows second-by-second observation of brain activity. At several American universities, economists and their collaborators in the neurosciences have been placing human subjects in such brain scanners and asking them to perform a variety of economic tasks and games.

For example, the idea that humans compute the "expected value" of future events is central to many economic models. Whether people will invest in shares or buy insurance depends on how they estimate the odds of future events weighted by the gains and losses in each case. Your pension, for example, might have a very low expected value if there is a large probability that bonds and shares will plunge just before you retire.

Brian Knutson, of Stanford University, carried out one recent brain-scan experiment to understand how humans compute such things. Subjects were asked to perform a task, in this case pressing a button during a short interval in which a certain shape was flashed on to a screen. In some trials, the subjects could win up to $5 if successful, while in others they would have to defend against a $5 loss. Before presenting the target, the researchers signalled to subjects which kind of trial they were in.

Brain activity in certain neural systems seemed to reveal a strong correlation with the amount of money at stake. Moreover, the prospects of gains and losses activated different parts of the brain. Traditional economists had long thought—or assumed—that the prospect of a $1,000 gain could compensate you for an equally likely loss of the same size. In subsequent trials, subjects were given another signal: one that provided an estimate of the odds of success. That allowed the researchers to identify the regions of the brain used for recognising an amount of money and for estimating the probability of winning (or losing) it. Having identified these regions, the hope is that future work can measure how the brain performs in situations such as share selection, gambling or deciding to participate in a pension scheme.

David Laibson, an economist at Harvard University, thinks that such experiments underscore the big role that expectations play in a person's well-being. Economists have usually assumed that people's well-being, or "utility", depends on their level of consumption, but it might be that changes in consumption, especially unexpected downward ones, as in these experiments, can be especially unpleasant.

Mr. Laibson's own work tries to solve a different riddle: why people seem to apply vastly different discount rates to immediate and short-term rewards compared with rewards occurring well into the future. People tend much to prefer, say, $100 now to $115 next week, but they are indifferent between $100 a year from now and $115 in a year and a week. In one recent experiment, Mr. Laibson and others found that the brain's response to short-term riches (in this case, gift certificates of $15 or $20) occurs largely in the limbic system, a region that governs emotion. By contrast, the prospect of rewards farther into the future triggers the prefrontal cortex, which is often associated with reason and calculation. Thus, choosing immediate economic gratification, by spending excessively on credit cards or not saving enough even though you "know better", could be a sign that the limbic system is in charge. Government policies, such as forced savings or "cooling off" periods for buying property or cars, may be one remedy.

And then there is trust and deception. Colin Camerer, of the California Institute of Technology, has conducted experiments in which brain-scanned participants play strategic games with anonymous partners. In these, a subject chooses his own actions and also tries to anticipate the choices of the other player. When players are doing the best that they can to "win" the game by anticipating their opponents' moves, their brains tend to show a high degree of co-ordination between the "thinking" and the "feeling" regions. Economic equilibrium, by this measure, is an identifiable "state of mind".

NEW WORDS

chariot/ˈtʃæriət/ *n.*	an ancient horse-drawn two-wheeled vehicle used in war, races, and processions 战车
obsess/əbˈses/ *v.*	to preoccupy the mind of excessively 迷住，使困扰
invest/inˈvest/ *v.*	to commit (money or capital) in order to gain a financial return 投资
assume/əˈsjuːm/ *v.*	to take for granted; suppose 假定，臆想；理所当然地认为
burgeon/ˈbəːdʒ(ə)n/ *v.*	to grow and flourish 萌芽
dub/dʌb/ *v.*	to give a name to facetiously or playfully 起绰号
poised/pɔizd/ *adj.*	completely ready to do or achieve something and about to do it 做好准备要……，摆好姿势要……；calm and composed 镇定沉着的
insight/ˈinsait/ *n.*	the capacity to discern the true nature of a situation;

Unit 15

	penetration 洞察力,穿透力;心智的敏锐
bout /baut/ n.	a contest between antagonists; a match 一场,一回;对手间的一次较量;一次比赛
functional /ˈfʌŋkʃənl/ adj.	capable of performing; operative 有功能的;在起作用的
collaborator /kəˈlæbəreitə(r)/ n.	people who work together, especially in a joint intellectual effort 合作者
scanner /ˈskænə/ n.	扫描器,扫描仪
perform /pəˈfɔːm/ v.	to take action in accordance with the requirements of; fulfill 履行;根据……需要而采取行动;满足
variety /vəˈraiəti/ n.	the quality or condition of being various or varied; diversity 多样化;多样性
share /ʃɛə/ n.	a part or portion belonging to, distributed to, contributed by, or owed by a person or group 股份
insurance /inˈʃuərəns/ n.	保险
estimate /ˈestimeit/ v.	to calculate approximately (the amount, extent, magnitude, position, or value of something) 推测,估计
odds /ɔdz/ n.	the likelihood of the occurrence of one thing rather than the occurrence of another thing, as in a contest 可能性,机会
pension /ˈpenʃən/ n.	退休金,抚恤金
probability /ˌprɔbəˈbiliti/ n.	the quality or condition of being probable; likelihood 可能性,或然性;可能的性质或状况
bond /bɔnd/ n.	债券
plunge /plʌndʒ/ v.	to descend steeply; fall precipitously 陡峭地下倾;突然地下降
press /pres/ v.	to exert steady weight or force against; bear down on 挤压,按,在……上按下
interval /ˈintəvəl/ n.	the amount of time between two specified instants, events, or states 间隔
trial /ˈtraiəl/ n.	the act or process of testing, trying, or putting to the proof 试验;检验、试用或验证的行为或过程

correlation/ˌkɔriˈleiʃən/ n.　an act of correlating or the condition of being correlated　相互关联；相关性

prospect/ˈprɔspekt/ n.　something expected; a possibility　期待；被期望的某物；可能性

activate/ˈæktiveit/ v.　to set in motion; make active or more active　使活动，使活泼；使活动起来

compensate/ˈkɔmpənseit/ v.　to make satisfactory payment or reparation to; recompense or reimburse　报酬；偿还；赔偿或补偿

subsequent/ˈsʌbsikwənt/ adj.　following in time or order; succeeding　随后的

identify/aiˈdentifai/ v.　to ascertain the origin, nature, or definitive characteristics of　确认，验明

underscore/ˌʌndəˈskɔː/ v.　to emphasize; stress　强调；加强

consumption/kənˈsʌmpʃən/ n.　the act or process of consuming　消耗；消耗的行为或过程

riddle/ˈridl/ n.　a question or statement requiring thought to answer or understand　谜（语）

discount/ˈdiskaunt/ n.　an amount deducted from the usual list price　折扣；从整个或标准的价格或债款的折扣

indifferent/inˈdifərənt/ adj.　without interest or concern　不在乎的，淡漠的，不关心的

trigger/ˈtrigə/ v.　to set off; initiate　引发，触发

remedy/ˈremidi/ n.　something that corrects an evil, a fault, or an error　补救办法；改正邪恶，过错或者错误的事物

deception/diˈsepʃən/ n.　the use of deceit, a trick　行骗，欺诈，骗局

strategic/strəˈtiːdʒik/ adj.　of or relating to strategy　战略的；战略的，与战略有关的

anonymous/əˈnɔniməs/ adj.　having an unknown or unacknowledged name　匿名的，姓氏不明的

anticipate/ænˈtisipeit/ v.　to look forward to, especially with pleasure; expect to prevent someone doing something by acting first　预感，预料；预防，先发制胜

equilibrium/ˌiːkwiˈlibriəm/ n.　a state of rest or balance between opposing forces, powers, or influences　平衡，均衡

Unit 15

PHRASES

have one's way: carry one's point, get what one wants 为所欲为,按照自己的意愿去做
a variety of: a group or collection containing different sorts of the same thing or people 多种的
carry out: fulfill, complete 完成,实现,贯彻,执行
up to: as far as, to and including 一直到,等于
at stake: at risk, in danger of being lost 濒临危险;得失攸关
know better: be wise or experienced enough to avoid making mistakes 有头脑,明事理
cool off: become calmer and less excited 变凉,平静下来

NOTE

gift certificate: (Am E) a special piece of paper that is worth a particular amount of money when it is exchanged for goods in a shop 奖券,礼券,赠券

EXERCISES

I. *Reading Comprehension*:

Choose the best answer to each question.

1. According to the author, modern economics has mostly been a one-horse show because _____.
   A. it concerns how people react to a certain economic situation
   B. it helps people to decide how much to produce
   C. it tells people whether to save or to invest
   D. it has been appealing to reason in solving problems
2. Which of the following is true of "neuroeconomics"?
   A. It is a subject studied by medical scientists.
   B. It studies how people are affected by economic situations.
   C. It is a subject which requires cooperation of economists and neural scientists.
   D. It is not a rigorous subject.
3. What are the human subjects most probably told to do in the research?
   A. To decide whether to invest in shares or buy insurance.
   B. To observe brain activity.

C. To tell the "expected value" of future events.

D. To participate in a pension scheme.

4. What is Brian Knutson's finding in his brain-scan experiment?

   A. Human brain has a region for recognizing an amount of money.

   B. How human subjects press a button during a short interval.

   C. Human subjects could win up to $5.

   D. Human subjects could defend against a $5 loss.

5. What is the problem David Laibson wanted to solve?

   A. Why people prefer immediate rewards to long-term rewards.

   B. How a reward of $100 differs from that of $115.

   C. The brain's responses to short-term riches differ from person to person.

   D. How trust contrasts with deception.

II. *Getting Information*:

Answer the following questions in English.

1. According to the author, what is the new technology that has made "neuroeconomics" research possible?

2. What is the idea that is central to many economic models?

3. What is Brian Knutson's brain-scan experiment for?

4. What did Brian Knutson think the future work would be?

5. Why does the author say that economic equilibrium is an identifiable "state of mind"?

III. *Vocabulary and Structure*:

A. Choose the correct word/phrase to fill into each sentence, using the proper form.

perform	estimate	invest	assume	plunge
compensate	identify	indifferent	anticipate	trigger

1. It was a high-level meeting that _____ bitter bureaucratic debates.

2. We _____ great pleasure from our visit to London.
3. It is quite _____ to me whether you go or stay.
4. The markings are so blurred that it is difficult to _____.
5. Nothing can _____ the young mother for the loss of her favorite daughter.
6. Sophisticated laser experiments are _____ regularly in the laboratory.
7. The disabled aircraft _____ to the ground and burst into flames.
8. I _____ you always get up at the same time.
9. The state has planned to _____ two millions in the dam.
10. While an author is yet living we _____ his powers by his worst performance.

B. Find the proper forms of the following words according to the given word class.
1. obsess   (n.) _____
2. invest   (n.) _____
3. insight   (a.) _____
4. functional   (n.) _____
5. collaborator   (v.) _____
6. probability   (a.) _____
7. consumption   (v.) _____
8. indifferent   (n.) _____
9. identify   (n.) _____
10. strategic   (n.) _____

C. Complete the following sentences with the missing prepositions or adverbs.
1. Although Plato compared the human soul _____ a chariot pulled by the two horses of reason and emotion, modern economics has mostly been a one-horse show.
2. A burgeoning new field dubbed "neuroeconomics" seems poised to provide fresh insights _____ how the two horses together produce economic behaviour.
3. Whether people will invest _____ shares or buy insurance depends on how they estimate the odds of future events weighted by the gains and losses in each case.
4. Before presenting the target, the researchers signalled to subjects which kind of trial they were _____.
5. Economists have usually assumed that people's well-being, or "utility", depends _____ their level of consumption.
6. Why do people seem to apply vastly different discount rates _____ immediate and

short-term rewards compared with rewards occurring well into the future.
7. People tend much to prefer, say, $100 now _____ $115 next week.
8. Colin Camerer has conducted experiments _____ which brain-scanned participants play strategic games with anonymous partners.
9. The prospect of rewards farther into the future triggers the prefrontal cortex, which is often associated _____ reason and calculation.
10. In some trials, the subjects could win up to $5 if successful, while in others they would have to defend _____ a $5 loss.

IV. ***Translation***:
A. Translate the following into Chinese.
1. In decisions from how much to produce to whether to save and invest, humans have been assumed to be coolly rational calculators of their own self-interest.

2. Whether people will invest in shares or buy insurance depends on how they estimate the odds of future events weighted by the gains and losses in each case.

3. Traditional economists had long thought—or assumed—that the prospect of a $1,000 gain could compensate you for an equally likely loss of the same size.

4. Having identified these regions, the hope is that future work can measure how the brain performs in situations such as share selection, gambling or deciding to participate in a pension scheme.

5. People tend much to prefer, say, $100 now to $115 next week, but they are indifferent between $100 a year from now and $115 in a year and a week.

B. Translate the following into English.
1. 他们认为价格要上涨。(assume)

2. 这个购物中心出售许多种商品。(a variety of)

3. 他们仅能大致估计出人群的规模。(estimate)

4. 史密斯先生被选为议员的希望不大。(prospect)
_____

5. 一个人失去了健康是不可弥补的。(compensate)
_____

6. 我立即认出了那件外套,它是我兄弟的。(identify)
_____

7. 这辆大型轿车耗油量很大。(consumption)
_____

8. 那名官员成功地完成了使命。(carry out)
_____

9. 我们期待再接到你们的来信。(anticipate)
_____

10. 允许学生有两个小时来完成考试。(up to)
_____

V. *Writing Task*:

Write about "**Neuroeconomics**" in some 120 words. Try to cover the following points:
1. Can studying the human brain revolutionize economics?
2. How can you compare "neuroeconomics" with traditional economics?
3. What do you think of the new developments of economics?

VI. *Oral Practice*:

Form a pair, and then talk about possible changes that "neuroeconomics" might bring about to traditional economics. Present your opinions to each other.

Part B Grammar

插入语 (Parenthesis)

插入语是句子的独立成分,客观上起状语的作用,通常用逗号与句子的主语部分隔开。作为插入语的有:副词、不定式、介词短语或短句。如:

· Telecommunication means, simply, communication from a distance.（副词作插入语）
· To put it briefly, the purpose is to process information.（不定式作插入语）
· At a distance, the field appears to be a sheet of green carpet.（介词短语作插入语）
· As you know, the center of the earth is very hot.（短句作插入语）

常用副词作插入语有：chiefly、generally、fortunately、briefly、hopefully、probably、similarly、perhaps、clearly、practically、actually、roughly

常用介词短语作插入语有：as a rule、in particular、in the same way、in short、in fact、in the long run、in part、for the most part、in a word

常用不定式作插入语有：to be brief、to be honest、to begin with、to tell the truth、to sum up、to be more precise、to put it briefly

常用短句作插入语有：as we know、as its name implies、as you see、as far as we know、as far as it goes、as it appears to me、as things are

练 习

1. 用插入语的方式翻译下面的句子。

(1) 显然，他没有努力学习。(obviously)

(2) 确切地说，他们五点钟到达那里。(to be exact)

(3) 由于这一原因，他无法参加会议。(for this reason)

(4) 无论如何，这个计划要做修改。(in any case)

(5) 首先，让我们复习一下第十课。(to begin with)

(6) 就此而论，计算机不能完全替代人。(as far as it goes)

(7) 一般来说，一周可以记住30个单词。(generally speaking)

(8) 同样，你也可以承担这项工作。(similarly)

(9) 正如大家所看到的那样，这条河已被严重污染了。(as everyone sees)

（10）简言之，这本书对考试是很有用的。(to be brief)

2. 将下列句子译成汉语。

(1) Frankly, I'm afraid your mother will be a little disappointed.

(2) Evidently, he was sensitive on this topic.

(3) I can't come, unfortunately.

(4) Hopefully, we'll win.

(5) Surprisingly, she has married again.

(6) I thought it would rain, and sure enough, it did.

(7) He's lived in France for years, but strangely enough, he can't speak a word of French.

(8) The rain was heavy—consequently the land was flooded.

(9) Oddly enough, I had no doubt that he would be glad to see me.

(10) Miraculously, no one was killed.

Part C   Supplementary Reading

When to Say No to Your Kids

How can you keep your child from developing the gimmies—or cure him if they've already set in? Here's what experts advise:

Teach kids not to rely on TV, computers and toys. If you're like most parents, such a thought sends waves of panic through you. Without their dolls, action figures, videos and electronic games, won't your kids drive you crazy?

Not if you engage them in meaningful activities, Lickona says, such as work that helps the family. Traditionally, he points out, kids on farms would milk cows, collect eggs and perform other duties, even at a very young age. Nowadays, however, we ask almost nothing of our children.

Lickona says parents can fend off the gimmies by creating a schedule of chores. Even four-year-olds can help clear breakfast dishes, feed the cat, water the plants and so on. Older children can make beds, work in the garden and sort laundry.

Don't feel it's up to you, however, to keep your child busy. Growing children have to figure out how to entertain themselves without expensive toys—or adults' help. If you restrict TV and computer time, they'll eventually discover something to do that doesn't require buying more things.

Don't buy goodies for your kids every time you go shopping. This is a practice often brought about by guilt. "Parents who work feel that because they're unavailable to their children so much of the day, they should somehow make it up to them," says New York City psychologist Dennis Shulman.

Buying gifts habitually may make you feel generous, but your children may begin to feel entitled to treats and demand them all the time.

Explain that money is a consideration. Make clear to your child right from the start that what you buy for him is a matter of heavy decision-making. Give him some idea of the financial thinking that goes into deciding whether you will buy him a bicycle.

But don't give children the "we're too poor" excuse if you can afford the item. If they see you indulging your own whims, they figure that you should indulge theirs too. Remind them that owning a lot of things is not crucial to happiness. Emphasize that some things are trashy and not worth buying. Drawing distinctions for your children will ultimately transform them into savvy consumers and disciplined savers later on.

If you think your child's request is worthwhile, give him a chance to earn the money to buy the item. Say something like, "I can't buy those designer jeans today. But I will if you help me in the kitchen every night this month." This also encourages your child to develop initiative and drive.

If you reject a child's request, keep your explanation simple. One day at a supermarket, I heard a father explain to his four-year-old son that the bag of potato chips the boy wanted was "not a good option because they aren't nutritious and contain fat and salt and are harmful to your health." At a drugstore, a mother told her daughter that she couldn't have a pack of barrettes because "having so many barrettes is irresponsible."

Such explanations sound civilized to adults, but to a child they are confusing and indefinite. Better to deliver a firm "no" and then offer the simplest explanation you can think of: "They're not good for you." Such a flat rejection gives a child no reason to think that crying, fussing or yelping will get him anywhere.

Once you say no, stick to it. Your response to the gimmies teaches children something important: "How things are gained and not gained," Shulman says. Letting a child have her own way after crying and whining tells her she can get ahead by making other people's lives miserable.

If you find yourself usually giving in, examine your own motives. "The primary reason is to avoid a scene," Shulman says. But keeping the peace comes at a high price—it teaches your child that fussing works. "You're much better off letting a scene happen," Shulman advises. "Even if your child cries piteously and onlookers think you're the wicked Witch of the West, you must stand by your decision."

"If necessary, leave the store," advises family therapist Michele Weiner-Davis of Woodstock, Ill. "Sometimes you have to inconvenience yourself to prove a point."

Your job as a parent is to help your children decide what's worth getting and then show them the right way to go about it. The important lesson they'll learn is that getting takes more effort than saying, "Gimme."

NEW WORDS

gimme/'gimi/	[口] = give me (或 give it to me)
panic/'pænik/ n.	unreasoning, uncontrolled, quickly spreading fear 恐慌,惊慌
fend/fend/ v.	to defend oneself from 挡开
chore/tʃɔː/ n. pl.	家庭杂务;日常零星工作
laundry/'lɔːndri/ n.	要洗的或已洗好的衣物
unavailable/ˌʌnəˈveiləbl/ a.	(of objects) unable to be used; that cannot be obtained 无法利用的,得不到的;达不到的
indulge/inˈdʌldʒ/ v.	to gratify; to give way to and satisfy (desires, etc.); to

	overlook the faults of; to allow oneself the pleasure of 放纵(感情、欲望);纵容,迁就
whim/ʜwim/ n.	sudden desire or idea, often something unusual or unreasonable 狂想,幻想,一时的兴致
trashy/'træʃi/ a.	worthless 废物似的;毫无价值的
savvy/'sævi/ a.	shrewdly intelligent 精明老练的;有见识的
nutritious/nju'triʃəs/ a.	nourishing; having high value as food 有营养的,滋养的
barrette/bə'ret/ n.	(妇女用的)条状发夹
fuss/fʌs/ v.	to act or behave in a nervous, restless, and anxious way over small matters 抱怨;小题大作地争辩
yelp/jelp/ v.	to utter a short, sharp cry (of pain, anger, excitement, etc.) 叫喊着说
whine/ʜwain/ v.	to utter complaints, especially about trivial things 嘀咕,发牢骚
scene/siːn/ n.	(incident characterized by an) emotional outburst 当众吵嘴,发脾气
piteously/'pitiəsli/ ad.	乞怜地;可怜地
therapist/'θerəpist/ n.	治疗学家

PHRASES

keep... from: prevent... from 阻止;使免于

up to somebody: the duty or responsibility of 该由……决定;适于……的

figure out: work out, understand by thinking 解决

make it up to somebody: compensate sb. for sth. missed or suffered, or for money, etc. spent 补偿某人

entitle to: give the right to 授权与,使……有资格

later on: at a later time; afterwards 以后;下回

get ahead: do well, succeed 成功,得逞

give in: yield 屈服,让步

be better off: be in a more advantageous position 不如……更好/有利,不妨

Unit 15

EXERCISES

I. Reading Comprehension:

Choose the best answer to each question.

1. According to the author, how do most parents keep their kids engaged?
    A. They keep their kids studying all the time.
    B. They tell their kids to milk cows and collect eggs.
    C. They'll see that their kids have many dolls, videos and electronic games to play with.
    D. They have to teach their kids how to do housework.
2. What does the author suggest in order to fend off the gimmies?
    A. Try to say "No" to the kids.
    B. Buy what the kids ask for.
    C. Give the kids detailed explanations.
    D. Create a schedule of chores.
3. According to Dennis Shulman, why do most parents buy goodies for their kids every time they go shopping?
    A. They have enough money.
    B. They know their kids like goodies.
    C. They feel sorry that they have so little time to be with their kids.
    D. They think it is a good way to keep their kids happy.
4. Why is it wrong buying gifts habitually?
    A. The kids may begin to feel that they deserve treats.
    B. That will cost parents too much money.
    C. The kids think it is unnecessary to buy gifts habitually.
    D. Parents do not have much time to do so.
5. Why does the author say "don't give children the 'we're too poor' excuse if you can afford the item"?
    A. Children will not trust what you say.
    B. Children will follow you in indulging their own whims.
    C. It is not favorable to tell a lie to children.
    D. It is not good to show you are poor.
6. Why does the author suggest that parents give their kids a chance to earn the money to

buy the item?

   A. Parents do not have enough money to pay for the item.

   B. That will help to set up co-operations between parents and their kids.

   C. That will encourage the kids to develop their own initiative and drive.

   D. By doing so the kids will understand how difficult it is to buy the item.

7. Why does the author maintain that parents keep their explanation simple if they reject a child's request?

   A. They try to make children understand their explanation.

   B. It is easy to give a simple explanation.

   C. The simple explanation will make children bother their parents no more.

   D. Children like simple explanations.

8. Why are parents supposed to stick to saying no from the beginning?

   A. Parents want to show their authority.

   B. They have no choice but to say no.

   C. Children will give in sooner or later.

   D. To tell children they cannot get ahead by making other people's lives miserable.

9. According to the author, why do parents usually give in to their child's request?

   A. Because they want their child to watch a scene.

   B. Because they want to avoid a quarrel in public.

   C. Because they think their child's request is reasonable.

   D. Because they let their child decide on their own.

10. In the author's view, the important lesson that a child is supposed to learn is _____.

    A. getting is better than saying, "Gimme"

    B. getting is no better than saying, "Gimme"

    C. getting is more difficult than saying, "Gimme"

    D. getting is less difficult than saying, "Gimme"

II. *Vocabulary and Structure*:

Fill in the blanks with appropriate form of the given phrases.

| give in | get ahead | rely on | figure out | up to | fend off |
| better off | keep... from | make it up to | entitle to | later on | point out |

1. She had to hold the boy tight, to _____ him _____ falling.

2. Hong Kong's prosperity _____ heavily _____ foreign business.
3. It is _____ parents to teach their children manners.
4. She had not yet _____ what she was going to do.
5. You missed the concert; never mind, we'll _____ you next time.
6. We mustn't _____ to threats.
7. His teacher _____ the incorrect English usages in the essay writing.
8. No one else but John _____ praise.
9. I'll tell you all about it _____.
10. You'd be _____ with a bicycle.

读者意见反馈表

亲爱的读者:

您好!非常感谢您选用我们的图书。为了今后能给您提供更优秀的外语图书,请您抽出宝贵的时间填写这份意见反馈表,并沿线剪下,寄至:100084 北京市海淀区双清路学研大厦 A 座 601 清华大学出版社外语分社。咨询电话:(010)62770175—3113,62794243(兼传真)。E-mail:qhwy@tup.tsinghua.edu.cn。如果您有特别好的意见,或需要哪方面的书,请予说明。我们可向您推荐并寄送清华大学出版社有关最新书目。

如果您还想购买我社其他图书,而当地不能如愿,请您与我们的邮购部联系。电话:(010)62786544 传真:(010)62779977。再次感谢您对我们的支持与爱护!

书名:《工程硕士研究生英语基础教程——学生用书》
第__印次　印刷年月:_____

读者个人资料
姓名:_____　性别:□男　□女　　年龄:_____
职业:_____　文化程度_____　　通讯地址:_____

您是如何得知这本书的:
□经人介绍　□书店　□出版社图书目录
□媒体的介绍(请指明)_____
□广告宣传　□其他_____

您从何处购得此书:
□书店　□网上书店　□邮购
□学校教材科　□其他_____

您购买过我社几本外语图书?
□一本　□两本　□三本　□四本以上

影响您选购图书的因素有(可复选):
□封面、装帧设计　　□书的内容
□内容提要、前言和目录　□价格
□作者或出版社名声　□广告宣传
□买过同系列其他书,感觉满意
□其他_____

您对本书封面设计的满意度:
□很满意　□满意　□一般　□不满意
改进建议_____

您对本书印刷质量的满意度:
□很满意　□满意　□一般　□不满意
改进建议_____

您对本书的总体满意度:
□很满意　□满意　□一般　□不满意

本书最令您满意的方面是(可复选):
□针对性强　□内容充实　□语言地道
□装帧精美　□实例丰富　□讲解详尽
□角度新颖　□有实用价值
□有欣赏价值　□有保留价值
□其他_____

您希望本书在哪些方面进行改进?
_____
_____

您希望我社外语图书有哪些改进?
_____
_____

您希望购买哪些方面的外语图书?
_____
_____

其他建议或要求:
_____
_____